DRIVE THRU THEOLOGY
A Busy Person's Guide for Understanding the Bible

by
Dr. Kelly Brady

EQUIP Publishing

DRIVE THRU THEOLOGY
A Busy Person's Guide for Understanding the Bible
Copyright @ 2026 by Kelly Brady
Fifth Edition. Printed in the U.S.A., Published by EQUIP

All rights reserved. No part of this publication may be reproduced, stored, or transmitted in any form by any means, electronic, mechanical, photocopy, recording, or otherwise, without prior written permission by the author.

All Scripture quotations, unless otherwise indicated, are taken from the HOLY BIBLE, NEW INTERNATIONAL VERSION®. Copyright © 1973, 1978, 1984 by International Bible Society. Used by permission of Zondervan. All rights reserved.

Scripture marked NASB are taken from the New American Standard Bible®, Copyright © 1960, 1962, 1963, 1968, 1971, 1972, 1973, 1975, 1977, 1995 by the Lockman Foundation. Used by permission.

Scripture marked ESV are from the Holy Bible, English Standard Version, copyright © 2001 by Crossway, a publishing ministry of Good New Publishers. Used by permission. All rights reserved.

Scripture quotations marked (NLT) are taken from the Holy Bible, New Living Translation, copyright © 1996, 2004, 2007 by Tyndale House Foundation. Used by permission of Tyndale House Publishers, Inc., Carol Stream, Illinois 60188. All rights reserved.

Scripture marked HCSB are taken from the Holman Christian Standard Bible®, Copyright © 1999, 2000, 2002, 2003, 2009 by Holman Bible Publishers. Used by permission. Holman Christian Standard Bible®, Holman CSB®, and HCSB® are federally registered trademarks of Holman Bible Publishers.

Scripture taken from the New King James Version®. Copyright © 1982 by Thomas Nelson, Inc. Used by permission. All rights reserved.

ISBN 13: 978-0-692-84890-6   ISBN 10: 0-692-84890-8

Also by Dr. Kelly Brady

FOLLOWING JESUS
Defining Discipleship in the 21st Century

WAIT…WHAT?
Biblical Teachings Worth Repeating

RESTORE
Experiencing the Power of Healing Fellowship

SHEPHERDING
The Elder Notebook of Glen Ellyn Bible Church

EQUIPPED: 2 Timothy 3:16-17
A Specialty Journal that Helps You Study Scripture

TABLE OF CONTENTS

Abortion	19
Addiction	21
Adultery	23
Angels	25
Anointing Oil	27
Anxiety	29
Apologetics	31
Arminianism	33
Ascension Day	35
Atonement	37
Baptism	39
Born Again	41
Calvinism	43
Church	44
Circumcision	46
Clean and Unclean in the Old Testament	48
Communion	50
Confession of Sin	52
Conviction	54
Creation Theories of Genesis 1	56
Cults	58
Deacon	59
Death	61
Demons and Exorcism	63
Denominationalism	65
Discerning God's Will	67
Discipleship	69
Discipline within the Church	71
Dispensationalism	73
Divorce	75
Elders	77

Election	79
How can I know if I am elect?	81
Evangelism	83
How can I share my faith with others?	85
Eschatology (End Times)	87
Faith	89
How are faith and good works related?	94
Fasting	95
Fear	97
Fellowship	99
Forgiveness	101
Fornication	103
Freedom from Sin	105
Gospel	107
Gospel and Its Exclusivity and Inclusivity	109
Grace	111
Healing	113
How much faith is needed for healing?	115
Hearing God's Voice	117
Heaven	119
Hell	121
How is eternal punishment justified?	123
How is Hell consistent with God's love?	125
Why is Hell populated, if God can save all?	127
Hiddenness of God	130
Holiness	132
Holy Spirit	134
What does "filled" with the Spirit mean?	136
Homosexuality	138
Incarnation	140
Israel and the Church	142
Jesus Christ	145
Jesus Christ's Deity	147

Jesus Christ's Humanity	149
Jesus Christ's Resurrection	151
Why should we believe Jesus was raised?	154
What benefit is the resurrection to the believing?	158
Jesus Christ's Return	163
Jesus Christ, Son of God	164
Jesus Christ, Son of Man	165
Judgment by God	167
Judgment of Others	169
Law	171
Lent	172
Marriage	174
Heterosexual Marriage as the Biblical Design	176
Mercy	181
Miracles	183
Modesty	185
Money	187
Names of God	190
Obedience	192
Original Sin and Imputed Righteousness	194
Peace	196
Pentecost	198
Polygamy	200
Prayer	202
Why prayer in Jesus' name?	204
Why might our prayers go unanswered?	206
Prayer and Laying on Hands	208
What does it mean to pray in the Spirit?	210
Prayer in the New Testament	212
The prayer of a righteous man	215
Problem of Evil	217
Puritan	219
Racism	221

Remarriage	224
Repentance	226
Resurrected Bodies	228
Rewards in Heaven	230
Sabbath	232
Salvation	233
Salvation and God's Sovereignty	235
Salvation and Our Assurance	237
Salvation and Our Perseverance	240
Salvation and Our Security	242
What happens in the process of salvation?	243
Satan	244
Scripture	245
Scripture's Authority	247
Scripture's Historicity	249
Scripture's Inerrancy	250
Scripture's Sufficiency	251
How can we accurately interpret the Scripture?	254
How do we answer Old Testament questions?	255
Why are there so many different Bible translations?	256
Service	257
Sexuality	258
Sin	260
Slavery	261
Speaking in Tongues	263
Why does God use tongues to communicate?	265
Spiritual Gifts and Sign Gifts	267
Spiritual Maturity	268
Spiritual Warfare	270
What does it mean to wear the armor of God?	273
Ten Commandments	275
Temptation	277
Tithing	278

Transgender	280
Trials and Suffering	282
Trinity	284
Wisdom	286
Women in Ministry	288
Work	293
Worship	295
Wrath of God	297
Glossary	**299**

To my wife,

Sherri

in whom I see and through whom I have experienced God's grace at work.

*All Scripture is God-breathed and is useful
for teaching, rebuking, correcting and training
in righteousness, so that the servant of God may be
thoroughly equipped for every good work.
2 Timothy 3:16-17 (NIV)*

INTRODUCTION

People have lots of questions about what the Bible teaches, but little time. *Drive Thru Theology* provides quick answers from the Bible for those on the go.

This book is designed as a quick reference tool, offering concise theological statements on a broad range of topics. Each of the theological topics addressed are listed alphabetically and are presented along with Scripture references. The theological statements are listed in *bold* type, followed by the verse/s that support that point of theology. Sprinkled throughout the book are also short answers to commonly asked questions about the Christian faith. Questions like: "How much faith is needed to receive healing?" and "Why might our prayers go unanswered?"

Both the theological statements and the answers offered to the commonly asked questions are not meant to be exhaustive. In other words, not every theological statement that could be made regarding a particular verse has been made. These are merely summary statements meant only to provide quick reference for people who have time enough only to do a little bit of reading. For this reason, the content of this book is meant only to be a starting point.

As a pastor, I am reminded daily that shepherds do not grow the grass. Shepherds simply point the sheep to where they can find the grass. This means that anytime we are caring for others spiritually, our job is primarily to point to the truth found in Scripture. Our job is not to try and create food, but rather direct them to the nourishment of Scripture. Ultimately, it is only the truth of God's Word that satisfies, sustains, and strengthens God's people.

It is tempting to offer our own words of wisdom when guiding others spiritually, or the popular psychology of the day, but the greatest need we have is to hear the truth of God's Word. It is the Scripture that is "useful," because it is the Scripture that is "God-breathed" (2 Timothy 3:16).

Abortion

Abortion is the termination of a pregnancy. Although Scripture does not identify exactly when life begins in the womb (e.g., conception or implantation), we do know from Scripture that God actively works within the womb to form individual human beings (Psalm 139:13-16). Further, we know that the taking of innocent life is murder (Exodus 20:13), which means that the wisest course of action is to protect and preserve all human life growing in the womb.

Scripture clearly indicates that the mystery of creating a living soul, a human being with a personality, character, and purpose, is sovereignly attended to by God as he works in the womb to bring humans into existence. Although the Bible is not a science book, and should not be interpreted as if it were, the Psalmist declares God's active participation in the process of making a life in the womb (Psalm 139:13-16). Job, who was made famous by his story of suffering in the Old Testament, said the same; God forms us in the womb (Job 31:15). We even learn in the book of Jeremiah that God knows us "before" we are formed in the womb (Jeremiah 1:5). Imagine that! God knows us before we are embodied. God knows our personality and our character and the plans he has for each of us before we are conceived. Finally, John the Baptist jumped in the womb at the sound of Mary's voice, which is an indication of personality and character and volition in the womb. (Luke 1:41).

Admittedly, while the human reproduction process involves a lot that we *can* understand scientifically, it also includes a lot of realities that we *cannot* understand spiritually, as God is at work in the womb doing what only he can do—creating a person in his image, a living, breathing, and eternal soul. Abortion is immoral, and thus sinful, because it interrupts the person-forming work of God that takes place in the womb.

Abortion is immoral, as being known by God in the womb demonstrates personhood.
Before I formed you in the womb I knew you, and before you were born I consecrated you. Jeremiah 1:5 (NASB)

For it was You who created my inward parts; You knit me together in my mother's womb. Psalm 139:13 (HCSB)

Did not He who made me in the womb make him, And the same one fashion us in the womb? Job 31:15 (NASB)

Abortion is immoral because perception and response on the part of unborn children demonstrates personhood.
But the two children struggled with each other in her womb. So she went to ask the Lord about it. "Why is this happening to me?" she asked. Genesis 25:22 (NLT)

When Elizabeth heard Mary's greeting, the baby leaped in her womb. Luke 1:41 (NIV)

Abortion is immoral because being sinful at conception implies personal responsibility, which demonstrates personhood.
Surely I was sinful at birth, sinful from the time my mother conceived me. Psalm 51:6 (NIV)

Abortion is immoral in that capital punishment was prescribed for those causing an abortion, demonstrating that an unborn child is to be considered fully human.
"If men struggle with each other and strike a woman with child so that she gives birth prematurely, yet there is no injury, he shall surely be fined as the woman's husband may demand of him, and he shall pay as the judges decide. But if there is any further injury, then you shall appoint as a penalty life for life, eye for eye, tooth for tooth, hand for hand, foot for foot, burn for burn, wound for wound, bruise for bruise. Exodus 21:22-25 (NASB)

Addiction

Addiction is physical and/or psychological dependence on an activity or substance, continuing in the activity despite its negative consequences, and lacking the ability to stop the activity. While Christians may become entangled in sin for a season, a lifestyle of addiction is contrary to the life of freedom from sin that Christians are offered through faith in Jesus Christ's resurrection.

Addiction is to be overcome by corrupting behavior.
For speaking out arrogant words of vanity they entice by fleshly desires, by sensuality, those who barely escape from the ones who live in error, promising them freedom while they themselves are slaves of corruption; for by what a man is overcome, by this he is enslaved. 2 Peter 2:18-19 (NASB)

Addiction is to be held captive by a sin.
Repent of your wickedness and pray to the Lord. Perhaps he will forgive your evil thoughts, for I can see that you are full of bitter jealousy and are held captive by sin." Acts 8:22-23 (NLT)

Addiction is a thankless posture of abusing creation.
For everything created by God is good, and nothing is to be rejected if it is received with gratitude. 1 Timothy 4:4 (NASB)

Addiction is an unprofitable use of one's body, as one fails to master their body to bring God glory.
All things are lawful for me, but not all things are profitable. All things are lawful for me, but I will not be mastered by anything. Food is for the stomach and the stomach is for food, but God will do away with both of them. Yet the body is not for immorality, but for the Lord, and the Lord is for the body. For you have been bought with a price: therefore glorify God in your body. 1 Corinthians 6:12-13, 20 (NASB)

Addiction is contrary to a Christian lifestyle because we are to grow in self-control through the Spirit.
Teach the older men to be temperate, worthy of respect, self-controlled, and sound in faith, in love and in endurance. Likewise, teach the older women to be reverent in the way they live, not to be slanderers or addicted to much wine, but to teach what is good. Titus 2:2-3 (NIV)

Addiction is contrary to a Christian lifestyle because Christians have the power to share in God's divine nature and escape the world's corruption.
By his divine power, God has given us everything we need for living a godly life. We have received all of this by coming to know him, the one who called us to himself by means of his marvelous glory and excellence. And because of his glory and excellence, he has given us great and precious promises. These are the promises that enable you to share his divine nature and escape the world's corruption caused by human desires. 2 Peter 1:3-4 (NLT)

Addiction is contrary to the Christian lifestyle, because Christians can do all things through Jesus' power.
I know how to be brought low, and I know how to abound. In any and every circumstance, I have learned the secret of facing plenty and hunger, abundance and need. I can do all things through him who strengthens me. Philippians 4:12-13 (ESV)

Addiction is contrary to a Christians lifestyle, because Christians have become slaves of righteousness.
Now you are free from your slavery to sin, and you have become slaves to righteous living. Because of the weakness of your human nature, I am using the illustration of slavery to help you understand all this. Previously, you let yourselves be slaves to impurity and lawlessness, which led ever deeper into sin. Now you must give yourselves to be slaves to righteous living so that you will become holy. Romans 6:18-19 (NLT)

Adultery

Adultery is a sin committed when a married person has sexual relations with someone other than their spouse. Adultery is prohibited in the Seventh Commandment (Exodus 20:14) and was also condemned by Jesus (Matthew 5:27), as well as the Apostle Paul (1 Corinthians 6:9, Galatians 6:19-20). Jesus even taught that to look at another person lustfully was to break the Seventh Commandment by committing the sin of adultery within one's heart.

> You have heard the commandment that says, 'You must not commit adultery.' But I say, anyone who even looks at a woman with lust has already committed adultery with her in his heart. Matthew 5:27-28 (NLT)

Jesus' point is that lust can grow in our heart long before we act on it, meaning there are very few who have not broken the spirit of the seventh commandment. Whether it is a lingering lustful stare, or even a longer sexual fantasy, according to Jesus both are sinful and committing adultery in one's heart. While we may not ever act on the sin outwardly, we are nonetheless guilty of the sin inwardly. Stating the Seventh Commandment's prohibition against adultery in the affirmative might read "Those who are married are to remain sexually faithful to their spouse, in body, mind and heart."

The Old Testament penalty for adultery was death, and it applied equally to both men and women (Leviticus. 20:10, Deuteronomy 22:22). Generally, it is understood that the penalty was severe because the offense was so damaging to the community of God's people. Breaking one's marriage vow weakens the fabric of the community of God's people as it undermines the unity within marriage, which was ultimately designed by God to reflect his loving relationship with his people.

For this reason, the sin of idolatry was described relationally as committing adultery, when God's people would act unfaithfully by worshiping gods other than Yahweh. Those who participated in idolatry were considered "spiritual adulterers" (Ezekiel 6:9, Hosea 4:13), giving their bodies, minds, and hearts to a god other than their Creator.

The call to "spiritual fidelity" is carried into the New Testament by the Apostle Paul, who explained that marriage is designed to be a metaphor of Jesus Christ's love, as the spiritual groom, for the church, his spiritual bride (Ephesians 5:31-32). The mysterious union between God and those trusting in Jesus as Savior is even compared to the mysterious union of a man and woman becoming one flesh in marriage through sexual relations. Christians are ultimately to live lives of fidelity (i.e., faithful service) in relationship with Jesus (James 4:4), just as those married are to remain faithful to their spouse sexually. Ultimately, marriage is to be a living, breathing, walking, and talking example of God's love for his people.

In fact, it is entirely possible that God did not *adopt* the metaphor of marriage to describe his desires for relational intimacy with his people, but rather that God *created* marriage for the purpose of representing his desires for relationship with his people. It was likely God's intention from the beginning of Creation that when people look at marriage, they are to see an example of Jesus' love for the Church and the Church's love for her Savior. For this reason, adultery is a serious sin that undermines the world's understanding of the unity between Jesus and the Church.

Angels

The word "angel" means "messenger," which gives some indication of their role. Stephen and Paul both note that the Old Testament law was delivered to humanity by angels (Acts 7:53, Galatians 3:19). Only a few of the names of angels are offered in Scripture. Michael is described as an "archangel," or "chief" angel (Jude 9), while Gabriel delivers special messages (Daniel 9:21, Luke 1:26).

Angels may appear in human bodies (Genesis 18:3, Numbers 22:31, Mark 16:5, Luke 24:4). However they are described as "spirit" beings (Hebrews 1:14), and for this reason are most often not seen by us (2 Kings 6:17). There is no record in the Bible of angels appearing as ghosts or with wings. While angels are spirit beings, they are not all-knowing (Matthew 24:36, 1 Peter 1:12) or all-powerful (Daniel 10:13), and they are not to be worshipped (Colossians 2:18).

Angels were created to serve God's purposes and people.
Are they not all ministering spirits sent out to serve for the sake of those who are to inherit salvation? Hebrews 1:14 (ESV)

See that you do not despise one of these little ones. For I tell you that in heaven their angels always see the face of my Father who is in heaven. Matthew 18:10 (ESV)

Angels were sent to carry out God's judgment.
Immediately an angel of the Lord struck him down, because he did not give God the glory, and he was eaten by worms and breathed his last. Acts 12:23 (ESV)

Some angels rebelled and received God's judgment.
And the angels who did not stay within their own position of authority, but left their proper dwelling, he has kept in eternal chains under gloomy darkness until the judgment of the great day. Jude 1:6 (ESV)

Angels can carry messages to people and defend people.
Do not neglect to show hospitality to strangers, for thereby some have entertained angels unawares. Hebrews 13:2 (ESV)

The angel said to them, "Fear not, for behold, I bring you good news of great joy that will be for all the people." Luke 2:10 (ESV)

But when the archangel Michael, contending with the devil, was disputing about the body of Moses, he did not presume to pronounce a blasphemous judgment, but said, "The Lord rebuke you." Jude 9 (ESV)

He made me understand, speaking with me and saying, "O Daniel, I have now come out to give you insight and understanding." Daniel 9:22 (ESV)

He struck Peter on the side and woke him, saying, "Get up quickly." And the chains fell off his hands. Acts 12:7 (ESV)

Anointing Oil

In the ancient world, anointing with oil was a widespread practice and was used in a broad range of applications, from medicinal to ceremonial. In the Old Testament, anointing with oil was most often used to set something or someone apart for service to God. For example, kings and priests were anointed with oil as they began their service, functionally set apart for leadership and ministry (1 Samuel 10:1). In the New Testament, the term Christ, or Messiah, means literally "anointed one," as Jesus was set apart for special service in God's Work of redemption (Matthew 1:16, Mark 8:29).

In our contemporary culture, it is not an uncommon practice for Christians to anoint the sick, by placing a little bit of oil on the forehead of those receiving prayer for healing (James 5:14-15). In this application, the oil is understood as representing God's healing presence brought through the Holy Spirit. In this way, the sick person is "set apart" for God's special care by the Holy Spirit in healing.

While anointing with oil is a centuries old tradition, it is important to understand that there is no special power in the oil itself. The power for healing comes from God's Spirit who blesses our obedience as we act in faith and do as directed in Scripture. It is also important to understand that anointing the sick with oil is not prescribed in the Bible as a substitute for medical treatment. People of faith can, and should, both receive medical treatment from a doctor, as well as act in faithful obedience to the Scripture and receive oil during prayer for healing.

Anointing oil was used to consecrate priests for service.
"Then you shall take the anointing oil and pour it on his head and anoint him. "You shall bring his sons and put tunics on them." Exodus 29:7-8 (NASB)

Anointing oil was used to consecrate kings for service.
Then Samuel took a flask of olive oil and poured it over Saul's head. He kissed Saul and said, "I am doing this because the Lord has appointed you to be the ruler over Israel, his special possession. 1 Samuel 10:1 (NLT)

Anointing oil was used by the Israelites in sacrifice.
"Whatever is needed, both young bulls, rams, and lambs for a burnt offering to the God of heaven, and wheat, salt, wine and anointing oil, as the priests in Jerusalem request, it is to be given to them daily without fail, that they may offer acceptable sacrifices to the God of heaven and pray for the life of the king and his sons. Ezra 6:9-10 (NASB)

Anointing the sick with oil was practiced by the disciples.
They went out and preached that men should repent. And they were casting out many demons and were anointing with oil many sick people and healing them. Mark 6:12-13 (NASB)

Anointing the sick with oil is commanded in James.
Is any one of you sick? He should call the elders of the church to pray over him and anoint him with oil in the name of the Lord. And the prayer offered in faith will make the sick person well; the Lord will raise him up. If he has sinned, he will be forgiven. James 5:14-15 (NIV)

Anxiety

Anxiety is a general feeling of uneasiness, which can range from simple feelings of nervousness to paralyzing feelings of dread. Often distinguished from feelings of fear, which are caused by the reality of a specific and identifiable danger that produces a fight or flight response, anxiety is most often fueled by a more generalized, and in many cases seldom realized, feeling of threat that produces an intense sense of helplessness or danger.

Anxiety is a common emotion that most people experience at one time or another, and it can have any number of causes, and even combination of causes, including traumatic experiences, underlying health issues, or difficult relationships and overwhelming circumstances. Whatever the cause though, when we continue feeling anxious over a long period of time it has negative effects upon us physically, mentally, and emotionally.

Unfortunately for many, identifying the causes of anxiety and alleviating feelings of anxiety can be difficult. For this reason, diagnosing and treating various anxiety related disorders is one of the most common cases in modern psychiatry.

Anxiety does not increase the control we have over life.
Consider the ravens: they neither sow nor reap, they have neither storehouse nor barn, and yet God feeds them. Of how much more value are you than the birds! And which of you by being anxious can add a single hour to his span of life? If then you are not able to do as small a thing as that, why are you anxious about the rest? Consider the lilies, how they grow: they neither toil nor spin, yet I tell you, even Solomon in all his glory was not arrayed like one of these. But if God so clothes the grass, which is alive in the field today, and tomorrow is thrown into the oven, how much more will he clothe you, O you of little faith! Luke 12:24-28 (ESV)

Anxiety is an opportunity to pray and know God's peace.
Do not be anxious about anything, but in everything by prayer and supplication with thanksgiving let your requests be made known to God. And the peace of God, which surpasses all understanding, will guard your hearts and your minds in Christ Jesus. Philippians 4:6-7 (ESV)

Anxiety may be overcome by giving our worries to God.
Give all your worries and cares to God, for he cares about you. 1 Peter 5:7 (NLT)

Anxiety can be a distraction from what is important.
And he said to his disciples, "Therefore I tell you, do not be anxious about your life, what you will eat, nor about your body, what you will put on. For life is more than food, and the body more than clothing. Luke 12:22-23 (ESV)

But the Lord answered her, "Martha, Martha, you are anxious and troubled about many things, but one thing is necessary. Mary has chosen the good portion, which will not be taken away from her." Luke 10:41-42 (ESV)

Anxiety may indicate a need to know more of God's love.
There is no fear in love, but perfect love casts out fear. For fear has to do with punishment, and whoever fears has not been perfected in love. 1 John 4:8 (ESV)

Apologetics

The word "apologetics" comes from the Greek word *apologia*, which means "to make a verbal defense" or to offer reasons for a belief. The Apostle Peter wrote that we are to be prepared to answer everyone who asks the "reason" (apologia) for the hope we have in Christ (1 Peter 3:15).

The work of apologetics implies that the Christian faith is reasonable—that there are good reasons, or rational explanations, to believe what we believe. At the same time, becoming a Christian will always require faith. In other words, it is impossible to argue someone into believing the claims of Christianity. Although we can rationally demonstrate that the Bible is a trustworthy and historically accurate source of information, we will never be able to prove that it is the inspired Word of God. Believing that the Bible is inspired is a tenet of faith, while believing that it is historically reliable is a deduction that can be made based upon evidence. Ultimately, having faith in the Bible as God's Word is the result of God's Spirit at work in our lives drawing us to faith.

Therefore, while we can, and should, work to answer people's questions about matters of faith, we cannot hope to convince anyone to believe. Only the Holy Spirit moves people to faith. For this reason, our role is to simply communicate the reasonable nature of the Christian faith. It is the Holy Spirit's role to convince people to believe.

Apologetics is a work for which we are to be prepared and we are to do with gentleness and respect for others.
Always be prepared to give an answer to everyone who asks you to give the reason for the hope that you have. But do this with gentleness and respect, keeping a clear conscience, so that those who speak maliciously against your good behavior in Christ may be ashamed of their slander. 1 Peter 3:15-16 (NIV)

While doing apologetics, Paul noted how many, who were still living at that time, saw Jesus resurrected.

After that, he appeared to more than five hundred of the brothers at the same time, most of whom are still living, though some have fallen asleep. Then he appeared to James, then to all the apostles, and last of all he appeared to me also, as to one abnormally born. 1 Corinthians 15:6-8 (NIV)

The work of apologetics leads people to faith only as the Holy Spirit convinces people of the truth of Scripture.

The man without the Spirit does not accept the things that come from the Spirit of God, for they are foolishness to him, and he cannot understand them, because they are spiritually discerned. 1 Corinthians 2:14 (NIV)

Arminianism

Arminianism is the theological system of James Arminius (1560-1609). While holding many beliefs in common with John Calvin, such as the belief that all humans are born sinful (Ephesians 2:1) and that Scripture is inspired by God (2 Timothy 3:16) and that it is without error, he differed with John Calvin on the role of man in salvation.

Arminianism teaches that salvation is the result of God's predestination of those whom he foreknew would themselves freely accept the offer of forgiveness provided through Jesus' death. This differs from Calvinism, which teaches that salvation is the result of God's predestination of those whom he foreknew and whom he sovereignly chose to be saved. In response to Calvinism, the followers of Arminius offered these five points of protest:

Universal Prevenient Grace. Grace given by God overcomes the effects of sin, providing the freedom needed to accept or reject salvation offered through faith in Jesus Christ.

Conditional Election. God elects to save only those whom he foreknew would accept Jesus Christ as Savior.

Unlimited Atonement. Christ died for all people, but those who are saved are only those whom God foreknew would freely choose to believe in Jesus as Savior.

Resistible Grace. God never forces his will upon people, but all are free to reject or accept the forgiveness offered in Jesus Christ's sacrificial death on the cross.

Uncertainty of Perseverance. Although the grace and power needed to persevere are available to all who believe, salvation can be lost by those who fail to persevere in faith.

While it should be noted that not all who identify with Arminianism affirm each of these five points, Arminianism is best known for its affirmation of man's will, which is thought to be freely exercised in the process of salvation. The Methodist, Wesleyan, Assemblies of God, and Pentecostal denominations are historically Arminian in theology.

Ascension Day

Ascension Day, which comes 40 days after Easter, is the day dedicated to remembering Jesus' ascension into heaven. Jesus' ascension marks the end of Christ's physical ministry on earth and the beginning of a ten-day period of waiting for the arrival of the Holy Spirit, which came at Pentecost.

Both Mark and Luke recount Jesus' ascension in their gospels (Mark 16:19, Luke 24:51). The book of Acts also reports events surrounding the ascension (Acts 1:1-11). After the ascension, the disciples waited in Jerusalem, as they had been instructed (Acts 1:4). During that historic ten-day waiting period they gave themselves constantly to prayer (Acts 1:14), and they were gathered in the Upper Room praying when the Holy Spirit descended in power on the day of Pentecost (Acts 2:1-13).

Jesus taught that the ascension had to take place before the Holy Spirit could be poured out at Pentecost (John 16:7). While it is true that Jesus physically left our world when he ascended into heaven, because of his continuing presence through the Holy Spirit, his power is available now to all believers (Acts 1:8). That is certainly something to celebrate! The ascension of Jesus opened the door to the coming of the Holy Spirit, God's presence with us.

Jesus' ascension is a part of his work of redemption.
And if I go and prepare a place for you, I will come again and receive you to Myself; that where I am, there you may be also. John 14:3 (NKJV)

"Most assuredly, I say to you, he who believes in Me, the works that I do he will do also; and greater works than these he will do, because I go to My Father. John 14:12 (NKJV)

Who is the one who condemns? Christ Jesus is the One who died, but even more, has been raised; He also is at the right hand of God and intercedes for us. Romans 8:34 (HCSB)

Jesus' ascension is another proof of his resurrection.
After He had suffered, He also presented Himself alive to them by many convincing proofs, appearing to them during 40 days and speaking about the kingdom of God. Acts 1:3 (HCSB)

Jesus' ascension foreshadows his bodily return.
After He had said this, He was taken up as they were watching, and a cloud took Him out of their sight. While He was going, they were gazing into heaven, and suddenly two men in white clothes stood by them. They said, "Men of Galilee, why do you stand looking up into heaven? This Jesus, who has been taken from you into heaven, will come in the same way that you have seen Him going into heaven." Acts 1:9-11 (HCSB)

Jesus' ascension had to precede the Holy Spirit's arrival.
Nevertheless I tell you the truth. It is to your advantage that I go away; for if I do not go away, the Helper will not come to you; but if I depart, I will send Him to you. John 16:7 (NKJV)

Jesus' ascension begins his exaltation and his reign.
Therefore, since He has been exalted to the right hand of God and has received from the Father the promised Holy Spirit, He has poured out what you both see and hear. Acts 2:33 (HCSB)

He demonstrated this power in the Messiah by raising Him from the dead and seating Him at His right hand in the heavens—far above every ruler and authority, power and dominion, and every title given, not only in this age but also in the one to come. And He put everything under His feet and appointed Him as head over everything for the church. Ephesians 1:20-22 (HCSB)

Atonement

Atonement is the act of removing sin, which makes possible relational reconciliation with God. Some have cleverly dissected the word into "at-one-ment," to help demonstrate its meaning. Sin is any action or attitude contrary to God's character and is revealed to us in the Law (1 John 3:4). Sin separates us from God, which creates the need for atonement.

In the Old Testament, making atonement involved shedding blood through animal sacrifice, as well as making offerings of grain and flour (Leviticus 1-4). Shedding of an innocent animal's blood atoned for human sin. In this way, application of animal blood to the altar, or in some cases the Israelites themselves, provided for a symbolic ransoming of human life (Leviticus 17:11).

On the Day of Atonement, the holiest day in the Israelite calendar, the High Priest made sacrifices for the sins of Israel (Leviticus 16). The sacrifices for sin offered on The Day of Atonement "paid" for the sins of Israel from the previous year. Ultimately, because it was impossible for the blood of animals to take away sins, the Old Testament sacrifices foreshadowed the perfect and complete atonement made available through faith in the blood of Jesus Christ (Romans 3:24-25, Hebrews 9:1-10:14).

Atonement is made through blood sacrifice.
The life of the body is in its blood. I have given you the blood on the altar to purify you, making you right with the Lord. It is the blood, given in exchange for a life, that makes purification possible. Leviticus 17:11 (NLT)

Atonement comes through Jesus, God's sacrificial lamb.
The next day John saw Jesus coming toward him and said, "Look! The Lamb of God who takes away the sin of the world! John 1:29 (NLT)

Get rid of the old "yeast" by removing this wicked person from among you. Then you will be like a fresh batch of dough made without yeast, which is what you really are. Christ, our Passover Lamb, has been sacrificed for us. 1 Corinthians 5:7 *(NLT)*

For you know that God paid a ransom to save you from the empty life you inherited from your ancestors. And the ransom he paid was not mere gold or silver. It was the precious blood of Christ, the sinless, spotless Lamb of God. 1 Peter 1:18-19 *(NLT)*

Atonement by Jesus' blood cleanses our conscience.
And since we have a great High Priest who rules over God's house, let us go right into the presence of God with sincere hearts fully trusting him. For our guilty consciences have been sprinkled with Christ's blood to make us clean, and our bodies have been washed with pure water. Hebrews 10:21-22 *(NLT)*

Atonement by Jesus' blood provides our forgiveness.
You have come to Jesus, the one who mediates the new covenant between God and people, and to the sprinkled blood, which speaks of forgiveness instead of crying out for vengeance like the blood of Abel. Hebrews 12:24 *(NLT)*

Atonement comes by faith in Jesus' sacrifice for our sin.
Yet God, with undeserved kindness, declares that we are righteous. He did this through Christ Jesus when he freed us from the penalty for our sins. For God presented Jesus as the sacrifice for sin. People are made right with God when they believe that Jesus sacrificed his life, shedding his blood. Romans 3:24-25 *(NLT)*

Baptism

Coming from a Greek root-word that means to plunge, immerse or sink, "baptism" denotes washing or covering in water. A common ritual in the Jewish community during the time of Jesus, baptism was observed by Jews who were returning to faith or by gentiles who were converting to Judaism. In these cases, it was a ritual that marked a repentance from sin, submission to God's law and identification with God's people, the Israelites. John the Baptist's ministry of baptism was an example of ancient Jewish baptism (Matthew 3:1-6).

As the New Testament unfolds, baptism continued to be a sign of repentance from sin, but became a symbol of dependence upon the Savior. Today, the act of submersion in water symbolizes one's identification with Jesus Christ's death and resurrection. As Jesus was buried in the ground, those trusting in Jesus for salvation are placed below the water during baptism, and just as Jesus was raised from the grave, those trusting in Jesus for salvation are raised out of the water. In this way, baptism is a public declaration of one's trust in the death of Jesus for the forgiveness of sin and resurrection of Jesus for eternal life. The act of immersion in water also symbolizes the cleansing we receive by faith in Jesus' shed blood. Just as water washes us clean of dirt, Jesus' blood washes off the stain of sin.

It is important to understand that we are not saved through baptism. Instead, baptism is meant to be a symbol of one's saving faith in Jesus' death and resurrection. We are saved by our faith in Jesus Christ's death and resurrection, apart from anything we do (Ephesians 2:8-9), including baptism. For this reason, every example of baptism in the New Testament comes after one has made a profession of faith in Jesus Christ.

Baptism was modeled by Jesus.
Then Jesus arrived from Galilee at the Jordan coming to John, to be baptized by him. Matthew 3:13 (NASB)

Baptism was commanded by Jesus.
Go therefore and make disciples of all the nations, baptizing them in the name of the Father and the Son and the Holy Spirit. Matthew 28:19 (NASB)

Baptism was practiced by the early church.
Peter replied, "Repent and be baptized, every one of you, in the name of Jesus Christ for the forgiveness of your sins. And you will receive the gift of the Holy Spirit. Acts 2:38 (NIV)

Baptism is an identification with Jesus' death and resurrection.
Or do you not know that all of us who have been baptized into Christ Jesus have been baptized into His death? Therefore we have been buried with Him through baptism into death, so that as Christ was raised from the dead through the glory of the Father, so we too might walk in newness of life. For if we have become united with Him in the likeness of His death, certainly we shall also be in the likeness of His resurrection. Romans 6:3-5 (NASB)

Baptism symbolizes God's deliverance from sin and death.
For Christ also died for sins once for all, the just for the unjust, so that He might bring us to God, having been put to death in the flesh, but made alive in the spirit; in which also He went and made proclamation to the spirits now in prison, who once were disobedient, when the patience of God kept waiting in the days of Noah, during the construction of the ark, in which a few, that is, eight persons, were brought safely through the water. Corresponding to that, baptism now saves you—not the removal of dirt from the flesh, but an appeal to God for a good conscience—through the resurrection of Jesus Christ, who is at the right hand of God, having gone into heaven, after angels and authorities and powers had been subjected to Him. 1 Peter 3:18-22 (NKJV)

Born Again

"Born again" is the phrase that best describes the beginning of the process of salvation. To enter the kingdom of God, Jesus said "you must be born again" (John 3:7). To be born again is to be made spiritually alive by the Holy Spirit (John 3:6). When we are biologically born, we are spiritually dead (Ephesians 2:1-4) and must be born again to be spiritually alive.

Much like our biological birth is the result of our parents' exercising their will, we are born again spiritually as God wills to bring us to new life (John 1:13). We are born again when the Spirit of God gives us new life, making those who are spiritually dead come to life. In this work, God's Spirit gives life to our spirit (John 3:6, James 1:18).

Although we are born again by God's will and his Spirit's work in our life, this is not to say that we do not participate in the process. While we do not cause our new birth, we do participate in it. Just as a baby participates in physical birth, by descending the birth canal, we participate in the process of our spiritual new birth by expressing our faith in Jesus Christ through repentance, which is an active turning away from sin, and confession of faith (Romans 10:9-10, Matthew 3:8-9, Acts 26:20).

Being born again is a requirement for entering heaven.
Jesus answered him, "Truly, truly, I say to you, unless one is born again he cannot see the kingdom of God." John 3:3 (ESV)

Being born again is to be reborn by God's Spirit.
That which is born of the flesh is flesh, and that which is born of the Spirit is spirit. John 3:6 (ESV)

Being born again is caused by God, not man.
Who were born, not of blood nor of the will of the flesh nor of the will of man, but of God. John 1:13 (ESV)

Being born again is to become a child of God.
But to all who did receive him, who believed in his name, he gave the right to become children of God. John 1:12 (ESV)

Being born again gives us the power to resist sin.
No one born of God makes a practice of sinning, for God's seed abides in him, and he cannot keep on sinning because he has been born of God. 1 John 3:9 (ESV)

Being born again provides power to overcome sin.
For everyone who has been born of God overcomes the world. And this is the victory that has overcome the world— our faith. 1 John 5:4 (ESV)

Being born again provides protection from the evil one.
We know that everyone who has been born of God does not keep on sinning, but he who was born of God protects him, and the evil one does not touch him. 1 John 5:18 (ESV)

Calvinism

Calvinism is the theological system associated with John Calvin (1509-1564). Calvin was a leader in the Protestant Reformation, the movement to reform the Roman Catholic Church. His most famous theological work is the *Institutes of the Christian Religion*. Calvinism is often contrasted with the theology of James Arminius, which is known as Arminianism. The five main theological points of Calvinism are most often referred to by the acrostic TULIP. They are:

- **Total Depravity.** Born in sin (Ephesians 2:1-4), a condition characterized by a corrupted mind, body and will. Originating with Adam and Eve, sin is passed to all in the womb (Romans 5:12-17). While this does not mean that humans are as depraved as they could be, it does mean that we are unable to act without sin's influence, and thus radically corrupted and unable to earn God's favor.
- **Unconditional Election.** God has chosen those whom he wanted to save, based solely upon his will, apart from any human action (Romans 9:15, 21; Ephesians 1:4-8).
- **Limited Atonement.** Christ's sacrificial death provides atonement for the sins of only those God has unconditionally elected to save (John 17:9, Ephesians 5:25).
- **Irresistible Grace.** All whom God has elected will respond to the offer of salvation (John 6:37, 44).
- **Perseverance of the Saints.** All who are saved by God's grace will persevere through faith to receive eternal life (John 6:39; Romans 8:30).

Many denominations are Calvinistic in their theology including: Reformed, Presbyterian, Baptist, and Congregational churches.

Church

The Church is all people whom God is saving through faith in the sacrifice of Jesus Christ (Ephesians 5:25). For this reason, the Church is an eternal community made up of those who will live forever, together with God (Hebrews 12:1). The Church is also a universal community that stretches throughout time and space, as all Christians are connected with each other through the fellowship of the Holy Spirit (1 Corinthians 12:13). Yet, the Church also has a local, visible, witness with which all Christians are to join in fellowship regularly (Hebrews 10:24-25). As the people of God, we are to come together for the purposes of reading Scripture publicly (1 Timothy 4:13), encouraging one another through song (Ephesians 5:19) and remembering Christ's sacrifice through baptism (Matthew 28:19) and communion (1 Corinthians 11:25).

The Church is the body of Christ of which Jesus is head.
And God placed all things under his feet and appointed him to be head over everything for the church, which is his body, the fullness of him who fills everything in every way. Ephesians 1:22-23 (NIV)

The Church is God's family and dwelling place.
So then you are no longer strangers and aliens, but you are fellow citizens with the saints, and are of God's household, having been built on the foundation of the apostles and prophets, Christ Jesus Himself being the cornerstone, in whom the whole building, being fitted together, is growing into a holy temple in the Lord, in whom you also are being built together into a dwelling of God in the Spirit. Ephesians 2:19-22 (NASB)

The Church is the bride of Christ.
Husbands, love your wives, just as Christ also loved the church and gave Himself for her, that He might sanctify and cleanse her with the washing of water by the word, that He might present her to Himself a glorious church,

not having spot or wrinkle or any such thing, but that she should be holy and without blemish. Ephesians 5:25-27 (NKJV)

The Church has been given authority and power.
I will give you the keys of the kingdom of heaven; and whatever you bind on earth shall have been bound in heaven, and whatever you loose on earth shall have been loosed in heaven. Matthew 16:19 (NASB)

The Church is the pillar and foundation of truth.
If I am delayed, you will know how people ought to conduct themselves in God's household, which is the church of the living God, the pillar and foundation of the truth. 1 Timothy 3:15 (NIV)

The Church grows as the Lord adds to those being saved.
And the Lord was adding to their number day by day those who were being saved. Acts 2:47 (NASB)

The Church is God's means for displaying his wisdom.
His intent was that now, through the church, the manifold wisdom of God should be made known to the rulers and authorities in the heavenly realms. Ephesians 3:10 (NIV)

The Church is headed by Christ and submits to Christ.
He is before all things, and in Him all things hold together. He is also head of the body, the church; and He is the beginning, the firstborn from the dead, so that He Himself will come to have first place in everything. Colossians 1:17-18 (NASB)

Church attendance is not to be forsaken and the Church is to prepare one another for the Day of Judgment.
Let us not give up meeting together, as some are in the habit of doing, but let us encourage one another—and all the more as you see the Day approaching. Hebrews 10:25 (NIV)

Circumcision

Circumcision is the removal of foreskin from the penis. According to Old Testament law, all Jewish males were to be circumcised eight days after birth. Circumcision was the symbol of the covenant between God and the Jews (Genesis 17:10), an indication of their acceptance and dependence upon God's promises to bless all the nations of the world through Abraham's descendants (Genesis 17:16).

Considering the *location* of this symbol on the body of the Jewish male, some insight can be gained about its significance for the Jewish people and its relationship to God's promises to Abraham. Placed on the male reproductive organ, circumcision served as an ever-present physical reminder to Abraham and Sarah of God's promise of descendants, as well as a later testimony to God's faithfulness to provide Abraham and Sarah with children (Genesis 22:18).

God's promise to Abraham has been fulfilled through Jesus Christ, as peoples from all nations enter into covenant relationship with God through faith in Jesus' death and resurrection. This is one reason that Matthew's and Luke's gospel trace Jesus' genealogy to Abraham, effectively linking Jesus with the promise given to Abraham.

Unfortunately, many Jews were physically circumcised, but spiritually untransformed. In the Old Testament book of Jeremiah, we read:

> Circumcise yourselves to the Lord; remove the foreskin of your hearts, O men of Judah and inhabitants of Jerusalem; lest my wrath go forth like fire, and burn with none to quench it, because of the evil of your deeds. Jeremiah 4:4 (ESV)

God wants his peoples' hearts to be marked by a love for him, not simply their body marked with a symbol. For this reason, there was some debate among the first Christians about whether circumcision was to continue as the mark of God's people. But the Apostle Paul settled the argument.

> But a Jew is one inwardly, and circumcision is a matter of the heart, by the Spirit, not by the letter. Romans 2:29 (ESV)

Paul's point is that we are "marked" as God's people when our hearts are transformed by a love for God, and he draws a direct link between the Old Testament symbol of circumcision and the New Testament symbol of baptism.

> In Christ you were also circumcised, in the putting off of the sinful nature, not with a circumcision done by the hands of men but with the circumcision done by Christ, having been buried with him in baptism and raised with him through your faith in the power of God, who raised him from the dead. Colossians 2:11-12 (NIV)

Today, the outward sign of the new covenant is baptism (1 Peter 3:20-22), which is the symbol of one's faith in Jesus's death and resurrection. While many continue to be circumcised for reasons other than religious, which is fine, Paul explains that if we trust in an outward conformity to the Old Testament law for our salvation, then the sacrifice of Jesus Christ is of no advantage to us.

> Look: I, Paul, say to you that if you accept circumcision, Christ will be of no advantage to you. Galatians 5:2 (ESV)

Paul is urging us to trust solely in the finished work of Jesus on the cross and his resurrection for salvation and to put no confidence in the works of our own flesh (Philippians 3:3).

Clean and Unclean in Old Testament Laws

"Clean" and "unclean" was a ceremonial designation, which indicated whether a person, animal or object was fit to enter the Tabernacle or Temple of God. To be clean was to be "pure" or "holy," and fit for God's presence. To be unclean was to be "impure" or "unholy," and unfit for God's presence. While being clean and unclean was simply a ceremonial designation, it had spiritual, physical, and relational implications.

Being unclean excluded one from the normal activities of life (Leviticus 7:20-21, Numbers 5:3, 9:6-13, Deuteronomy 26:14), and from entering the Tabernacle or Temple (Leviticus 21:1-4, 11-12). To continue in uncleanliness placed individuals, as well as all Israel, under God's judgment and potentially in a position to receive God's condemnation (Leviticus 15:31, Leviticus 17:16, Leviticus 18:25).

The ordinary state of the Israelites was clean, but a person could become unclean by touching the carcasses of or eating meat from unclean animals (Leviticus 11), giving birth or helping deliver a child (Leviticus 12), contracting a skin disease or having mold in one's house (Leviticus 13), and discharging almost any bodily fluid (Leviticus 15), as well as touching a dead human body (Numbers 5:2).

The steps in purification (i.e., becoming clean again after being made unclean) varied, depending upon the severity of one's uncleanliness. Contracting a skin disease was one of the most severe types of uncleanliness and required that a person be placed outside the camp. One could only reenter after being purified outside the camp, which included sacrificing certain animals, washing their clothes, and shaving off all of their hair (even their eyebrows). These tasks were to be done over a seven-day period (Leviticus 14:1-9). On the eighth day, once they had reentered the community, more sacrifices were made and they were to be anointed with oil by the priest (Leviticus 14:10-32).

The purification process always involved a waiting period of some amount of time, whether inside or outside the camp. Due to Jesus' birth, Mary waited the allotted 40 days before traveling from Bethlehem to the Temple in Jerusalem for purification (Leviticus 12:1-8, Luke 2:22).

The lesson taught by the system of purification is that God is holy and humans are contaminated by sin. Everyone must be purified to approach God, and purification was made by offering the prescribed sacrifices (Leviticus 5:1-5, 16:16-22). In fact, it was the prohibition against eating the blood of an animal that reminded Israel of the necessity of blood sacrifice in cleansing sinful humanity (Leviticus 17:10-14).

Ultimately, it is the reality of uncleanliness that helps us understand our need for the final and perfect sacrifice of Jesus (John 6:53-54). Paul wrote that the law is a "tutor" leading us to an understanding of our need for faith in Jesus' sacrificial death (Galatians 3:24). The good news of the gospel is that the purity that the law was unable to provide, God has provided to all those who have faith in Jesus Christ (Romans 3:21-24).

Interestingly, Jesus was very clear about his respect for God's law (Matthew 5:17), while at the same time not allowing the reality of uncleanliness to prevent him from caring for others. Jesus often made physical contact with those who were unclean. He touched lepers (Matthew 8:1-4, Mark 1:40-45, Luke 17:11-17). He also touched dead bodies (Matthew 9:25, Mark 5:41, Luke 8:54), and on several occasions brought those who had died back to life. He also allowed a prostitute to touch him (Luke 7:36-38), as well as a woman who had been menstruating for twelve years (Matthew 9:20-22, Mark 5:27). Jesus was clearly not defiled when he came into contact with those who were unclean, and he went through no ceremonial purification. Rather, those who came near to him were all cleansed and healed. In other words, Jesus' holiness made the unclean, clean.

Communion

Communion is the meal of remembrance shared by all trusting in Jesus' death for salvation. The word "Communion" denotes the connection, or fellowship, created between those having faith in Jesus. Established by Jesus on the night before his crucifixion (1 Corinthians 11:23), Communion is often referred to as the Last Supper or the Lord's Supper, Communion is also referred to as the Eucharist, which is derived from a Greek word meaning "thanksgiving" (1 Corinthians 11:24), as participants give thanks for Jesus' sacrifice.

Consisting simply of bread and drink, the Communion meal commemorates Jesus' broken body (bread) and shed blood (drink), and is the replacement meal for the Jewish meal of remembrance called the Passover (Exodus 11-12). As the replacement meal for Passover, Communion's remembrance of Jesus' shed blood and broken body is described as a picture of the traditional Passover sacrifice of a lamb (1 Corinthians 5:7).

In the Old Testament, the Passover meal served as a reminder of God's miraculous deliverance of his people from the tenth plague, which was brought against Egypt (Exodus 12:13). Israelite families who smeared the blood of a slain lamb on the doorposts of their house were protected from God's wrath, which was poured out on Egypt during the tenth plague.

In a similar way, Jesus became the sacrificial lamb, spilling his blood, to protect us from certain death because of God's wrath against our sinfulness. And just as the Passover meal was given by God to the Israelites as a celebration of God's deliverance from death in the tenth plague, communion was given by Jesus to his followers as a celebration of God's deliverance from the death brought to us through our sin. For this reason, when Christians regularly partake of Communion together, it is an effective means for proclaiming the good news of the forgiveness of sin through Jesus Christ (1 Corinthians 11:26).

Communion was established by Jesus during Passover.
He said, "Go into the city to a certain man and say to him, 'The Teacher says, My time is at hand. I will keep the Passover at your house with my disciples.'" Matthew 26:18 (ESV)

Jesus instituted Communion the night before his death.
And He took bread, gave thanks and broke it, and gave it to them, saying, "This is My body which is given for you; do this in remembrance of Me." Likewise He also took the cup after supper, saying, "This cup is the new covenant in My blood, which is shed for you. Luke 22:19-20 (NKJV)

Communion is a reminder of Jesus' sacrifice on the cross.
On the night when he was betrayed, the Lord Jesus took some bread and gave thanks to God for it. Then he broke it in pieces and said, "This is my body, which is given for you. Do this to remember me." In the same way, he took the cup of wine after supper, saying, "This cup is the new covenant between God and his people—an agreement confirmed with my blood. Do this to remember me as often as you drink it." For every time you eat this bread and drink this cup, you are announcing the Lord's death until he comes again. 1 Corinthians 11:23-26 (NLT)

Communion is a means for proclaiming the Lord's death.
For whenever you eat this bread and drink this cup, you proclaim the Lord's death until he comes. 1 Corinthians 11:26 (NIV)

Communion is to be taken only after self-examination.
So anyone who eats this bread or drinks this cup of the Lord unworthily is guilty of sinning against the body and blood of the Lord. That is why you should examine yourself before eating the bread and drinking the cup. For if you eat the bread or drink the cup without honoring the body of Christ, you are eating and drinking God's judgment upon yourself. 1 Corinthians 11:27-29 (NLT)

Confession of Sin

Confession is the act of acknowledging or admitting. Sin is any attitude or action contrary to the character of God. Confession of sin includes either the acknowledgment of specific sins or the admission of one's sinfulness in general.

When we sin, we break God's law (1 John 3:4), offending God, as well as often offending other people in the process. For this reason, we are directed in Scripture to not only confess our sin to God, but also to one another. The good news of the gospel is that when we confess our sin to God we are promised his forgiveness. And when we confess our sin to one another we are directed to extend forgiveness to one another, just as God has shown us forgiveness (Colossians 3:13).

Confession of sin brings God's forgiveness.
I acknowledged my sin to you, and I did not cover my iniquity; I said, "I will confess my transgressions to the LORD," and you forgave the iniquity of my sin. Psalm 32:5 (ESV)

Confessing of sin brings God's compassion.
He who conceals his transgressions will not prosper, but he who confesses and forsakes them will find compassion. Proverbs 28:13 (NASB)

Confession of sin brings God's cleansing.
If we confess our sins, he is faithful and just to forgive us our sins and to cleanse us from all unrighteousness. 1 John 1:9 (ESV)

Confession of sin was a part of John the Baptist's ministry.
Then Jerusalem and all Judea and all the region about the Jordan were going out to him, and they were baptized by him in the river Jordan, confessing their sins. Matthew 3:5-6 (ESV)

Confession of sin accompanies repentance and leads to salvation.
Also many of those who were now believers came, confessing and divulging their practices. Acts 19:18 (ESV)

Confession of sin is to take place one to another.
Therefore, confess your sins to one another and pray for one another, that you may be healed. The prayer of a righteous person has great power as it is working. James 5:16 (ESV)

Confession of sin is to be a part of healing prayer.
Therefore, confess your sins to one another and pray for one another, that you may be healed. The prayer of a righteous person has great power as it is working. James 5:16 (ESV)

Confession of sin is to take precedence over worship.
Therefore if you are presenting your offering at the altar, and there remember that your brother has something against you, leave your offering there before the altar and go; first be reconciled to your brother, and then come and present your offering. Matthew 5:23-24 (NASB)

Conviction

Conviction is a firmly held belief, and Jesus described the Holy Spirit's work as that of convicting humanity of some very particular truths. Jesus said about the Holy Spirit,

> He will convict the world concerning sin and righteousness and judgment: concerning sin, because they do not believe in me; concerning righteousness, because I go to the Father, and you will see me no longer; concerning judgment, because the ruler of this world is judged. John 16:8-11 (ESV)

Here, the word "convict" is best understood from a legal perspective. Much like a jury might be persuaded to believe the facts in a case by an attorney, the Holy Spirit convicts, or "convinces," people of their sinfulness, and the certainty of coming judgement because of their sinfulness, as well as their need for forgiveness through faith in the righteousness of Jesus.

This means biblical conviction is different from our feelings of conviction. Biblical conviction is a firmly held belief, which is based upon convincing evidence provided by the Holy Spirit. Having feelings such as shame because of our sinfulness, or fear about coming judgement, or even love for Jesus are appropriate and may accompany conviction. However, these feelings are not the same as conviction. Conviction brought by the Holy Spirit is an affirmation of the factual evidence that sin exists, judgement is coming, and Jesus' death alone is sufficient to cover our sin.

Drawing a distinction between our feelings and biblical conviction is important because our feelings often change, while the facts about sin, judgment, and our need for faith in the righteousness of Jesus do not change. Further, distinguishing between one's feelings and the facts is important because in some cases one's feelings may not align with the facts.

For example, one may feel no shame regarding particular sin, all the while remaining condemned by God because of those same sins. Or one might feel fear of condemnation for sin, when in reality standing forgiven by God through faith in Jesus. Many people are haunted by feelings of shame and fear, even after repenting of sin and trusting in Jesus for forgiveness. The good news of the gospel is that the reality of God's love shown towards us is independent of one's feelings.

The good news is that our condemnation before God because of sin, as well as God's love shown toward us even in our sinful state, are facts that we can base our lives upon regardless of how we feel. While feelings of shame and fear may remind us of our condemnation because of our sin, in the end these feelings are overcome by the realities of the gospel, and over time those feelings may be replaced with feelings of love and peace and joy through faith in Jesus.

Biblical conviction is also more than simply knowledge of right and wrong. Conviction involves moral knowledge, but biblical conviction goes far beyond simply affirming godliness and condemning ungodliness. Biblical conviction includes both an understanding and embracing of truth. In other words, biblical conviction always results in a change of our perspective, as well as a change of behavior. Biblical conviction always results in a willful effort to honor God with one's life.

Distinguishing between ethical knowledge and biblical conviction is vital because behaving morally is not synonymous with being convicted by the Holy Spirit. There are lots of highly moral people who have not been convicted by the Holy Spirit. While conviction involves a recognition of sinful behavior and the condemnation we deserve as a result, biblical conviction ultimately leads us toward a posture of trust in the righteousness of Jesus. In other words, the goal of conviction brought by the Holy Spirit is never simply better behavior, but rather greater trust in the only One who is truly moral, Jesus.

Creation Theories of Genesis 1

Christians offer many different interpretations of Genesis 1. Although there is room for disagreement there is also essential doctrine for all Christians to embrace. For example, all Christians must embrace God as Creator (Genesis 1:1, Colossians 1:16, Hebrews 11:3), and humanity as uniquely created in God's image, distinct from all other animals (Genesis 1:26-27, Genesis 9:6, Ephesians 4:24). The following is a summary of John Walton's interpretation from the book, *The Lost World of Genesis One* (IVP).

Beyond affirming essential doctrines, we must be careful not to assume that what we want to know about God's creative work is what the ancient author addressed. As moderns with a scientific worldview, we most often want to know *how* God created (e.g., intelligent design or evolution). However, in the ancient world the questions surrounding creation were about *who* created and *why* they created. We must be careful not to impose our scientific questions on the ancient text, but rather accept the answers provided to the questions they were asking.

A distinction between the "how" and the "why" of creation, is clearly seen in the Hebrew verb translated in Genesis 1:1 as "created," which is never used to describe the act of making material. Instead, this word always refers to organizing existing material so that it is functional. While it is true that God did in fact make all material (Hebrews 11:3), that is not what Genesis 1 is necessarily describing. Rather, Genesis 1 describes the organization of all materials for a particular purpose and person, namely God and his glory. Just as an artist might hover over a dark canvas ordering the colors applied to the canvas for a particular purpose, God hovered over the darkness of the cosmos and ordered the materials of the universe for his glory (Genesis 1:2). Understanding the non-scientific view of the ancient world, as well as the meaning of keywords, the passage communicates what God intended.

The first act of creation was separating night from day (Genesis 1:3-4). But how can we have daylight without the Sun? Again, Genesis 1 is not a scientific explanation of creation, but rather an organizing of the cosmos for functionality, and the single greatest organizing element in creation is "time." During day one God separated night from day, which is to say that he created time.

Similarly, the second day of creation separated the waters above from the waters below, creating the sea and the sky, whose functional impact on the globe was creating weather (Genesis 1:6-8). Separating the sea from the sky created wind and rain, which drive our weather patterns.

On day three God gathered the waters below into one place, creating dry land whose purpose is to support vegetation (Genesis 1:9-11). God hovered over the cosmic mess and created a functional universe, so we have night and day (time), sky and sea (weather), and dry land (agriculture). What was previously formless is now functional and must be filled with functionaries, those who will bring God glory through their service.

On the fourth day, God filled what he had formed on the first day, the night and the day, with the Sun, Moon and the stars. The function of time now has heavenly lights that serve as the functionaries. On the fifth day, God filled what he formed on the second day, the sea and the sky, with the functionaries of fish and birds. And on the sixth day, God filled what he formed on the third day, dry land, with animals of every kind, as well as with mankind, who is uniquely created to bear his image (Genesis 1:27, Colossians 1:16).

Having made the world functional (i.e., days 1-3) and having filled it with functionaries (i.e., days 4-6), God rested from all his work on day seven, receiving the glory he alone is due. From an ancient author's and ancient audience's perspective this interpretation addresses the most urgent questions of who and why we were created.

Cults

The word "cult" is derived from the Latin term *cultus*, which means to "care." In the ancient world a cult was a group of people dedicated to the "care" of a particular deity through various worship rituals. For example, each of the ancient Greek gods (e.g., Zeus and Apollo) had cultic worshippers who were dedicated to their veneration. The Imperial Cult of Rome supported the worship of Roman emperors, and Rome labeled any who refused to participate in this particular cult as traitors, which brought great persecution upon the earliest Christians.

In our modern context "cult" has come to mean something much different. Today, a cult is defined by Christians as any group whose beliefs and/or actions have perverted the teachings of historic Christianity. The Apostle Paul warned that these groups would come and wrote to alert pastor Timothy of their deceptions (1 Timothy 4:1-2, 2 Timothy 4:3-4).

Rather than altogether rejecting the claims of Christianity, as other major world religions do, cults adopt a portion of Christian theology, while making select changes to essential beliefs. Some essential teachings that are most often twisted by cults are: the doctrine of the Trinity, the role and relationship of the Holy Spirit within the Trinity, the deity of Jesus, the bodily death and resurrection of Jesus, and the immortality of the human soul.

For example, many cults will accept Jesus as a great teacher, but reject his claim to deity. In their attempt to make this claim fit with the teachings of Scripture they will change subtle aspects of the biblical text. This is common in John 1:1, which is often translated by cultists as "the Word was *a* God," rather than the accepted and grammatically accurate translation, which reads "the Word *was* God." Some of the most recognized cults include: The Way International, Unification Church (Moonies), Hare Krishna, Mormonism (Latter Day Saints), and Jehovah's Witnesses.

Deacon

The word "deacon" is a translation of a Greek word that means servant. Jesus used this Greek word to describe his service through suffering and death on the cross for the forgiveness of sin (Matthew 20:28, Mark 10:45).

In the New Testament, deacon may refer to virtually any type of service, whether offering personal assistance to others or administrative oversight within the church. The role of deacon is most clearly exemplified in Acts 6:1-7, as the earliest Christians selected seven men to provide oversight in the daily distribution of food to the poor. In 1 Timothy 3:8-13 the Apostle Paul offers a list of the character requirements for holding this office. In that the ability to teach and lead is not specifically mentioned as qualifications for the role of deacon, most have viewed this role as a support role to elder leadership. While many churches may not refer to those serving as a "deacon," every church will need men and women filling this role.

Deacons were a part of the earliest church organization.
I am writing to all of God's holy people in Philippi who belong to Christ Jesus, including the elders and deacons. Philippians 1:1 (NLT)

Deacons were both male and female in the early church.
I commend to you our sister Phoebe, who is a deacon in the church in Cenchrea. Welcome her in the Lord as one who is worthy of honor among God's people. Help her in whatever she needs, for she has been helpful to many, and especially to me. Romans 16:1-2 (NLT)

Deacons must demonstrate good character to serve.
In the same way, deacons must be well respected and have integrity. They must not be heavy drinkers or dishonest with money. They must be committed to the mystery of the faith now revealed and must live with a clear conscience. 1 Timothy 3:8-9 (NLT)

Deacons must pass a character evaluation before serving.
Before they are appointed as deacons, let them be closely examined. If they pass the test, then let them serve as deacons. 1 Timothy 3:10 (NLT)

A deacon's spouse must demonstrate good character.
*In the same way, their wives must be respected and must not slander others. They must exercise self-control and be faithful in everything they do.
1 Timothy 3:11 (NLT)*

Deacons who serve well are to be respected.
A deacon must be faithful to his wife, and he must manage his children and household well. Those who do well as deacons will be rewarded with respect from others and will have increased confidence in their faith in Christ Jesus. 1 Timothy 3:12-13 (NLT)

Death

Death is the end of all biological function, which includes all physical movement and metabolism. The human experience of death is the result of sin's entry into the world (Romans 5:12, Romans 6:23), which was not God's intended design for humanity. God is the source of all life (Romans 4:17, Colossians 1:15-16) and it was God who placed the Tree of Life in the Garden of Eden (Genesis 2:9), from which humanity was to eat and live eternally.

While our death is no more a surprise to God than our birth (Psalms 139:16), death is a difficult subject for most people to discuss. Death causes feelings of fear for many, but the Bible encourages us to consider our death and offers comfort to all those trusting in Jesus' resurrection for eternal life.

Death is certain and we should live with this awareness.
Death is the destiny of every man; the living should take this to heart. Ecclesiastes 7:2 (NIV)

Death brings Christians into God's presence.
Jesus answered him, "I tell you the truth, today you will be with me in paradise." Luke 23:43 (NIV)

We are confident, I say, and would prefer to be away from the body and at home with the Lord. 2 Corinthians 5:8 (NIV)

Death is the result of sin, but Jesus provides life.
For the wages of sin is death, but the gift of God is eternal life in Christ Jesus our Lord. Romans 6:23 (NIV)

So then as through one transgression there resulted condemnation to all men, even so through one act of righteousness there resulted justification of life to all men. Romans 5:18 (NASB)

Death is not to be feared by Christians.
Even though I walk through the valley of the shadow of death, I fear no evil, for You are with me; Your rod and Your staff, they comfort me. Psalm 23:4 (NASB)

Death is a gain for Christians, as we go to be with Christ.
For to me, to live is Christ and to die is gain. If I am to go on living in the body, this will mean fruitful labor for me. Yet what shall I choose? I do not know! I am torn between the two: I desire to depart and be with Christ, which is better by far; but it is more necessary for you that I remain in the body. Philippians 1:21-24 (NIV)

Death can be the result of obedience to God's commands.
Do not be afraid of what you are about to suffer. I tell you, the devil will put some of you in prison to test you, and you will suffer persecution for ten days. Be faithful, even to the point of death, and I will give you the crown of life. Revelation 2:10 (NIV)

Demons and Exorcism

Demons are spirit beings, associated with Satan, who attack people (1 Peter 5:8). Their origin is not clear, but some believe they are angels who rebelled against God (Matthew 25:41). In the New Testament, demons are often described as "unclean" or "evil" spirits (Mark 1:26, 5:2-3, 7:26, Acts 5:16), and their activities are expected to increase in the last days (I Timothy 4:1, Revelation 16:13-14).

"Exorcism" is the term used for removing demons from a person (Mark 5:15). The common biblical description for having a demon is "possession," but this word is misleading. Christians cannot be "possessed" (i.e., owned) by a demon, as they are children of God and are possessed by the Holy Spirit (1 John 3:10, 1 Corinthians 6:19). Demons are not presented as owners in Scripture, but rather as invaders. The Greek words translated as possession are *daimonizomai* or *echein daimonion*, which mean "to be under the influence of a demon" or "to have a demon." Therefore, a more accurate description is to say that someone is "demonized," meaning they have a demon influencing them. Much like a burglar invades a home, we may be invaded and/or influenced by demons, and the continuum of influence can range from mild to severe, even life threatening. For this reason, the Bible tells Christians to stop giving a place to the devil (Ephesians 4:27) and to resist the devil's influence (James 4:7).

Demons were cast out of people by the name of Jesus.
The seventy-two returned with joy, saying, "Lord, even the demons are subject to us in your name!" Luke 10:17 (ESV)

Demons are not to be feared by Christians.
Behold, I have given you authority to tread on serpents and scorpions, and over all the power of the enemy, and nothing shall hurt you. Luke 10:19 (ESV)

Demons bring destruction to those they influence.
And when Jesus had stepped out of the boat, immediately there met him out of the tombs a man with an unclean spirit. He lived among the tombs. And no one could bind him anymore, not even with a chain, for he had often been bound with shackles and chains, but he wrenched the chains apart, and he broke the shackles in pieces. No one had the strength to subdue him. Night and day among the tombs and on the mountains he was always crying out and cutting himself with stones. Mark 5:2-5 (ESV)

Demons were cast out of people by Jesus and his disciples.
But if it is by the Spirit of God that I cast out demons, then the kingdom of God has come upon you. Matthew 12:28 (ESV)

And proclaim as you go, saying, 'The kingdom of heaven is at hand.' Heal the sick, raise the dead, cleanse lepers, cast out demons. Matthew 10:7-8 (ESV)

Then some of the itinerant Jewish exorcists undertook to invoke the name of the Lord Jesus over those who had evil spirits, saying, "I adjure you by the Jesus whom Paul proclaims." Seven sons of a Jewish high priest named Sceva were doing this. But the evil spirit answered them, "Jesus I know, and Paul I recognize, but who are you?" And the man in whom was the evil spirit leaped on them, mastered all of them and overpowered them, so that they fled out of that house naked and wounded. Acts 19:13-16 (ESV)

Demons author the "wisdom" accepted in the world.
Such "wisdom" does not come down from heaven but is earthly, unspiritual, demonic. James 3:15 (NIV)

Demons can perform signs and lead people astray.
They are demonic spirits that perform signs, and they go out to the kings of the whole world, to gather them for the battle on the great day of God Almighty. Revelation 16:14 (NIV)

Denominationalism

A denomination is a subgroup. For the first fifteen hundred years of Church history there were no denominations. Today there are many. We wrongly assume that having different denominations indicates that there is little doctrinal agreement among Christians. That is not the case. In fact, denominations were originally formed to preserve the unity among Christians. Allowing for disagreement over certain "non-essential" doctrines, the existence of denominations demonstrates that there is unity among Christians on "essential" doctrines.

Historically, non-essential doctrines have been defined as any doctrine that does not bear directly on salvation. For example, some have wanted the freedom to celebrate communion or to baptize, believing the Bible prescribed a particular form for these practices. Denominationalism allows for differences in these types of worship practices without disunity. In this way, denominationalism allows for a distinction to be drawn between what may seem to some an important theological conviction (e.g., mode of baptism), and what is a vital theological conviction (e.g., deity of Jesus). Denominations allow for important differences of opinion, while preserving unity on vital beliefs.

Picture denominations like branches on a tree. Although each branch is distinct and separated from the other branches, they all stem from a single trunk. In the case of denominations, the trunk from which all branches stem is the Apostles' teaching (Acts 2:42). Some of the essential doctrinal beliefs that all Christian denominations embrace are: the deity of Jesus, the bodily death and resurrection of Jesus, the Trinity, and the return of Jesus.

Some of the main denominations are Roman Catholicism, Eastern Orthodoxy, Anglicanism (Episcopalian),

Presbyterianism, Lutheranism, Methodism, Pentecostalism and Baptist. Roman Catholicism is the oldest denomination.

Several of these Christian denominations are often referred to as "Protestant" denominations, which is a name derived from their common theological heritage in the sixteenth century "protest" against certain Roman Catholic abuses of power. This period of protest is known as the Reformation, as members of the Roman Catholic Church called for reforms in governance and theology. Frustrated by Roman Catholic resistance, new denominations formed.

While these new Protestant denominations varied in the degree to which they differed with Roman Catholic theology and practice, they were generally formed around a doctrinal emphasis on 1) the authority and supremacy of the Bible in all matters of faith and practice, 2) justification by grace alone through faith alone in Jesus Christ, and 3) the priesthood of all believers.

These three doctrinal foundations stood in stark contrast to Roman Catholic doctrine that teaches 1) a combination of both Scriptural and Papal authority in matters of faith and practice, 2) justification by grace, faith and sacramental observance, and 3) the priesthood as a separate class of believers called by God to lead the church.

Some of the larger Protestant denominations include: Methodist, Baptist, Congregational, Lutheran, Presbyterian, and Pentecostal. And while all Protestant branches of the Christian faith have historically affirmed the essential doctrinal beliefs of the faith, some Protestant denominations have begun to stray from their orthodox theological heritage. For this reason, it is wise when selecting a community of faith with which to worship, that one investigates their theology, making sure that the church is a good match for one's beliefs.

Discerning God's Will

The "will" of God is mentioned often in Scripture and is described as having both hidden and revealed elements. Those intentions known only by God are described as his "hidden" will, while those intentions made known to humanity through Scripture represent his "revealed" will (Deuteronomy 29:29). Concerning our being saved through faith in Jesus Christ, the Apostle Paul wrote that which was once hidden has now been fully revealed as God's will for mankind (Ephesians 1:9).

Beyond God's will in salvation though, possibly the single most common prayer request made is for understanding God's will regarding specific situations in life, particularly when facing major life decisions. The good news is that God wants us to know his will. At the same time, God has not provided a blueprint for our lives, a specific set of instructions detailing every step we are to take in every situation. Instead, God has provided what is better described as a game plan, or boundaries within which we are to operate. Living according to God's game plan means living a lifestyle of obedience to God's commands, and those who live within these boundaries are better enabled to discern God's particular will in a specific situation.

Discerning God's will requires obeying Jesus' teaching.
If anyone chooses to do God's will, he will find out whether my teaching comes from God or whether I speak on my own. John 7:17 (NIV)

Discerning God's will is made possible by the Holy Spirit.
Likewise the Spirit also helps in our weaknesses. For we do not know what we should pray for as we ought, but the Spirit Himself makes intercession for us with groanings which cannot be uttered. Now He who searches the hearts knows what the mind of the Spirit is, because He makes intercession for the saints according to the will of God. Romans 8:26-27 (NKJV)

Discerning God's will comes as we renew our mind.
Do not conform any longer to the pattern of this world, but be transformed by the renewing of your mind. Then you will be able to test and approve what God's will is—his good, pleasing and perfect will. Romans 12:2 (NIV)

Discerning God's will means being sanctified.
It is God's will that you should be sanctified: that you should avoid sexual immorality. 1 Thessalonians 4:3 (NIV)

Discerning God's will includes embracing faith.
Be joyful always; pray continually; give thanks in all circumstances, for this is God's will for you in Christ Jesus. 1 Thessalonians 5:16-18 (NIV)

Discerning God's will is God's desire for us and will include being filled with the Spirit.
So then do not be foolish, but understand what the will of the Lord is. And do not get drunk with wine, for that is dissipation, but be filled with the Spirit, speaking to one another in psalms and hymns and spiritual songs, singing and making melody with your heart to the Lord; always giving thanks for all things in the name of our Lord Jesus Christ to God, even the Father; and be subject to one another in the fear of Christ. Ephesians 5:17-21 (NASB)

Discipleship

A disciple is a follower, and discipleship is the practice of following a particular person. In the first-century world disciples were those who detached themselves from their own way of life and reattached themselves to a *rabbi* (teacher), committing themselves to his service and to becoming like him in every possible way. So complete was a disciple's commitment to the rabbi that it became the defining element of their character, and the nature of what it means to be a disciple of Jesus has not changed in over 2000 years.

Accepting the invitation to follow Jesus in the twenty-first century is still to be a first-century commitment. Jesus is still looking for men and women who will disrupt their lives, attach themselves to him in the most intimate of relationships, and begin reflecting his person and carrying out his purposes in their everyday lives. While the experience of discipleship may look dramatically different in the twenty-first century, the nature of discipleship has not changed in over two millennia.

Discipleship was practiced among the ancient prophets.
Bind up the testimony; seal the teaching among my disciples. Isaiah 8:16 (ESV)

As John's disciples were leaving, Jesus began talking about him to the crowds. "What kind of man did you go into the wilderness to see? Was he a weak reed, swayed by every breath of wind? Matthew 11:7 (NLT)

Discipleship results from Jesus revealing himself to us.
Then the disciples came and said to him, "Why do you speak to them in parables?" And he answered them, "To you it has been given to know the secrets of the kingdom of heaven, but to them it has not been given. Matthew 13:10-11 (ESV)

You did not choose me, but I chose you and appointed you that you should go and bear fruit. John 15:16 (ESV)

Discipleship means prioritizing a relationship with Jesus.
If anyone comes to me and does not hate his own father and mother and wife and children and brothers and sisters, yes, and even his own life, he cannot be my disciple. Luke 14:25-26 (ESV)

As disciples, our relationship with Jesus is familial.
Who is my mother, and who are my brothers?" And stretching out his hand toward his disciples, he said, "Here are my mother and my brothers! For whoever does the will of my Father in heaven is my brother and sister and mother." Matthew 12:48-49 (ESV)

Our discipleship is confirmed as we bear fruit.
By this my Father is glorified, that you bear much fruit and so prove to be my disciples. John 15:8 (ESV)

You did not choose me, but I chose you and appointed you so that you might go and bear fruit —fruit that will last—and so that whatever you ask in my name the Father will give you. John 15:16 (NIV)

Discipleship means receiving Jesus' commission to go.
Jesus came and said to them, "All authority in heaven and on earth has been given to me. Go therefore and make disciples of all nations, baptizing them in the name of the Father and of the Son and of the Holy Spirit, teaching them to observe all that I have commanded you. And behold, I am with you always, to the end of the age." Matthew 28:18-20 (ESV)

Discipleship is demonstrated by the love we show others.
By this all people will know that you are my disciples, if you have love for one another." John 13:35 (ESV)

Discipline within the Church

Discipline within the Church is the process of helping correct sinful attitudes and actions of other Christians, as well as working to restore the damage done to relationships by sinful behavior. Church discipline has both informal and formal aspects, with most discipline happening at an informal level.

Informally, discipline happens any time Scripture is taught, in that God's Word is useful for correcting, rebuking, and encouraging one another (2 Timothy 4:2). Formally, discipline is to follow a biblically prescribed process, being done first in private (one-to-one), then before other witnesses (one-to-a-few), and then finally the entire church (one-to-many) (Matthew 18:15-17). The goal at each step in the process is to turn one from their sin and bring them to repentance (Galatians 6:1-2).

Our posture in discipline must be one of humility, admitting that we are all sinners saved by grace and recognizing the unique temptation to correct minor issues in other's lives while ignoring greater issues within ourselves (Matthew 7:1-5). At the same time, we are not to shy away from discipline, understanding the direct link between our actions on earth and the spiritual reality in heaven (Matthew 18:18-20). Instead, we are to discipline others without fear, convinced that unaddressed sin compromises the Church's witness (1 Corinthians 5:6-7).

Discipline has as its goal teaching and salvation.

You must call a meeting of the church. I will be present with you in spirit, and so will the power of our Lord Jesus. Then you must throw this man out and hand him over to Satan so that his sinful nature will be destroyed and he himself will be saved on the day the Lord returns.
1 Corinthians 5:4-5 (NLT)

Among them are Hymenaeus and Alexander, whom I have handed over to Satan to be taught not to blaspheme. 1 Timothy 1:20 (NIV)

Discipline is needed as some reject sound doctrine.
For the time will come when they will not endure sound doctrine; but wanting to have their ears tickled, they will accumulate for themselves teachers in accordance to their own desires, and will turn away their ears from the truth and will turn aside to myths. 2 Timothy 4:3-4 (NASB)

Discipline is to be done gently by the spiritual.
Brothers, if someone is caught in a sin, you who are spiritual should restore him gently. But watch yourself, or you also may be tempted. Carry each other's burdens, and in this way you will fulfill the law of Christ. Galatians 6:1-2 (NIV)

The Lord's bond-servant must not be quarrelsome, but be kind to all, able to teach, patient when wronged, with gentleness correcting those who are in opposition, if perhaps God may grant them repentance leading to the knowledge of the truth, and they may come to their senses and escape from the snare of the devil, having been held captive by him to do his will. 2 Timothy 2:24-26 (NASB)

Discipline was practiced by early church leaders.
But Peter said, "Ananias, why has Satan filled your heart to lie to the Holy Spirit and to keep back some of the price of the land? While it remained unsold, did it not remain your own? And after it was sold, was it not under your control? Why is it that you have conceived this deed in your heart? You have not lied to men but to God." And as he heard these words, Ananias fell down and breathed his last; and great fear came over all who heard of it. The young men got up and covered him up, and after carrying him out, they buried him. Acts 5:1-6 (NASB)

Dispensationalism

Dispensationalism is a theological system that divides biblical history into different periods (i.e., dispensations), and describes God as working with mankind uniquely in each period. It was popularized by John Nelson Darby (1800-1882), who was a leader in the Plymouth Brethren Movement.

Fundamental to dispensationalism is the divide between the period of God's work in and through Israel and the period of God's work in and through the Church. This divide is crucial as it influences the dispensational interpretation of God's work at the end of time when Jesus Christ returns to set up his millennial kingdom. The dispensational view stands in contrast to historic "replacement" theology, which teaches that the church is the replacement of Israel as the people of God and the fulfillment and receiver of the Old Testament promises to Israel. Dispensationalists believe that God has yet to complete his work with Israel and they teach that God will finish a unique and separate work with both Israel and the Church.

While there has been some disagreement between dispensationalists on exactly how many dispensations there have been in history, ranging from as many as eight to as few as three, all Christians agree that there have been at least two unique periods to God's work of redemption in history, as all Christians divide God's work between the Old Testament and the New Testament. The seven classic dispensations are:

- **The Dispensation of Innocence**. The period beginning with creation, but before the fall of humanity into sin (Genesis 1-2).

- **The Dispensation of Conscience**. The period beginning with the fall of humanity into sin and lasting until Noah's deliverance from the flood in the Ark (Genesis 3-9).

- **The Dispensation of Government.** The period beginning with Noah and lasting until Abraham, as man began to establish himself on the earth (Genesis 10-11)

- **The Dispensation of Patriarchal Rule.** The period beginning with Abraham and lasting until Moses, as God first called the Israelites to worship him (Genesis 12-Exodus 19).

- **The Dispensation of Mosaic Law.** The period beginning with the Law given to Moses and lasting until the birth of Jesus Christ, including the writings of the Old Testament law, history, poetry and prophets (Exodus 20-Malachi 4).

- **The Dispensation of Grace.** The period beginning with Christ's establishment of the new covenant through his death and the gathering of the Church to himself, as described in the four Gospels and the book of Acts.

- **The Dispensation of the Millennial Kingdom.** The period beginning with Jesus Christ's return to rapture his Church and establish his 1000-year reign on the earth. This period has not started yet.

Divorce

Divorce is the legal dissolution of a marriage. While the Bible does not encourage divorce in any situation, it does guide and care for those seeking a divorce.

In that marriage is designed as an indissoluble union, divorce is always outside God's desire for a married couple (Matthew 19:6). This means that divorce is never morally neutral and is always the product of sin, whether in one or both spouse's lives (Matthew 19:8). For this reason, Paul wrote plainly that divorce should not happen among God's people (1 Corinthians 7:10-11).

Although there is much debate among Christians over the biblical permissibility of divorce, specifically in situations involving adultery, abandonment, and/or abuse (Matthew 5:32, 19:9; 1 Corinthians 7:15), we know that God always desires reconciliation between spouses (1 Corinthians 7:10-11). For this reason, the church should not recommend divorce, but should rather encourage patience and hope in God's ability to heal and restore marriage relationships (2 Corinthians 5:18).

At the same time, because divorces do occur within Christ's community, the church has a responsibility to care for the divorced. Therefore, while the church is to work for the preservation of all marriages, it is also to eagerly extend grace to those who fail in marriage, realizing that God longs to do a work of repair and restoration in every person's life.

Divorce was not a part of God's original design.
Some Pharisees came to him to test him. They asked, "Is it lawful for a man to divorce his wife for any and every reason?" "Haven't you read," he replied, "that at the beginning the Creator 'made them male and female,' and said, 'For this reason a man will leave his father and mother and be united to his wife, and the two will become one flesh'? So they are no longer two, but one. Therefore what God has joined together, let man not separate." Matthew 19:3-6 (NIV)

Divorce is a product of hardheartedness.
"Why then," they asked, "did Moses command that a man give his wife a certificate of divorce and send her away?" Jesus replied, "Moses permitted you to divorce your wives because your hearts were hard. But it was not this way from the beginning." Matthew 19:7-8 (NIV)

Divorce was prohibited by Paul, but when spouses do divorce they are to remain unmarried or be reconciled.
To the married I give this command (not I, but the Lord): A wife must not separate from her husband. But if she does, she must remain unmarried or else be reconciled to her husband. And a husband must not divorce his wife. 1 Corinthians 7:10-11 (NIV)

Divorce law in the Old Testament aimed at protecting women against the possibility of being divorced for trivial reasons.
"When a man takes a wife and marries her, and it happens that she finds no favor in his eyes because he has found some uncleanness in her, and he writes her a certificate of divorce, puts it in her hand, and sends her out of his house, when she has departed from his house, and goes and becomes another man's wife, if the latter husband detests her and writes her a certificate of divorce, puts it in her hand, and sends her out of his house, or if the latter husband dies who took her as his wife, then her former husband who divorced her must not take her back to be his wife after she has been defiled; for that is an abomination before the Lord, and you shall not bring sin on the land which the Lord your God is giving you as an inheritance. Deuteronomy 24:1-4 (NKJV)

Elders

Elders were the leaders in the early church. While there are three different words used interchangeably to describe the Elder role, each word refers to different functions of the same office. The three terms are: elder (Greek *presbuteros*), which carries the sense of one who is older and wiser, overseer (Greek *episkopos*), which designates management responsibilities, and pastor (Greek *poimen*), which means shepherd.

The Apostle Peter uses all three words in a single New Testament passage writing, "Therefore, I exhort the elders (*presbuteros*) among you...shepherd (*poimen*) the flock of God, exercising oversight (*episkos*)" (1 Peter 5:1-2). Elders are to govern the church (*presbuteros*), exercising authority and managing ministry (*episkopos*), as well as caring for people spiritually (*poimen*).

Elders are shepherds of God's flock, serving as examples.
And now, a word to you who are elders in the churches. I, too, am an elder and a witness to the sufferings of Christ. And I, too, will share in his glory when he is revealed to the whole world. As a fellow elder, I appeal to you: Care for the flock that God has entrusted to you. Watch over it willingly, not grudgingly—not for what you will get out of it, but because you are eager to serve God. Don't lord it over the people assigned to your care, but lead them by your own good example. And when the Great Shepherd appears, you will receive a crown of never-ending glory and honor.
1 Peter 5:1-4 (NLT)

Elders are to watch for those who would distort the truth.
So guard yourselves and God's people. Feed and shepherd God's flock— his church, purchased with his own blood—over which the Holy Spirit has appointed you as elders. I know that false teachers, like vicious wolves, will come in among you after I leave, not sparing the flock. Even some men from your own group will rise up and distort the truth in order to draw a following. Watch out! Remember the three years I was with you—my

constant watch and care over you night and day, and my many tears for you. Acts 20:28-31 (NLT)

Elders must have the desire and character for leadership.
The saying is trustworthy: If anyone aspires to the office of overseer, he desires a noble task. Therefore an overseer must be above reproach, the husband of one wife, sober-minded, self-controlled, respectable, hospitable, able to teach, not a drunkard, not violent but gentle, not quarrelsome, not a lover of money. He must manage his own household well, with all dignity keeping his children submissive, for if someone does not know how to manage his own household, how will he care for God's church? He must not be a recent convert, or he may become puffed up with conceit and fall into the condemnation of the devil. Moreover, he must be well thought of by outsiders, so that he may not fall into disgrace, into a snare of the devil.
1 Timothy 3:1-7 (ESV)

Elders were appointed in each congregation by Paul.
Paul and Barnabas appointed elders for them in each church and, with prayer and fasting, committed them to the Lord, in whom they had put their trust. Acts 14:23 (NIV)

Elders are to pray for the sick, anointing them with oil.
Is any one of you sick? He should call the elders of the church to pray over him and anoint him with oil in the name of the Lord. James 5:14 (NIV)

Elders must be able to teach and endure opposition.
The Lord's bond-servant must not be quarrelsome, but be kind to all, able to teach, patient when wronged, with gentleness correcting those who are in opposition, if perhaps God may grant them repentance leading to the knowledge of the truth, and they may come to their senses and escape from the snare of the devil, having been held captive by him to do his will.
2 Timothy 2:24-26 (NASB)

Election

Election refers to the doctrine of God's sovereign selection of some for salvation through faith in Jesus Christ (Ephesians 1:4). Election is the outcome of God's will (Ephesians 1:1-11), apart from human effort (Romans 9:11, Ephesians 2:8-9), always leads to salvation (Romans 8:29-30) and results in God's glory (Ephesians 1:6).

Of course, many ask, "How is God just, in electing to save only some, when he is able to save all?" Even the Apostle Paul, when describing election asked, "Is God unjust?" (Romans 9:14). Paul answered this question by explaining that God is just in saving only some because he always acts for his glory, even in the condemnation of those he has the power to save.

Do we define justice, as any and every action that brings God glory? Or is justice determined as that which best serves humanity? To demonstrate the primacy of God's glory in all things, Paul highlights God's work in and through Pharaoh. God told Pharaoh "I raised you up for this very purpose, that I might display my power in you and that my name might be proclaimed in all the earth" (Romans 9:17). While it can be hard to accept that any and everything that brings God glory is in fact just, faith is trusting what we know about God (e.g., God is loving and good.) rather than distrusting what we do not understand (i.e., Why is God only saving some?).

It's not uncommon for God's sovereign election in the work of salvation to cause some to question the goodness of the gospel. But the doctrine of God's sovereign election of some to salvation is good news for several reasons. First, it affirms that anyone can be saved, as one's election is separate from anything one does (Ephesians 2:8-9), whether good or bad. This means that no one is beyond salvation (i.e., too sinful to be saved) and that no one is good enough to be saved on their own merit. Instead, the Bible teaches that we are "dead" in our sins and only God can act to bring us to new life spiritually (Ephesians 2:1).

The doctrine of election is also good news because it provides security in salvation. If one had provided in any way for one's own salvation, then one's faith is weakened by any weakness that one possesses. But, because God freely chooses to save apart from anything anyone has done, is doing, or will do, one's faith is completely secure. The good news of the gospel is that God has laid hold of us and holds on to us. We have not laid hold of God, nor are we responsible for holding on to God (John 6:39, John 10:28-29).

The doctrine of election is also good news because it identifies God's mercy and demonstrates the importance of showing mercy. Christians have received God's unmerited favor, and our showing compassion toward others is an essential indication that we have received God's compassion offered in Jesus Christ (Matthew 25:31-46).

The doctrine of election is also good news because it provides a better understanding of the urgency in prayer (John 15:5). We learn in Scripture that God not only ordains the end (i.e., someone's salvation), but also the means by which they are saved, which includes prayer (Luke 10:2). Thus, the doctrine of election integrates God's sovereignty with man's volition.

The doctrine of election is also good news because it provides freedom. Others coming to faith does not depend on the communicator's eloquence or brilliance, but on Gods' activity. We can boldly proclaim the truth of God's Word, much like a farmer sows seed, knowing that unless God's Spirit acts no one will come to salvation (1 Corinthians 3:7). Our role is simply to communicate the gospel. God's role is to convert sinners. Thus, we can relax (1 Corinthians 2:14). The difference between the saved and those unsaved is that God has provided understanding to the saved.

Finally, the doctrine of election is good news because it increases evangelistic urgency. When we realize that God cared enough to pursue us, and not because we were deserving, then we are compelled to share the Gospel with greater urgency.

How can we know if we are elect?

The "elect" are those whom God has chosen to save through faith in Jesus Christ (Ephesians 1:4). For this reason, election is always the outcome of God's will (Ephesians 1:1-11) and not based upon any human action (Romans 9:11, Ephesians 2:8-9). Although we have no power over whether we are elect (God is doing the choosing), we *can* know whether we are a part of the elect. In fact, the Apostle John explained that this was the very purpose for which he wrote one of his New Testament letters, so that we might know that we are saved (1 John 5:13).

First, we can know that we are elect based upon the promises of Scripture. In this respect, the knowledge of and confidence in being elect is separate from our feelings, and rests solely on the trustworthy character of God to keep his Word. For example, in Scripture we read that "all who call upon the name of the Lord" are saved (Acts 2:21). Jesus is "the Lord" and "to call" upon his name is a poetic way to describe trusting in his life, death and resurrection for the forgiveness of sin and life eternal (Acts 16:31). Scripture also teaches that "If you declare with your mouth, 'Jesus is Lord,' and believe in your heart that God raised him from the dead, you will be saved" (Romans 10:9). In other words, if we act upon Scripture's directives regarding salvation, then we can know that we are elect, because Scripture is completely dependable.

We can also know that we are elect based upon our desire for salvation. The Apostle John described this as having a "testimony" in one's heart (1 John 5:10). In a similar vein, the Apostle Paul wrote that the elect have God's Spirit "in" their hearts (Galatians 4:6-7). In other words, the idea of a person wanting to be elect by God for salvation, but being unable to express faith in Jesus and follow after Jesus, is absolutely foreign to the Bible. Jesus said, "everyone who asks receives" (Matthew 7:8), and we know that no one asks to be saved apart from being drawn by God (John 6:44, Romans 3:10-18), as those without faith in Jesus are blind to their need for faith in Jesus, until the Spirit opens them to their need (2 Corinthians 4:4). In short, if someone has a desire for salvation, then it is only because God has elected them to salvation (Acts 11:18).

Finally, we can also know that we are elect if our actions show that we have faith in Jesus. Scripture is clear that those who are elect will follow Jesus' teachings (1 John 2:3). This does not mean that we must be perfect, living lives without any sin, but rather that those who are elect will demonstrate their election through actions of faith in following after Jesus (James 2:14). In short, however small or insignificant, the elect will demonstrate the faith in action. Our actions do not save us, but all who are being saved have actions that demonstrate their salvation.

Admittedly, much about God's purposes in election are mysterious, but we can know whether we are elect, based upon Scripture, the desire of our heart and our actions.

Evangelism

The term "evangelism" comes from the Greek word *evangelion*, which means "good news," and from which we get the word "gospel," as well as the word evangelical. Evangelicals are those who believe the Gospel (i.e., the good news) is the "power of God for salvation" (Romans 1:16) and proclaim it publicly.

In Mark 1:14 we read that Jesus went about "proclaiming the good news *(evangelion)* of God." This means that God was the first evangelist, lovingly pursuing humanity out of his kindness and compassion, and providing for us the forgiveness of sin through faith in Jesus Christ.

Evangelism begins with God, who calls us to repentance.
The word of the Lord came to Jonah the son of Amittai saying, "Arise, go to Nineveh the great city and cry against it, for their wickedness has come up before Me." Jonah 1:1-2 (NASB)

But God showed his great love for us by sending Christ to die for us while we were still sinners. Romans 5:8 (NLT)

But do not let this one fact escape your notice, beloved, that with the Lord one day is like a thousand years, and a thousand years like one day. The Lord is not slow about His promise, as some count slowness, but is patient toward you, not wishing for any to perish but for all to come to repentance. 2 Peter 3:8-9 (NASB)

Evangelism was at the heart of Jesus' mission.
For the Son of Man came to seek and to save what was lost. Luke 19:10 (NIV)

Evangelism is at the center of disciple-making.
Go therefore and make disciples of all the nations, baptizing them in the name of the Father and of the Son and of the Holy Spirit, teaching them to

observe all things that I have commanded you; and lo, I am with you always, even to the end of the age." Amen. Matthew 28:19-20 (NKJV)

Evangelism is an activity for which the world is waiting.
"Do you not say, 'Four months more and then the harvest'? I tell you, open your eyes and look at the fields! They are ripe for harvest."
John 4: 35 (NIV)

Evangelism succeeds as God enables people to see the light.
And even if our gospel is veiled, it is veiled to those who are perishing, in whose case the god of this world has blinded the minds of the unbelieving so that they might not see the light of the gospel of the glory of Christ, who is the image of God. For we do not preach ourselves but Christ Jesus as Lord, and ourselves as your bond-servants for Jesus' sake. For God, who said, "Light shall shine out of darkness," is the One who has shone in our hearts to give the Light of the knowledge of the glory of God in the face of Christ.
2 Corinthians 4:3-6 (NASB)

Evangelism requires laborers for whom we are to pray.
After this the Lord appointed seventy-two others and sent them on ahead of him, two by two, into every town and place where he himself was about to go. And he said to them, "The harvest is plentiful, but the laborers are few. Therefore pray earnestly to the Lord of the harvest to send out laborers into his harvest. Go your way; behold, I am sending you out as lambs in the midst of wolves." Luke 10:1-3 (ESV)

Evangelism will continue until every nation hears.
And they sang a new song, saying, "Worthy are You to take the book and to break its seals; for You were slain, and purchased for God with Your blood men from every tribe and tongue and people and nation.
Revelation 5:9 (NASB)

How can I share my faith with others?

Sharing our faith with others is often easier when we have a relationship with the person. However, many times the Apostles also preached to crowds of people whom they did not know (Acts 2:14). At the same time, the Apostles never shared their faith without including Scripture. Failing to offer Scripture when sharing our faith, increases the probability that we are sharing only our personal experience and/or opinion.

When sharing our faith with others one-to-one, it is often best to begin by asking questions. Asking questions allows us to get to know others and invites a dialogue. Below is a question-and-answer framework for sharing one's faith that allows you to ask important questions and offer answers based upon Scripture.

Have you heard the story of God's love for mankind?
God loves us, even though we are sinful, and sent his Son to die on a cross as a sin sacrifice. The Bible says:

> *God demonstrates his own love for us in this: while we were still sinners, Christ died for us. Romans 5:8 (NIV)*

Do you think of yourself as a sinner in need of saving?
Sin is any action or attitude contrary to God's character (e.g., lying, stealing, cheating, hating). The Bible says:

> *All have sinned and fall short of the glory of God. Romans 3:23 (NIV)*

Do you see the deadly effects of sin in your life?
God is the author of life. Death comes because of sin, because God separates himself from what is sinful. Even though sin brings death, God offers us eternal life by believing in Jesus Christ's death and resurrection. The Bible says:

> *The wages of sin is death, but the gift of God is eternal life in Christ Jesus our Lord. Romans 6:23 (NIV)*

Do you know how to receive eternal life?
We can receive eternal life by believing that God sent his Son, Jesus, as a sacrifice for our sin, dying the death that we deserve for our sinfulness. The Bible says:

> *For God so loved the world that he gave his one and only Son, that whoever believes in him shall not perish but have eternal life. John 3:16 (NIV)*

> *If we confess our sins, He is faithful and righteous to forgive us our sins and to cleanse us from all unrighteousness.*
> *1 John 1:9 (NASB)*

Would you let me lead you in a prayer of confession?
There is nothing magical about the prayer below. It is simply a means for confessing our sinfulness, expressing our belief in Jesus and receiving forgiveness. You can simply repeat the words after me. Let's pray together.

> Heavenly Father,
> We thank you for your love for us. I recognize that I am a sinner and that my sin has brought death into my life. Thank you for the life offered through Jesus' death and resurrection, to all those who believe. I believe and I ask that you forgive my sin and that I would receive the eternal life promised through Jesus Christ. Help me now to live a life that honors you. In Jesus' name I pray. Amen.

Eschatology (End Times)

Eschatology is the study of last things, or those things that will unfold at the end of time, including Jesus' return, the final judgment, and the new creation. It is both a foundational and often confusing area of study, and it seems wisest to acknowledge that elements of eschatology are purposely veiled from our understanding. For example, the date of the return of Christ is purposely not revealed in Scripture, intentionally kept a mystery by God. On this topic, Jesus said,

> But about that day or hour no one knows, not even the angels in heaven, nor the Son, but only the Father. Matthew 24:36 (NIV)

While not everything is revealed about all that will unfold at the end of time and while there is a lot of debate about specifics passages, evangelical Christians agree that 1) Christ will return bodily and visibly, 2) all people will be raised from the dead and be judged by God, and 3) evil beings specifically, as well as humans who oppose God will be defeated.

With regard to Jesus' final return and ultimate reign on earth, most people's view on how things will unfold is determined by their interpretation of the millennial reign of Christ (i.e., the thousand-year reign), which is mentioned in Revelation 20:1-6. In this passage, John describes the binding of Satan, as well as the raising and co-reigning of the Christian martyrs. John writes: "…they will be priests of God and of Christ and will reign with him for a thousand years" (Revelation 20:6). With regard to the nature of the millennial reign of Jesus, there are generally three theological camps.

> **Amillennialism** is the view of those who believe that the thousand-year reign of Christ mentioned in the book of Revelation is not a literal thousand-year period, but

rather a figurative time frame describing the current Church age. Amillennialists typically interpret all the numbers in the book of Revelation as symbolic, and the thousand-year reign of Christ symbolizes a time where the gospel is preached with tremendous success, and the influence of Christ is growing globally. The growing success of gospel and the growth and influence of the church results in Christ's Kingdom coming in full and establishing his rule on earth. This is the more common interpretive framework of Reformed theologians.

Postmillennialism is the view of those who believe that Jesus will return after a golden "millennial age" in which the Church makes significant advances in the world with the Gospel. For Postmillennialists the one-thousand-year reign of Christ is not necessarily a literal time period, but a long era of gospel success and global transformation. The success of the gospel's preaching and the growth of Christ's influence brings great revival and social reform, which lead to Christ's return.

Premillennialism is the view of those who believe that Jesus will return before the millennial age, raising from the dead those Christians who have died and glorifying the bodies of Christians who are alive, to establish a thousand-year reign on earth. For Premillennialists the one-thousand-year reign of Christ is a literal period of time, which comes before the final judgment and ushers in a golden age of peace and justice.

Faith

Just as we need oxygen for physical life, we need faith for spiritual life. Apart from faith, a Christian cannot live spiritually, any more than we live physically without oxygen. By faith we are born again, and by faith we continue to live daily. Like oxygen, God provides the faith needed for our spiritual lives. And just as some have stronger bodies, better able to utilize oxygen, some Christians are stronger in the utilization of faith. Jesus said to the sleeping disciples, "the spirit is willing, but the flesh is weak" (Matthew 26:41). God's call is to strengthen ourselves through discipline so that they can better live by faith.

Faith is being certain of what we cannot see.
Now faith is being sure of what we hope for and certain of what we do not see. Hebrews 11:1 (NIV)

We live by faith, not by sight. 2 Corinthians 5:7 (NIV)

Faith is necessary to please God with our lives.
But my righteous one will live by faith. And if he shrinks back, I will not be pleased with him. Hebrews 10:38 (NIV)

And without faith it is impossible to please God, because anyone who comes to him must believe that he exists and that he rewards those who earnestly seek him. Hebrews 11:6 (NIV)

Faith in Jesus brings forgiveness of sin and salvation.
Some men brought to him a paralytic, lying on a mat. When Jesus saw their faith, he said to the paralytic, "Take heart, son; your sins are forgiven." Matthew 9:2 (NIV)

Jesus said to the woman, "Your faith has saved you; go in peace." Luke 7:50 (NIV)

Faith is necessary for receiving physical healing.
And he did not do many miracles there because of their lack of faith. Matthew 13:58 (NIV)

Then Jesus said to the centurion, "Go! It will be done just as you believed it would." And his servant was healed at that very hour. Matthew 8:13 (NIV)

Then Jesus answered, "Woman, you have great faith! Your request is granted." And her daughter was healed from that very hour. Matthew 15:28 (NIV)

"Go," said Jesus, "your faith has healed you." Immediately he received his sight and followed Jesus along the road. Mark 10:52 (NIV)

By faith in the name of Jesus, this man whom you see and know was made strong. It is Jesus' name and the faith that comes through him that has given this complete healing to him, as you can all see. Acts 3:16 (NIV)

He listened to Paul as he was speaking. Paul looked directly at him, saw that he had faith to be healed. Acts 14:9 (NIV)

And the prayer offered in faith will make the sick person well; the Lord will raise him up. If he has sinned, he will be forgiven. James 5:15 (NIV)

Faith is required for answered prayer.
If you believe, you will receive whatever you ask for in prayer. Matthew 21:22 (NIV)

"Have faith in God," Jesus answered. "I tell you the truth, if anyone says to this mountain, 'Go, throw yourself into the sea,' and does not doubt in his heart but believes that what he says will happen, it will be done for him. Therefore I tell you, whatever you ask for in prayer, believe that you have received it, and it will be yours. Mark 11:22-24 (NIV)

Faith, even small amounts, can produce great miracles.
The apostles said to the Lord, "Increase our faith!" He replied, "If you have faith as small as a mustard seed, you can say to this mulberry tree, 'Be uprooted and planted in the sea,' and it will obey you. Luke 17:5-6 (NIV)

"If you can'? said Jesus. "Everything is possible for him who believes." Mark 9:23 (NIV)

Faith is given to different people in different measures.
For by the grace given me I say to every one of you: Do not think of yourself more highly than you ought, but rather think of yourself with sober judgment, in accordance with the measure of faith God has given you. Romans 12:3 (NIV)

We have different gifts, according to the grace given us. If a man's gift is prophesying, let him use it in proportion to his faith. Romans 12:6 (NIV)

Accept him whose faith is weak, without passing judgment on disputable matters. Romans 14:1 (NIV)

Faith is to grow over time.
Our hope is that, as your faith continues to grow, our area of activity among you will greatly expand. 2 Corinthians 10:15 (NIV)

Night and day we pray most earnestly that we may see you again and supply what is lacking in your faith. 1 Thessalonians 3:10 (NIV)

We ought always to thank God for you, brothers, and rightly so, because your faith is growing more and more, and the love every one of you has for each other is increasing. 2 Thessalonians 1:3 (NIV)

Faith came to some as they saw Jesus work miracles.
This, the first of his miraculous signs, Jesus performed at Cana in Galilee. He thus revealed his glory, and his disciples put their faith in him. John 2:11 (NIV)

Believe me when I say that I am in the Father and the Father is in me; or at least believe on the evidence of the miracles themselves. John 14:11 (NIV)

Faith that is saving will produce works of obedience.
By faith Abraham, when God tested him, offered Isaac as a sacrifice. Hebrews 11:17 (NIV)

What good is it, my brothers, if a man claims to have faith but has no deeds? Can such faith save him? James 2:14 (NIV)

As the body without the spirit is dead, so faith without deeds is dead. James 2:26 (NIV)

Faith comes by hearing God's Word.
Even as he spoke, many put their faith in him. John 8:30 (NIV)

Consequently, faith comes from hearing the message, and the message is heard through the word of Christ. Romans 10:17 (NIV)

Faith in Jesus brings our justification and righteousness.
This righteousness from God comes through faith in Jesus Christ to all who believe. There is no difference. Romans 3:22 (NIV)

Know that a man is not justified by observing the law, but by faith in Jesus Christ. So we, too, have put our faith in Christ Jesus that we may be justified by faith in Christ and not by observing the law, because by observing the law no one will be justified. Galatians 2:16 (NIV)

Faith in Jesus is a gift given by God.
For it is by grace you have been saved, through faith—and this not from yourselves, it is the gift of God. Ephesians 2:8 (NIV)

Let us fix our eyes on Jesus, the author and perfecter of our faith. Hebrews 12:2 (NIV)

Just as Jannes and Jambres opposed Moses, so also these men oppose the truth—men of depraved minds, who, as far as the faith is concerned, are rejected. 2 Timothy 3:8 (NIV)

Listen, my dear brothers: Has not God chosen those who are poor in the eyes of the world to be rich in faith and to inherit the kingdom he promised those who love him? James 2:5 (NIV)

Faith that is strong is to be imitated by others.
Don't let anyone look down on you because you are young, but set an example for the believers in speech, in life, in love, in faith and in purity. 1 Timothy 4:12 (NIV)

Remember your leaders, who spoke the word of God to you. Consider the outcome of their way of life and imitate their faith. Hebrews 13:7 (NIV)

Faith can be destroyed by errant teaching.
*As I urged you when I went into Macedonia, stay there in Ephesus so that you may command certain men not to teach false doctrines any longer nor to devote themselves to myths and endless genealogies. These promote controversies rather than God's work—which is by faith.
1 Timothy 1:3-4 (NIV)*

Turn away from godless chatter and the opposing ideas of what is falsely called knowledge, which some have professed and in so doing have wandered from the faith. Grace be with you. 1 Timothy 6:21 (NIV)

How are faith and good works related?

Faith is like oxygen. Just as we need oxygen for physical life, we need faith for spiritual life. And much like oxygen is provided by God and supports physical life, faith is provided by God and supports spiritual life. Paul wrote:

> For it is by grace you have been saved, through faith — and this is not from yourselves, it is the gift of God— not by works, so that no one can boast.
> Ephesians 2:8-9 (NIV)

"Works" are any thoughts, attitudes or actions pleasing to God. And just as we need oxygen for our bodies to operate, we need faith to produce good works. Faith provided by God produces a life of good works (John 3:1-16). Paul wrote that we were created "to do good works" (Ephesians 2:10).

How are faith and good works related? Faith in Jesus Christ precedes and produces good works. A life of good works does not save us. But saving faith will always produce a life of good works. We are saved by God's grace through faith, apart from anything that we do, but genuine faith will always lead to doing good works, by which we may be recognized as spiritually alive (Matthew 7:20). For this reason, "faith by itself, if it is not accompanied by action, is dead" (James 2:17, NIV)

Unfortunately, many wrongly believe that a life of good works can somehow produce faith, resulting in salvation. But good works can no more produce spiritual life, than physical activity can produce oxygen resulting in physical life. Spiritual activity without faith is dead, just as physical activity without oxygen is dead.

Fasting

Fasting is to go without food and/or drink, in order to seek God. In fasting we acknowledge that we have a need for God that is greater than our need for nourishment (Matthew 4:4). It is important to note that every example of fasting in the Bible is joined with the activity of prayer. To fast without praying is simply to diet.

While fasting does not compel God to act according to our prayers, it can help us to hear his voice, obey and pray in accordance with his will. While we are certainly free to broaden our fasting to include abstinence from other activities (e.g., watching television or shopping), the fasting mentioned in the Bible was primarily abstaining from food.

Fasting was practiced by those seeking God in prayer.
So I gave my attention to the Lord God to seek Him by prayer and supplications, with fasting, sackcloth and ashes. Daniel 9:3 (NASB)

Fasting was practiced by Jesus before being tempted.
Then Jesus was led up by the Spirit into the wilderness to be tempted by the devil. And after He had fasted forty days and forty nights, He then became hungry. And the tempter came and said to Him, "If You are the Son of God, command that these stones become bread." But He answered and said, "It is written, 'MAN SHALL NOT LIVE ON BREAD ALONE, BUT ON EVERY WORD THAT PROCEEDS OUT OF THE MOUTH OF GOD.'" Matthew 4:1-4 (NASB)

Fasting reminds us of the sustaining nature of obedience.
But he said to them, "I have food to eat that you know nothing about." Then his disciples said to each other, "Could someone have brought him food?" "My food," said Jesus, "is to do the will of him who sent me and to finish his work." John 4:32-34 (NIV)

Fasting was an essential part of early church worship.
While they were worshiping the Lord and fasting, the Holy Spirit said, "Set apart for me Barnabas and Saul for the work to which I have called them." Acts 13:3 (NIV)

Fasting is to be fueled by a longing for Jesus.
Jesus answered, "How can the guests of the bridegroom fast while he is with them? They cannot, so long as they have him with them. But the time will come when the bridegroom will be taken from them, and on that day they will fast. Mark 2:19-20 (NIV)

Fasting in secret is rewarded by God.
When you fast, do not look somber as the hypocrites do, for they disfigure their faces to show men they are fasting. I tell you the truth, they have received their reward in full. But when you fast, put oil on your head and wash your face, so that it will not be obvious to men that you are fasting, but only to your Father, who is unseen; and your Father, who sees what is done in secret, will reward you. Matthew 6:16-18 (NIV)

Fasting that God desires results in compassion.
"Is this not the fast which I choose, to loosen the bonds of wickedness, to undo the bands of the yoke, and to let the oppressed go free and break every yoke? "Is it not to divide your bread with the hungry and bring the homeless poor into the house; when you see the naked, to cover him; and not to hide yourself from your own flesh? "Then your light will break out like the dawn, and your recovery will speedily spring forth; and your righteousness will go before you; the glory of the LORD will be your rear guard. "Then you will call, and the LORD will answer; you will cry, and He will say, 'Here I am.' If you remove the yoke from your midst, the pointing of the finger and speaking wickedness, and if you give yourself to the hungry and satisfy the desire of the afflicted, then your light will rise in darkness and your gloom will become like midday." Isaiah 58:6-10 (NASB)

Fear

Fear is the felt response to a real or perceived threat. It is one of the most powerful human emotions. Of course, not all fear is bad. Fearing God is a demonstration of wisdom, as God is the creator and sustainer of all things and by God all humanity will be judged, giving an account for our sinful actions and attitudes. To fear God is to possess a reverential awe for who he is and all that he has done. Fear of God most often leads to faithfulness during difficult circumstances, as God supplies power to those who fear him, enabling those who fear him to honor him with their lives.

While fearing man or the difficult circumstances of life can be an understandable and appropriate response in certain situations, some fear may be caused by a lack of faith in God's provision and lead to faithlessness. Through prayer we must wrestle with whether the fear we feel is rooted in a lack of faith, asking God to strengthen our faith in all circumstances.

Fear of God is appropriate and the beginning of wisdom.
The fear of the LORD is the beginning of wisdom; all those who practice it have a good understanding. His praise endures forever! Psalm 111:10 (ESV)

The fear of the LORD is the beginning of knowledge; fools despise wisdom and instruction. Proverbs 1:7 (ESV)

Fear of God is demonstrated in staying away from evil.
Then the Lord asked Satan, "Have you noticed my servant Job? He is the finest man in all the earth. He is blameless—a man of complete integrity. He fears God and stays away from evil." Job 1:8 (NLT)

Fear of circumstances is not what God wants for us.
For God gave us a spirit not of fear but of power and love and self-control. 2 Timothy 1:7 (ESV)

Fear of God resulted in the early church's growth.
The church then had peace throughout Judea, Galilee, and Samaria, and it became stronger as the believers lived in the fear of the Lord. And with the encouragement of the Holy Spirit, it also grew in numbers. Acts 9:31 (NLT)

Fear of circumstances is overcome by God's peace.
Peace I leave with you; my peace I give to you. Not as the world gives do I give to you. Let not your hearts be troubled, neither let them be afraid. John 14:27 (ESV)

Fear of circumstances can be overcome through the knowledge that God is our help.
So we can confidently say, "The Lord is my helper; I will not fear; what can man do to me?" Hebrews 13:6 (ESV)

Fear of circumstances is cast out by God's perfect love.
There is no fear in love, but perfect love casts out fear. For fear has to do with punishment, and whoever fears has not been perfected in love. 1 John 4:18 (ESV)

Fear of circumstances is overcome by God's comfort.
Even though I walk through the valley of the shadow of death, I will fear no evil, for you are with me; your rod and your staff, they comfort me. Psalm 23:4 (ESV)

Fear in life cannot separate us from God's love.
And I am convinced that nothing can ever separate us from God's love. Neither death nor life, neither angels nor demons, neither our fears for today nor our worries about tomorrow—not even the powers of hell can separate us from God's love. Romans 8:38 (NLT)

Fellowship

The New Testament Greek word translated as "fellowship" means "to participate." Although ordinary gatherings are described as fellowship (e.g., ice cream socials and church picnics), fellowship is a supernatural reality experienced as we *participate* by faith in the death and resurrection of Jesus Christ. The Apostle John wrote of fellowship that:

> We proclaim to you what we ourselves have actually seen and heard so that you may have fellowship with us. And our fellowship is with the Father and with his Son, Jesus Christ. 1 John 1:3 (NLT)

Paul proclaimed the life, death and resurrection of Jesus, that we might have fellowship, that we might participate in God's presence. However, Christian fellowship is much more than simply mental affirmation to doctrine. Note that Paul's desire is that through proclamation those who believe may have fellowship with God the Father and God the Son, Jesus Christ, as well as with one another.

This means that fellowship is a supernatural reality experienced as we believe what has been proclaimed about Jesus. Jesus himself said of his followers, "For where two or three gather together as my followers, I am there among them" (Matthew 18:20, NLT). How can Jesus' presence be with us and connecting those who gather in his name? The Apostle Paul explained:

> When you believed in Christ, he identified you as his own by giving you the Holy Spirit, whom he promised long ago. The Spirit is God's guarantee that he will give us the inheritance he promised and that he has purchased us to be his own people. He did this so we would praise and glorify him. Ephesians 1:13-14 (NLT)

Through faith in Jesus Christ all Christians physically receive (i.e., participate in) God's Spirit, who connects them with God and other Christians, and as we walk in the light of Jesus' teachings, we enjoy the fellowship with one another.

> This is the message we heard from Jesus and now declare to you: God is light, and there is no darkness in him at all. So we are lying if we say we have fellowship with God but go on living in spiritual darkness; we are not practicing the truth. But if we are living in the light, as God is in the light, then we have fellowship with each other, and the blood of Jesus, his Son, cleanses us from all sin. 1 John 1:5-7 (NLT)

Biblical fellowship is much more than simply participating in a social activity together. Friends can share food, but that does not mean that they are "walking in the light" and sharing in God's presence. Too often we mistake the fun of friendship for the supernatural event that is biblical fellowship. Fellowship is also more than simply enduring hard times together. Soldiers can form a bond by standing side-by-side in battle, but that does not necessarily mean that they are sharing in God's presence. Too often we confuse the company that misery loves with biblical fellowship. We can form valuable bonds, as we labor alongside others, and still miss out on sharing together in God's presence. Fellowship is experienced only as we live "in the light" of Jesus' person, emulating his character, conduct and concerns in every situation.

For this reason, we are warned in New Testament to avoid participating (i.e., fellowshipping) in one another's sins and wickedness (1 Timothy 5:22, 2 John 11), as well as the connection that comes by participating in demonic activities (1 Corinthians 10:16, 2 Corinthians 6:14). Instead, we are told to "walk in the light" (1 John 1:7), just as Jesus is in the light, and we are promised fellowship and forgiveness as a result.

Forgiveness

Forgiveness is to release someone from the debt they owe because of an offense they have committed against you. The Bible teaches that we are born into sin, deserving of God's wrath, and needing his forgiveness (Romans 5:12, Ephesians 2:3). We experience forgiveness by trusting in the message that Jesus died to pay the debt that we owed for the sin that we committed against God (John 3:16, Romans 6:23, Ephesians 2:8-10).

No religion, except Christianity, teaches that God completely forgives sin (Hebrews 10:17), stands ready to do so (Luke 15:11-32) and has provided a means by which we may be forgiven (John 3:16). God sent Jesus to pay our debt, purchasing our forgiveness by giving his life as a ransom for many (Romans 3:22-25, Romans 4:25, Hebrews 9:26).

Those receiving God's forgiveness are to forgive others (Matthew 18:22, Luke 17:4). Christians are to live with a posture of eagerness to forgive, just as they have been eagerly forgiven by God (Matthew 18:35).

Forgiveness is received by all who trust in Jesus' death as payment for their sin.
For the wages of sin is death, but the free gift of God is eternal life through Christ Jesus our Lord. Romans 6:23 (NLT)

Then he says, "I will never again remember their sins and lawless deeds." And when sins have been forgiven, there is no need to offer any more sacrifices. Hebrews 10:17-18 (NLT)

Forgiving others is a part of receiving God's forgiveness.
For if you forgive men when they sin against you, your heavenly Father will also forgive you. But if you do not forgive men their sins, your Father will not forgive your sins. Matthew 6:14-15 (NIV)

Forgive as the Lord forgave you. Colossians 3:13 (NIV)

"But when the man left the king, he went to a fellow servant who owed him a few thousand dollars. He grabbed him by the throat and demanded instant payment. "His fellow servant fell down before him and begged for a little more time. 'Be patient with me, and I will pay it,' he pleaded. But his creditor wouldn't wait. He had the man arrested and put in prison until the debt could be paid in full. "When some of the other servants saw this, they were very upset. They went to the king and told him everything that had happened. Then the king called in the man he had forgiven and said, 'You evil servant! I forgave you that tremendous debt because you pleaded with me. Shouldn't you have mercy on your fellow servant, just as I had mercy on you?' Then the angry king sent the man to prison to be tortured until he had paid his entire debt. "That's what my heavenly Father will do to you if you refuse to forgive your brothers and sisters from your heart." Matthew 18:28-35 (NLT)

Forgiving others reflects God's mercy toward us.
For He Himself is kind to ungrateful and evil men. "Be merciful, just as your Father is merciful. Luke 6:35-36 (NASB)

Get rid of all bitterness, rage, anger, harsh words, and slander, as well as all types of evil behavior. Instead, be kind to each other, tenderhearted, forgiving one another, just as God through Christ has forgiven you. Ephesians 4:31-32 (NLT)

Then Peter came and said to Him, "Lord, how often shall my brother sin against me and I forgive him? Up to seven times?" Jesus said to him, "I do not say to you, up to seven times, but up to seventy times seven. Matthew 18:21-22 (NASB)

Fornication

Fornication, in the narrowest sense of the word, is sexual intercourse between a man and a woman who are not married to each other. The Greek word translated as "fornication" in the New Testament is *porneia*, which has a breadth of meaning that can reference virtually any act of sexuality outside of a monogamous marriage relationship (e.g., premarital sex, adultery, incest, homosexuality, even lust). For this reason, most contemporary translations of the Bible have opted to replace the word "fornication" with the broader term of "sexual immorality."

Fornication is a sin that grows out of the heart.
For out of the heart proceed evil thoughts, murders, adulteries, fornications, thefts, false witness, blasphemies. Matthew 15:19 (NKJV)

Fornication is a sin from which we are to repent.
For I fear lest, when I come, I shall not find you such as I wish, and that I shall be found by you such as you do not wish; lest there be contentions, jealousies, outbursts of wrath, selfish ambitions, backbitings, whisperings, conceits, tumults; lest, when I come again, my God will humble me among you, and I shall mourn for many who have sinned before and have not repented of the uncleanness, fornication, and lewdness which they have practiced. 2 Corinthians 12:20-21 (NKJV)

Fornication is of the flesh, and not God's kingdom.
Now the works of the flesh are evident, which are: adultery, fornication, uncleanness, lewdness, idolatry, sorcery, hatred, contentions, jealousies, outbursts of wrath, selfish ambitions, dissensions, heresies, envy, murders, drunkenness, revelries, and the like; of which I tell you beforehand, just as I also told you in time past, that those who practice such things will not inherit the kingdom of God. Galatians 5:19-21 (NKJV)

Fornication is not fitting among God's people.
But fornication and all uncleanness or covetousness, let it not even be named among you, as is fitting for saints; neither filthiness, nor foolish talking, nor coarse jesting, which are not fitting, but rather giving of thanks. Ephesians 5:3-4 (NKJV)

Fornication is a sin that we are to put to death.
Therefore put to death your members which are on the earth: fornication, uncleanness, passion, evil desire, and covetousness, which is idolatry. Because of these things the wrath of God is coming upon the sons of disobedience, in which you yourselves once walked when you lived in them. Colossians 3:5-7 (NKJV)

Fornication can symbolize the act of forsaking God.
For all the nations have drunk of the wine of the wrath of her fornication, the kings of the earth have committed fornication with her, and the merchants of the earth have become rich through the abundance of her luxury." For all the nations have drunk of the wine of the wrath of her fornication, the kings of the earth have committed fornication with her, and the merchants of the earth have become rich through the abundance of her luxury." Revelation 18:3 (NKJV)

Freedom from Sin

Scripture teaches that all of humanity is born captive to sin (Romans 5:12). We are sinners not because we sin, but rather we sin because we are sinners. We are sinners by nature (Ephesians 2:3). The good news of the gospel is that through faith in Jesus we are made new creatures (2 Corinthians 5:17), receiving a new nature, which can now live increasingly free from sinful attitudes and actions.

Freedom from sin comes through faith in Jesus.
For the death that He died, He died to sin once for all; but the life that He lives, He lives to God. Even so consider yourselves to be dead to sin, but alive to God in Christ Jesus. Romans 6:10-11 (NASB)

Freedom from sin is made possible by God's grace.
For sin shall not be your master, because you are not under law, but under grace. Romans 6:14 (NIV)

Freedom from sin is experienced as we offer our body as instruments of righteousness.
Do not offer the parts of your body to sin, as instruments of wickedness, but rather offer yourselves to God, as those who have been brought from death to life; and offer the parts of your body to him as instruments of righteousness. Romans 6:12-13 (NIV)

You have been set free from sin and have become slaves to righteousness. I put this in human terms because you are weak in your natural selves. Just as you used to offer the parts of your body in slavery to impurity and to ever-increasing wickedness, so now offer them in slavery to righteousness leading to holiness. Romans 6:18-19 (NIV)

Freedom from sin strength in Christ.
I can do everything through him who gives me strength. Philippians 4:12-13 (NIV)

Freedom from sin is participating in the divine nature.
For by these He has granted to us His precious and magnificent promises, so that by them you may become partakers of the divine nature, having escaped the corruption that is in the world by lust. 2 Peter 1:4 (NASB)

Freedom from sin means carrying out the Spirit's desires.
But I say, walk by the Spirit, and you will not carry out the desire of the flesh. For the flesh sets its desire against the Spirit, and the Spirit against the flesh; for these are in opposition to one another, so that you may not do the things that you please. But if you are led by the Spirit, you are not under the Law. Galatians 5:16-18 (NASB)

Freedom from sin means seeing our body as dead to sin.
Therefore consider the members of your earthly body as dead to immorality, impurity, passion, evil desire, and greed, which amounts to idolatry. For it is because of these things that the wrath of God will come upon the sons of disobedience, and in them you also once walked, when you were living in them. Colossians 3:5-7 (NASB)

Freedom from sin means putting on the new self.
But now you also, put them all aside: anger, wrath, malice, slander, and abusive speech from your mouth. Do not lie to one another, since you laid aside the old self with its evil practices, and have put on the new self who is being renewed to a true knowledge according to the image of the One who created him--a renewal in which there is no distinction between Greek and Jew, circumcised and uncircumcised, barbarian, Scythian, slave and freeman, but Christ is all, and in all. So, as those who have been chosen of God, holy and beloved, put on a heart of compassion, kindness, humility, gentleness and patience; bearing with one another, and forgiving each other, whoever has a complaint against anyone; just as the Lord forgave you, so also should you. Beyond all these things put on love, which is the perfect bond of unity. Colossians 3:8-14 (NASB)

Gospel

The word Gospel means "good news," and it comes from the Greek word *Evangelion,* from which we get the word evangelical. Evangelicals are those who believe the Gospel is the "power of God for salvation" (Romans 1:16) and place a priority on proclaiming it publicly. In Mark 1:14 we read that Jesus went about "proclaiming the good news (*evangelion*) of God."

First, the Gospel is a declaration of God's historic work to save his people, through the sacrificial death of Jesus, as a fulfillment of Old Testament prophecy. This means that the Gospel is not simply a New Testament message. The Gospel is an ages old message, foretold in the Old Testament Law and through the Old Testament Prophets. Paul alludes to the historic work of God when he writes that "now a righteousness from God, apart from law, has been made known, to which the Law and the Prophets testify" (Romans 3:21). In fact, the Apostle Peter writes that Jesus was chosen for sacrifice from before the creation of the world. (1 Peter 1:20). And Jesus used the Old Testament to explain his gospel ministry.

> And beginning with Moses and all the Prophets, he explained to them what was said in all the Scriptures concerning himself. John 24:27 (NIV)

Second, the Gospel is also an affirmation that Jesus is both Savior and Lord, and the only way to the Father. Peter stood on the streets of Jerusalem and closed his message with this declaration, "Let all Israel be assured of this: God has made this Jesus, whom you crucified, both Lord and Christ" (Acts 2:36). Jesus said, "I'm the way, and the truth and the life, no one comes to the Father except through me" (John 14:6). The message of the Gospel is never presented as simply one option among many religions. The Gospel is presented as the only option leading to life. The gospel states "Salvation is found in no one else, for there is no other name under heaven given to men by which we must be saved" (Acts 4:12).

Finally, the Gospel is an invitation to confess and repent of our sin (Romans 6:23), and to receive God's forgiveness and avoid his wrath (Romans 1:18). Essential to the Gospel is the doctrine of God's certain judgment and coming wrath because of mankind's sinfulness (Hebrews 4:13). Without a thorough understanding of what we are being "saved" from, it is impossible to receive salvation itself. If the Gospel is simply a message of self-help or self-improvement, then Jesus didn't need to die. If the Gospel is simply a message of self-help or self-improvement, then Jesus only needed to teach and counsel and console those who were suffering. But Jesus died on a cross, spilling his blood as a sin sacrifice. He absorbed God's wrath against mankind, the punishment that was due each of us. Below is one of the most succinct explanations of the Gospel offered in Scripture.

> But now apart from the Law the righteousness of God has been manifested, being witnessed by the Law and the Prophets, even the righteousness of God through faith in Jesus Christ for all those who believe; for there is no distinction; for all have sinned and fall short of the glory of God, being justified as a gift by His grace through the redemption which is in Christ Jesus; whom God displayed publicly as a propitiation in His blood through faith This was to demonstrate His righteousness, because in the forbearance of God He passed over the sins previously committed; for the demonstration, I say, of His righteousness at the present time, so that He would be just and the justifier of the one who has faith in Jesus. Romans 3:21-26 (NASB)

Gospel and Its Exclusivity and Inclusivity

The gospel is exclusive in that it claims one can only be saved by believing that Jesus Christ is the Son of God, who died in our place for the forgiveness of our sin and was raised three days later that we might have eternal life (John 3:16). In this way, the gospel excludes all other religious teachings about salvation. While other religions certainly possess some truths, which are helpful in life, the gospel claims that life itself is found only as we place our faith in Jesus Christ's substitutionary death and certain resurrection.

At the same time, the gospel is also inclusive in that anyone who wants to be saved can be saved. No one who wants to believe that Jesus Christ is the Son of God, who died for the forgiveness of our sin and was raised from the grave three days later, is excluded from salvation. Anyone and everyone is invited to believe, regardless of their race, gender, social status or immorality.

While the means of salvation are exclusive, coming only by God's grace through faith in Jesus Christ, the experience of salvation is inclusive, anyone who wants to be saved can be saved. This is the "good news" of the gospel and a unique element of the gospel's message. Salvation is a gift, offered to all who would believe (Ephesians 2:8-9). In this respect the gospel is far more inclusive than any other world religion, not requiring conformity to certain moral standards before being offered the hope of eternal life, but rather including all who are willing to accept Jesus as God's perfect moral standard and sacrifice on their behalf.

The exclusivity of the gospel was taught by Jesus.
"You can enter God's Kingdom only through the narrow gate. The highway to hell is broad, and its gate is wide for the many who choose that way. But the gateway to life is very narrow and the road is difficult, and only a few ever find it. Matthew 7:13-14 (NLT)

Jesus answered, "I am the way and the truth and the life. No one comes to the Father except through me. John 14:6 (NIV)

The exclusivity of the Gospel was taught in the church.
Salvation is found in no one else, for there is no other name under heaven given to men by which we must be saved." Acts 4:12 (NIV)

The inclusivity of the Gospel was announced by Jesus.
"Come to Me, all who are weary and heavy-laden, and I will give you rest. Take My yoke upon you and learn from Me, for I am gentle and humble in heart, and YOU WILL FIND REST FOR YOUR SOULS. For My yoke is easy and My burden is light." Matthew 11:28-30 (NASB)

The inclusivity of the Gospel was taught in the church.
This righteousness from God comes through faith in Jesus Christ to all who believe. There is no difference, for all have sinned and fall short of the glory of God, and are justified freely by his grace through the redemption that came by Christ Jesus. Romans 3:22-24 (NIV)

Grace

Grace is an underserved blessing or favor. The experience of God's grace is at the center of Christianity (1 Peter 5:10), and dependence upon God's grace is essential for salvation (1 Corinthians 15:10).

Historically, a distinction has been drawn between "common" grace and "special" grace. Common grace is the blessing of God bestowed upon all humanity. For example, God graciously sends rain and causes the sun to shine upon both the just and the unjust (Matthew 5:45). Common grace is also demonstrated in the domestic and civil order established by God in the world. God provided both marriage and government for the purposes of helping humanity fulfill its purposes, as well as restraining sinfulness (Genesis 2:24, Romans 13:1-5).

While common grace is given to all humanity, God's special grace is given only to those whom God is saving through faith in Jesus Christ. In dispensing special (i.e., saving) grace, God takes the initiative, bringing spiritually dead people to new life to bless them through faith in Jesus (Romans 5:6-10, Ephesians 2:1-5, 1 John 4:10).

God's special grace is powerful and effective.
Everyone the Father gives Me will come to Me, and the one who comes to Me I will never cast out. For I have come down from heaven, not to do My will, but the will of Him who sent Me. This is the will of Him who sent Me: that I should lose none of those He has given Me but should raise them up on the last day. John 6:37-39 (HCSB)

For those He foreknew He also predestined to be conformed to the image of His Son, so that He would be the firstborn among many brothers. And those He predestined, He also called; and those He called, He also justified; and those He justified, He also glorified. Romans 8:29-30 (HCSB)

I am sure of this, that He who started a good work in you will carry it on to completion until the day of Christ Jesus. Philippians 1:6 (HCSB)

But by God's grace I am what I am, and His grace toward me was not ineffective. However, I worked more than any of them, yet not I, but God's grace that was with me. 1 Corinthians 15:10 (HCSB)

God's special grace is irresistible.

But when God, who from my birth set me apart and called me by His grace, was pleased to reveal His Son in me, so that I could preach Him among the Gentiles, I did not immediately consult with anyone. Galatians 1:15-16 (HCSB)

For He chose us in Him, before the foundation of the world, to be holy and blameless in His sight. In love He predestined us to be adopted through Jesus Christ for Himself, according to His favor and will, to the praise of His glorious grace that He favored us with in the Beloved. Ephesians 1:4-6 (HCSB)

God's special grace is sufficient to meet our needs.

For you are saved by grace through faith, and this is not from yourselves; it is God's gift—not from works, so that no one can boast. For we are His creation, created in Christ Jesus for good works, which God prepared ahead of time so that we should walk in them. Ephesians 2:8-10 (HCSB)

But He said to me, "My grace is sufficient for you, for power is perfected in weakness." Therefore, I will most gladly boast all the more about my weaknesses, so that Christ's power may reside in me. 2 Corinthians 12:9 (HCSB)

Anyone who believes in Him is not condemned, but anyone who does not believe is already condemned, because he has not believed in the name of the One and Only Son of God. John 3:18 (HCSB)

Healing

Healing is God's ultimate will for his people (3 John 2, Revelation 21:4) and will include all aspects of our person, spiritual, physical, and psychological. While complete healing will not be fully experienced until heaven, God reveals himself as the healer of his people (Exodus 15:26, Psalms 103:3).

Physical and psychological healing was a primary sign of Jesus' ministry as God's Savior (Luke 7:22-23), a significant element of his earliest disciples' ministry (Matthew 10:1-5, Mark 6:7-13, Luke 9:1-6, Luke 10:9), as well as being a part of the early church's ministry (Acts 14:3, Acts 19:12). Healing was also made a permanent provision of the church's ministry as believers were commissioned to pray for healing (James 5:16), and the Holy Spirit provided some with gifts of healing (1 Corinthians 12:9, 28, 30).

Healing comes to us by Jesus' suffering on our behalf.
Surely our griefs He Himself bore, and our sorrows He carried; Yet we ourselves esteemed Him stricken, smitten of God, and afflicted. But He was pierced through for our transgressions, He was crushed for our iniquities; the chastening for our well-being fell upon Him, and by His scourging we are healed. Isaiah 53:4-5 (NASB)

He Himself bore our sins in His body on the cross, so that we might die to sin and live to righteousness; for by His wounds you were healed. 1 Peter 2:24 (NASB)

Healing power flowed to those who touched Jesus.
And wherever he went—into villages, towns or countryside—they placed the sick in the marketplaces. They begged him to let them touch even the edge of his cloak, and all who touched him were healed. Mark 6:56 (NIV)

And all the people were trying to touch Him, for power was coming from Him and healing them all. Luke 6:19 (NASB)

Healing was a part of the ministry of the Apostles.
They went out and preached that men should repent. And they were casting out many demons and were anointing with oil many sick people and healing them. Mark 6:12-13 (NASB)

Healing flowed through Paul in extraordinary ways.
God was performing extraordinary miracles by the hands of Paul, so that handkerchiefs or aprons were even carried from his body to the sick, and the diseases left them and the evil spirits went out. Acts 19:11-12 (NASB)

Healing power from Jesus must be present to heal others.
One day as he was teaching, Pharisees and teachers of the law, who had come from every village of Galilee and from Judea and Jerusalem, were sitting there. And the power of the Lord was present for him to heal the sick. Luke 5:17 (NIV)

Healing prayer is to be a part of the ministry of elders.
Is anyone among you sick? Then he must call for the elders of the church and they are to pray over him, anointing him with oil in the name of the Lord. James 5:14 (NASB)

Healing comes from God as we turn to him from sin.
If my people, who are called by my name, will humble themselves and pray and seek my face and turn from their wicked ways, then will I hear from heaven and will forgive their sin and will heal their land. 2 Chronicles 7:14 (NIV)

Healing gifts are given to some by the Spirit for ministry.
To another gifts of healing by that one Spirit. 1 Corinthians 12:9 (NIV)

Healing is only and ultimately guaranteed in heaven.
And He will wipe away every tear from their eyes; and there will no longer be any death; there will no longer be any mourning, or crying, or pain; the first things have passed away. Revelation 21:4 (NASB)

How much faith is needed for healing?

While it is true that faith is an essential part of receiving healing (Matthew 15:28, Mark 5:34, Acts 3:16), it is not required that the sick person himself possess the faith. Frankly, God can heal even when the sick person does not even recognize him (John 5:13) and does not possess the ability to exercise faith (John 11:44), or by utilizing the faith of those who are not sick (James 5:14-15). When the sick person himself does need faith for healing, the good news is that very little is required. Jesus said:

> If you have faith as small as a mustard seed, you can say to this mulberry tree, 'Be uprooted and planted in the sea,' and it will obey you. Luke 17:6 (NIV)

A mustard seed is a tiny seed. Jesus' point was that the tiniest amount of faith can be used by God to do mighty things. Not only is very little faith needed to receive healing, but it is also true that faith itself is a gift from God. In the New Testament book of Hebrews, we read that Jesus is the "author and the perfecter" of our faith (Hebrews 12:2). Faith comes from God. For example, after healing a lame beggar, Peter explained that the faith needed for healing was supplied by Jesus.

> By faith in the name of Jesus, this man whom you see and know was made strong. It is Jesus' name and the faith that comes through him that has given this complete healing to him, as you can all see. Acts 3:16 (NIV)

Faith is not something that we can manufacture, but something that only God can provide. What are we to do if we lack faith? We are to ask. While it is true that faith comes only from God, this does not mean that we are without responsibility or opportunity. God is sovereign, providing healing as well as the required faith to receive healing, but we are also invited to ask for what we desire. Jesus said:

> Ask, and it will be given to you; seek, and you will find; knock, and it will be opened to you. For everyone who asks receives, and he who seeks finds, and to him who knocks it will be opened. Matthew 7:7-8 (NASB)

In the gospel of Mark, we read of a father's desperate plea for more faith, as he seeks his son's healing.

> So He asked his father, "How long has this been happening to him?" And he said, "From childhood. And often he has thrown him both into the fire and into the water to destroy him. But if You can do anything, have compassion on us and help us." Jesus said to him, "If you can believe, all things *are* possible to him who believes." Immediately the father of the child cried out and said with tears, "Lord, I believe; help my unbelief!" Mark 9:21-24 (NKJV)

Lots of Christians refuse to pray for the sick, but that is simply not an option. We are told in Scripture to pray for one another's healing, and that the prayer offered in faith will make the sick person well (James 5:14-16).

We must remember that God is at work in the lives of his people, even when he does not heal them. We must also remember that Jesus chastised those who demanded he perform signs and wonders in order for them to believe (John 4:48). We are not to base on our faith in God on being healed, but rather on the finished work of Jesus' death and resurrection, which will ultimately bring certain healing. The good news is all those who have faith in Jesus are guaranteed healing in heaven (Revelation 2:14).

Hearing God's Voice

God spoke to Abraham, Jacob and Moses directly (Genesis 17:22, Genesis 35:13, Exodus 3:4), while Ananias, Peter and Paul heard God's voice through visions (Acts 9:10, Acts 10:15, Acts 18:19). God speaks to comfort and protect his people, as well as to offer correction and guidance (Job 33:14-18). Not only does God speak, but the Bible also teaches that we can hear his voice and follow his lead.

Hearing God's voice often comes with practice, and as others help us learn to recognize his voice.
The LORD called Samuel a third time, and Samuel got up and went to Eli and said, "Here I am; you called me." Then Eli realized that the LORD was calling the boy. So Eli told Samuel, "Go and lie down, and if he calls you, say, 'Speak, LORD, for your servant is listening.' " So Samuel went and lay down in his place. 1 Samuel 3:8-9 (NIV)

Hearing God's voice means listening for a gentle sound.
So He said, "Go forth and stand on the mountain before the LORD " And behold, the LORD was passing by! And a great and strong wind was rending the mountains and breaking in pieces the rocks before the LORD; but the LORD was not in the wind. And after the wind an earthquake, but the LORD was not in the earthquake. After the earthquake a fire, but the LORD was not in the fire; and after the fire a sound of a gentle blowing. When Elijah heard it, he wrapped his face in his mantle and went out and stood in the entrance of the cave And behold, a voice came to him and said, "What are you doing here, Elijah?" 1 Kings 19:11-13 (NASB)

God's people can hear God's voice.
His disciples asked him what this parable meant. He said, "The knowledge of the secrets of the kingdom of God has been given to you, but to others I speak in parables, so that, "'though seeing, they may not see; though hearing, they may not understand.' Luke 8:9-10 (NIV)

Hearing God's voice means listening to Scripture.

For David himself, speaking under the inspiration of the Holy Spirit, said, 'The LORD said to my LORD, Sit in the place of honor at my right hand until I humble your enemies beneath your feet.' Mark 12:36 (NLT)

Long ago God spoke many times and in many ways to our ancestors through the prophets. And now in these final days, he has spoken to us through his Son. God promised everything to the Son as an inheritance, and through the Son he created the universe. Hebrews 1:1-2 (NLT)

Above all, you must realize that no prophecy in Scripture ever came from the prophet's own understanding, or from human initiative. No, those prophets were moved by the Holy Spirit, and they spoke from God. 2 Peter 1:20-21 (NLT)

Hearing God's voice is a function of the Holy Spirit.

But you have received the Holy Spirit, and he lives within you, so you don't need anyone to teach you what is true. For the Spirit teaches you everything you need to know, and what he teaches is true—it is not a lie. So just as he has taught you, remain in fellowship with Christ. 1 John 2:27 (NLT)

Hearing God's voice leads to following Jesus.

The watchman opens the gate for him, and the sheep listen to his voice. He calls his own sheep by name and leads them out. When he has brought out all his own, he goes on ahead of them, and his sheep follow him because they know his voice. But they will never follow a stranger; in fact, they will run away from him because they do not recognize a stranger's voice." John 10:3-5 (NIV)

Heaven

Heaven is a place of beauty, described as having streets of gold, walls encrusted with jewels, and gates made of giant pearls (Revelation 21:1-27). While this description need not be taken literally, heaven is certainly a place of physical splendor. Heaven is also a place of physical activity. The Bible describes heaven as a place we will experience physically (Romans 8:23). While we will not participate bodily in all the activities that we do on earth (Matthew 22:30, Mark 12:25, Luke 20:35), we will engage in many activities (Matthew 25:20-21, 1 Corinthians 6:3, Revelation 5:9). For example, Jesus describes the faithful as rewarded in heaven with the opportunity to exercise governing authority (Luke 19:17).

Ultimately though, heaven is the place where God's people will dwell fully in God's presence (Matthew 5:16, Matthew 18:10, John 14:2, 1 Corinthians 13:12, Revelation 21:3-4). Heaven is beautiful and fully engaging, because God's presence is finally and fully made available to us.

Heaven was Jesus' dwelling place before the incarnation.
For I have come down from heaven to do the will of God who sent me, not to do my own will. John 6:38 (NLT)

Heaven is where Jesus returned to and where he lives.
While he was blessing them, he left them and was taken up to heaven. Luke 24:51 (NLT)

Here is the main point: We have a High Priest who sat down in the place of honor beside the throne of the majestic God in heaven. Hebrews 8:1 (NLT)

For Christ did not enter into a holy place made with human hands, which was only a copy of the true one in heaven. He entered into heaven itself to appear now before God on our behalf. Hebrews 9:24 (NLT)

Heaven is where Christians go immediately after death.
Jesus answered him, "I tell you the truth, today you will be with me in paradise." Luke 23:43 (NIV)

We are confident, I say, and would prefer to be away from the body and at home with the Lord. 2 Corinthians 5:8 (NIV)

Heaven is being prepared by Jesus for Christians.
"In My Father's house are many dwelling places; if it were not so, I would have told you; for I go to prepare a place for you." "If I go and prepare a place for you, I will come again and receive you to Myself, that where I am, there you may be also." John 14:2-3 (NASB)

Now we know that if the earthly tent we live in is destroyed, we have a building from God, an eternal house in heaven, not built by human hands. 2 Corinthians 5:1 (NIV)

Heaven is the place of life eternal.
We always thank God, the Father of our Lord Jesus Christ, when we pray for you, since we heard of your faith in Christ Jesus and of the love that you have for all the saints, because of the hope laid up for you in heaven. Colossians 1:3-5 (ESV)

Heaven is the home of all Christians.
But we are citizens of heaven, where the Lord Jesus Christ lives. And we are eagerly waiting for him to return as our Savior. Philippians 3:20 (NLT)

Heaven, whether in part or in full, was seen by Paul.
I know a man in Christ who fourteen years ago--whether in the body I do not know, or out of the body I do not know, God knows--such a man was caught up to the third heaven. And I know how such a man--whether in the body or apart from the body I do not know, God knows--was caught up into Paradise and heard inexpressible words, which a man is not permitted to speak. 2 Corinthians 12:2-4 (NASB)

Hell

Hell is the place of eternal conscious physical punishment, reserved for all who are not righteous (Matthew 25:41). Of course, the trouble is that none are righteous (Romans 3:10), and thus all are deserving of Hell. All are born separated from God by their sinfulness and spiritually dead, and we escape Hell only as we are made alive and reunited with God through faith in Jesus (Ephesians 2:1-5). This process of being made alive was described by Jesus as being born again (John 3:3-21). A belief in Hell is commonly regarded as primitive or foolish and thus rejected by many. But to reject Hell is to reject a core teaching of Jesus and the Apostles.

Jesus taught that Hell is a place of eternal conscious physical punishment.

He is ready to separate the chaff from the wheat with his winnowing fork. Then he will clean up the threshing area, gathering the wheat into his barn but burning the chaff with never-ending fire. Matthew 3:12 (NLT)

Then they will go away to eternal punishment, but the righteous to eternal life. Matthew 25:46 (NIV)

And if your eye causes you to sin, gouge it out. It's better to enter the Kingdom of God with only one eye than to have two eyes and be thrown into hell, 'where the maggots never die and the fire never goes out.' Mark 9:47-48 (NLT)

They will throw them into the blazing furnace, where there will be weeping and gnashing of teeth. Matthew 13:42 (NIV)

In hell, where he was in torment, he looked up and saw Abraham far away with Lazarus by his side. So he called to him, 'Father Abraham, have pity on me and send Lazarus to dip the tip of his finger in water and cool my tongue, because I am in agony in this fire. Luke 16:23-24 (NIV)

"Then he will say to those on his left, 'Depart from me, you who are cursed, into the eternal fire prepared for the devil and his angels." Matthew 25:41 (NIV)

Jesus taught that Hell is the place of God's condemnation.
If you call someone an idiot, you are in danger of being brought before the court. And if you curse someone, you are in danger of the fires of hell. Matthew 5:22 (NLT)

But I will warn you whom to fear: fear the One who, after He has killed, has authority to cast into hell; yes, I tell you, fear Him! Luke 12:5 (NASB)

You snakes! You brood of vipers! How will you escape being condemned to hell? Matthew 23:33 (NIV)

The disciples affirmed Hells' existence.
They are wild waves of the sea, foaming up their shame; wandering stars, for whom blackest darkness has been reserved forever. Jude 13 (NIV)

God is just: He will pay back trouble to those who trouble you and give relief to you who are troubled, and to us as well. This will happen when the Lord Jesus is revealed from heaven in blazing fire with his powerful angels. He will punish those who do not know God and do not obey the gospel of our Lord Jesus. They will be punished with everlasting destruction and shut out from the presence of the Lord and from the glory of his might. 2 Thessalonians 1:6-9 (NIV)

But the cowardly, the unbelieving, the vile, the murderers, the sexually immoral, those who practice magic arts, the idolaters and all liars—they will be consigned to the fiery lake of burning sulfur. Revelation 21:8 (NIV)

How is eternal punishment justified?

Scripture teaches that those who die without trusting in Jesus' death for the forgiveness of sin are eternally punished (2 Thessalonians 1:8). This is a difficult reality, and one that can raise a lot of questions. In wrestling with this reality, many ask how *eternal* punishment is warranted for a *finite* amount of sin. Being finite, humans can only commit a limited number of sins, yet Hell is described as eternal punishment. How is this justified?

First, eternal punishment is justified because of the weight of sin's offensiveness to God. Ironically, we have trouble grasping the weight of our sin's offensiveness because our sin blinds us to some degree (2 Corinthians 4:3-4). This is most clearly seen in how we wince at descriptions of God's temporal judgment against human sin. For example, many consider God's judgment against Lot's wife, whom God turned into a pillar of salt (Genesis 19:6), and Nadab and Abihu, whom God consumed with fire (Leviticus 10:1-2), and Achan, whom God ordered to be stoned (Joshua 7:24-25), as excessively harsh and thus unjustified. Yet, sin is described in Scripture as "rebellion," "lawlessness," and "wickedness" (Leviticus 16:21, 1 John 3:4). Not surprisingly, these are words that few embrace as personal descriptors of their sinful behavior.

One of the best pictures of the weight of sin's offensiveness is provided in the prescribed slaughter of animals in the book of Leviticus (Leviticus 4:35, 5:10). Trying to physically picture the sacrificial rituals described in the Old Testament is gruesome. Imagine the bloodletting at the dedication of the Temple, in which thousands of animals were slaughtered (1 Kings 8:63). Ultimately, the most poignant picture of sin's offensiveness before God is the description of Jesus' suffering and death on the cross, which the Apostle Paul rightly labels as a stumbling block to many (1 Corinthians 1:23). Many recoil at the notion that a man, who was perfect in his moral character, had to suffer and die for our forgiveness.

Secondly, eternal punishment is justified because of God's holiness (Isaiah 6:3, Revelation 4:8). We have a tendency to not only diminish the gravity of our sin's offensiveness to God, but also to diminish the exalted status of God. When Scripture describes God as holy, it is not describing an attribute of God, as much as the sum of all of God's attributes, his moral purity, his limitless knowledge, his infinite beauty, and his unending power, etc. Together these attributes make God holy, that is to say unique and unparalleled in the universe. God's holiness implies a "separateness" on God's part. God is set apart by his holiness, and our sinfulness is uniquely offensive to him because of his holiness.

Perhaps the best example of why God's holiness justifies eternal punishment for sin is seen in our own judicial system. We intuitively judge the nature of crimes committed against citizens within the general population as less offensive than crimes committed against heads of state. For example, punching a President is a far greater offense than punching one's neighbor, because of the exalted position of the President. Anyone who punches the President is rightly punished more severely than someone who punches an average citizen. Similarly, eternal punishment is justifiable, when we understand both the offensiveness of our sin and the holiness of the One against whom we have sinned.

In the end, the reality of eternal punishment accentuates the beauty of the gospel, as only a God of infinite holiness could bear the weight of human sinfulness, and only a man of perfect moral character could sufficiently ransom us from God's just judgment.

How is Hell consistent with God's love?

God is love, which means love is not defined primarily by human experience (including the experience of being eternally punished), but by the person and purposes of God (1 John 4:8). To put a finer point on it, love is not a concept outside of God to which he conforms. In other words, God is not simply loving, but love and lovingness is a reality which he defines. If love were a reality external to God, to which he conformed, then there would be a law or reality greater than God, which is impossible. Because God's person defines what it means to be loving, whatever God does is loving, even when eternally punishing some in Hell.

Further, while we can act loving one moment and unloving the next, God does not have that ability. This means that God is never at risk for compromising his character or having to choose between the various attributes of his character (e.g., justice and love). God is at all times able to act with both perfect justice and complete love, even when eternally punishing some in Hell. In the Old Testament book of Exodus we learn of God's ability to both mete out justice and demonstrate love in all situations, as he described himself to Moses.

> And he passed in front of Moses, proclaiming, "The LORD, the LORD, the compassionate and gracious God, slow to anger, abounding in love and faithfulness, maintaining love to thousands, and forgiving wickedness, rebellion and sin. Yet he does not leave the guilty unpunished; he punishes the children and their children for the sin of the parents to the third and fourth generation. Exodus 34:6-7 (NIV)

We often have trouble understanding how eternal punishment is consistent with God's loving character, because not only do we lack God's integrity (i.e., we are sometimes loving and at other times unkind), we also lack the necessary information for making eternal judgments. We are finite with limited understanding of both justice and love. This means that while we can make temporal judgments (e.g., sending someone to jail for murder), we lack all the needed information to judge matters of eternal consequence. Job complained to God that he was suffering unjustly. God responded by reminding Job of his finite perspective. Then Job humbly admitted:

> I know that you can do all things; no plan of yours can be thwarted. You asked, 'Who is this that obscures my counsel without knowledge?' Surely I spoke of things I did not understand, things too wonderful for me to know. "You said, 'Listen now, and I will speak; I will question you, and you shall answer me.' My ears had heard of you but now my eyes have seen you. Therefore I despise myself and repent in dust and ashes.
> Job 42:1-6 (NIV)

Having a finite perspective, our affirmations of faith often possess a corresponding admission of ignorance. This is true for all faiths. Atheistic materialists affirm by faith all that exists is only that which can be known with the five senses. At the same time, they must admit their ignorance regarding how "something" came from "nothing." Too many, consider only the affirmations of belief in a particular faith system, and never consider the corresponding admissions of ignorance. In fact, we ought to be on guard against any person that fails to admit ignorance at some level.

In the end, Christians are confident in not only the affirmations made within Scripture (e.g., God is both perfectly loving and just in all his judgments), but also at peace with the corresponding admissions of ignorance (e.g., we do not have enough information to completely understand all of God's decisions on eternal matters).

Why is Hell populated, if God could save all?

If God can save everyone from Hell, why is he saving only some? The Apostle Paul wrestled with this question, and while he did not provide a direct answer, he did provide an indirect answer, reminding his readers of the Old Testament story of twin brothers born to Rebekah, one named Jacob and the other Esau.

> Yet, before the twins were born or had done anything good or bad—in order that God's purpose in election might stand: not by works but by him who calls—she was told, "The older will serve the younger." Just as it is written: "Jacob I loved, but Esau I hated." Romans 9:11-13 (NIV)

Paul's explanation of why God is only saving some is described as "unconditional election." Apart from what either brother had done, whether "good or bad," God chose Jacob. God's election of Jacob was not conditioned upon Jacob's behavior. Similarly, God's rejection of Esau was not conditioned upon Esau's behavior. Paul's point is that the same is happening in salvation. God is unconditionally electing some for salvation.

Of course, Paul anticipated objections. The first objection is that of fairness, and Paul wrote, "What then shall we say? Is God unjust?" (Romans 9:14). In other words, how is it fair that God is electing to save only some, when he could save all? Paul's answer is fascinating, and it is one that redefines our understanding of justice. Paul responds that God's decision to save only some is fair because it will result in his glory. In other words, justice is defined not by what we perceive as fair, but rather by what brings God glory. To illustrate his point, Paul explains that Pharaoh was raised to power for the glory of God.

> For Scripture says to Pharaoh: "I raised you up for this very purpose, that I might display my power in you and that my name might be proclaimed in all the earth." Romans 9:17 (NIV)

Paul's explanation forces us to assess whether we believe God's purposes to bring himself glory are the greatest good. Determining what is fair and what is unfair always requires a standard. The challenge for humanity is that we often want to determine, or even want to be, the standard of fairness and justice. Paul is clear that God's glory is the standard for justice (Romans 9:17-18).

The second objection addressed by Paul is, "How can God blame us?" In other words, if God is electing to save only those whom he chooses, and no one can resist God's will, then on what basis is someone condemned to Hell? Paul answers the question by writing:

> But who are you, O man, to talk back to God? "Shall what is formed say to him who formed it, 'Why did you make me like this?' " Does not the potter have the right to make out of the same lump of clay some pottery for noble purposes and some for common use? Romans 9:20-21 (NIV)

While much in my life might tempt us to believe that we have freewill, much in life also reminds us that we are not ultimately free. For example, we didn't choose to be born, or to whom we were born. We also didn't choose when to be born or where to be born. Clearly, while I can choose whom to marry and where to go to college, there are some very significant matters over which we have no control, including our eternal destiny. Some are made by God for "noble purposes" and some for "common use." Paul drove this point home with two of the deepest verses in all of Scripture.

> What if God, choosing to show his wrath and make his power known, bore with great patience the objects of his wrath—prepared for destruction? What if he did this to make the riches of his glory known to the objects of his mercy, whom he prepared in advance for glory—even us, whom he also called, not only from the Jews but also from the Gentiles? Romans 9:22-24 (NIV)

Although these two verses appear as questions, they are rhetorical. They are designed not to ask a question, but to proclaim a truth. If God has chosen to show his wrath and power toward those prepared for destruction and the riches of his glory toward those whom he is saving, then who are we to question him! Simply put, God is God and we are not! In the end, we can be comforted by the knowledge that eternal punishment preserves humanity's moral agency, while at the same time resulting in God's glory. God rightly condemns some to Hell because of their sinfulness, and God brings himself glory by saving some from the consequences of their sins.

How is this good news some might ask? This is good news because it affirms that anyone can be saved! No one is too bad or too weak that they can't be saved because our salvation does not depend upon us (Ephesians 2:8-9). Second, the is good news because it provides security in salvation. The good news of the Gospel is that God has laid hold of us, and God holds on to us. Jesus said that he would "lose none of those" whom the Father has given him (John 6:39, John 10:28-29). Thirdly, this is good news because it clearly identifies God's mercy. Christians are those who have received mercy and for that reason ministry to the poor and the sick and the jailed and the homeless and orphans is the greatest demonstration of what we have experienced. Mercy isn't coincidental to Christian faith. It is an essential indication that we have received God's mercy through faith in Jesus Christ (John 13:34-35).

Hiddenness of God

The "hiddenness" of God refers to mankind's inability to know God apart from God revealing himself. While all humans possess a sense that God exists, based upon evidence in nature (Romans 1:20) and the conviction of conscience (Romans 2:15), we are still unable to know God personally, apart from his intervention (Ephesians 2:4-5).

Being hidden from humanity was not God's original intention. God's hiddenness is a product of our sin. Because of sin, we see imperfectly, or vision is clouded (1 Corinthians 13:12). The good news is that the barrier of sin has been overcome through Jesus Christ's birth, death, and resurrection (John 1:18, Ephesians 3:3-4), and all those who trust in Christ for salvation can know God.

Being hidden from humanity was not God's original plan.
When the cool evening breezes were blowing, the man and his wife heard the Lord God walking about in the garden. So they hid from the Lord God among the trees. Then the Lord God called to the man, "Where are you?" Genesis 3:8-9 (NLT)

God's hiddenness is a product of our sinfulness.
So the Lord God banished them from the Garden of Eden, and he sent Adam out to cultivate the ground from which he had been made. Genesis 3:23 (NLT)

God's hiddenness is seen in Jesus' use of parables.
He replied, "You are permitted to understand the secret of the Kingdom of God. But I use parables for everything I say to outsiders, so that the Scriptures might be fulfilled: 'When they see what I do, they will learn nothing. When they hear what I say, they will not understand. Otherwise, they will turn to me and be forgiven.' Mark 4:11-12 (NLT)

Then he opened their minds to understand the Scriptures.
Luke 24:45 (ESV)

God's hiddenness is evident in the condemnation of some.
Then one said to Him, "Lord, are there few who are saved?" And He said to them, "Strive to enter through the narrow gate, for many, I say to you, will seek to enter and will not be able."' Luke 13:23-24 (NKJV)

The hiddenness of God is overcome by faith in Jesus.
But the people's minds were hardened, and to this day whenever the old covenant is being read, the same veil covers their minds so they cannot understand the truth. And this veil can be removed only by believing in Christ. 2 Corinthians 3:14 (NLT)

The hiddenness of God shows that salvation is a gift.
But because of his great love for us, God, who is rich in mercy, made us alive with Christ even when we were dead in transgressions—it is by grace you have been saved. Ephesians 2:4-5 (NIV)

God reveals himself as we seek him.
"Ask and it will be given to you; seek and you will find; knock and the door will be opened to you. For everyone who asks receives; he who seeks finds; and to him who knocks, the door will be opened. Matthew 7:7-8 (NIV)

Draw near to God and He will draw near to you. James 4:8 (NASB)

God's hiddenness will one day be completely overcome.
Now we see things imperfectly, like puzzling reflections in a mirror, but then we will see everything with perfect clarity. All that I know now is partial and incomplete, but then I will know everything completely, just as God now knows me completely. 1 Corinthians 13:12 (NLT)

Holiness

Holiness is not a single attribute of God, but rather a statement about his being. Holiness is the outcome of the sum of all of God's attributes, his moral purity, knowledge, beauty, power, etc. Together these attributes make God holy, that is to say unique and unparalleled in nature and separated from all other beings. Holiness implies a "separateness," as God's combination of perfect attributes makes him unique from all other creatures in the universe. Christians are commanded to be holy, which is a command to live a life separated from ungodliness, a life increasingly marked by the character, conduct and concerns of God.

Holiness is a description of God and is sung as his praise.
And the four living creatures, each one of them having six wings, are full of eyes around and within; and day and night they do not cease to say, "HOLY, HOLY, HOLY is THE LORD GOD, THE ALMIGHTY, WHO WAS AND WHO IS AND WHO IS TO COME." *Revelation 4:8 (NASB)*

Holiness is the call of God upon his people's lives.
As obedient children, do not conform to the evil desires you had when you lived in ignorance. But just as he who called you is holy, so be holy in all you do; for it is written: "Be holy, because I am holy." 1 Peter 1:14-16 (NIV)

Holiness comes to us through Jesus Christ.
It is because of him that you are in Christ Jesus, who has become for us wisdom from God—that is, our righteousness, holiness and redemption. Therefore, as it is written: "Let him who boasts boast in the Lord." 1 Corinthians 1:30-31 (NIV)

Holiness comes from offering ourselves to righteousness.
I put this in human terms because you are weak in your natural selves. Just as you used to offer the parts of your body in slavery to impurity and to ever-increasing wickedness, so now offer them in slavery to righteousness leading to holiness. Romans 6:19 (NIV)

Holiness is a call to purity.
Since we have these promises, dear friends, let us purify ourselves from everything that contaminates body and spirit, perfecting holiness out of reverence for God. 2 Corinthians 7:1 (NIV)

Holiness is the reason we have been born again.
You were taught, with regard to your former way of life, to put off your old self, which is being corrupted by its deceitful desires; to be made new in the attitude of your minds; and to put on the new self, created to be like God in true righteousness and holiness. Ephesians 4:22-24 (NIV)

Holiness is the product of God's grace teaching us.
For the grace of God that brings salvation has appeared to all men. It teaches us to say "No" to ungodliness and worldly passions, and to live self-controlled, upright and godly lives in this present age. Titus 2:11-12 (NIV)

Holiness is the purpose of God's discipline in our lives.
Moreover, we have all had human fathers who disciplined us and we respected them for it. How much more should we submit to the Father of our spirits and live! Our fathers disciplined us for a little while as they thought best; but God disciplines us for our good, that we may share in his holiness. Hebrews 12:9-10 (NIV)

Holiness is the life prepared for judgment.
*Since everything will be destroyed in this way, what kind of people ought you to be? You ought to live holy and godly lives as you look forward to the day of God and speed its coming. That day will bring about the destruction of the heavens by fire, and the elements will melt in the heat.
2 Peter 3:11-12 (NIV)*

Holy Spirit

The Holy Spirit is God. The Bible teaches that God is one, with three distinct persons (i.e., Father, Son and Holy Spirit), each person within the Trinity is fully God and distinct in essence. This is known as Trinitarianism, and it means that all of God's attributes (e.g., his eternality, omniscience, omnipresence) are fully present in all three persons of the Trinity, who each have distinct and complementary roles within salvation history.

The Holy Spirit is God, a member of the Trinity.
Therefore go and make disciples of all nations, baptizing them in the name of the Father and of the Son and of the Holy Spirit. Matthew 28:19 (NIV)

There is one body and one Spirit—just as you were called to one hope when you were called—one Lord, one faith, one baptism; one God and Father of all, who is over all and through all and in all. Ephesians 4:4-6 (NIV)

The Holy Spirit physically dwells with Christians.
"He who believes in Me, as the Scripture said, 'From his innermost being will flow rivers of living water.'" But this He spoke of the Spirit, whom those who believed in Him were to receive; for the Spirit was not yet given, because Jesus was not yet glorified. John 7:38-39 (NASB)

Or do you not know that your body is a temple of the Holy Spirit who is in you, whom you have from God, and that you are not your own? 1 Corinthians 6:19 (NASB)

The Holy Spirit gives power, guidance, and gifts.
But you will receive power when the Holy Spirit comes on you; and you will be my witnesses." Acts 1:8 (NIV)

So I say, live by the Spirit, and you will not gratify the desires of the sinful nature. Galatians 5:16 (NIV)

God also testifying with them, both by signs and wonders and by various miracles and by gifts of the Holy Spirit according to His own will. Hebrews 2:4 (NASB)

The Holy Spirit's presence in us guarantees our salvation.
In Him, you also, after listening to the message of truth, the gospel of your salvation--having also believed, you were sealed in Him with the Holy Spirit of promise, who is given as a pledge of our inheritance, with a view to the redemption of God's own possession, to the praise of His glory. Ephesians 1:13-14 (NASB)

The Holy Spirit gives life to those trusting in Christ.
You, however, are not in the flesh but in the Spirit, if in fact the Spirit of God dwells in you. Anyone who does not have the Spirit of Christ does not belong to him. But if Christ is in you, although the body is dead because of sin, the Spirit is life because of righteousness. If the Spirit of him who raised Jesus from the dead dwells in you, he who raised Christ Jesus from the dead will also give life to your mortal bodies through his Spirit who dwells in you. Romans 8:9-11 (ESV)

The Holy Spirit produces righteousness in our lives.
But the fruit of the Spirit is love, joy, peace, patience, kindness, goodness, faithfulness, gentleness, self-control; against such things there is no law. Galatians 5:22-23 (NASB)

The Holy Spirit is given as a helper who teaches us.
"But the Helper, the Holy Spirit, whom the Father will send in My name, He will teach you all things, and bring to your remembrance all that I said to you. John 14:26 (NASB)

What does "filled" with the Spirit mean?

Being filled with the Holy Spirit is to be uniquely empowered by his presence, and Paul commands all Christians to be filled.

> And don't get drunk with wine, which leads to reckless actions, but be filled by the Spirit: speaking to one another in psalms, hymns, and spiritual songs, singing and making music from your heart to the Lord, giving thanks always for everything to God the Father in the name of our Lord Jesus Christ, submitting to one another in the fear of Christ. Ephesians 5:18-21 (HCSB)

According to Paul, filling by the Holy Spirit can and should be an ongoing and repeated occurrence in the lives of Christians.

When we are born again, it is a singular event, much like being born biologically is a singular event. It happens once and, in an instant, and our adoption, that is our new relationship with God, is sealed by receiving the Holy Spirit as a deposit (Ephesians 1:13-14). When we are born again God gives us his presence, depositing his Holy Spirit within us, guaranteeing our redemption, much like a parent would deposit money in a bank, guaranteeing their children's inheritance.

But, being filled by the Spirit is something different than the initial reception of the Holy Spirit at the time of spiritual new birth. Being filled is the experience of being uniquely empowered by the Holy Spirit. For example, in the New Testament book of Acts we read that the Apostle Peter was filled with the Holy Spirit on multiple occasions (Acts 2:4, Acts 4:8, Acts 4:31). And Stephen, although he was selected to be a deacon because he was known as a man "full of the Spirit" (Acts 6:3, 5), received a fresh filling of the Holy Spirit during his persecution (Acts 7:55).

This means that it is entirely possible to have the Holy Spirit and not be filled with his influence and power in our lives. It is entirely possible to be "saved," that is born again, sealed, and set apart for the day of redemption, but to be weak and ineffective as Christians. God's desire is that his Holy Spirit's presence fill us entirely, influencing every attitude and action we have, which will bring blessings into our lives and glory to God. Blessings, according to Paul, that include renewed worship, thanksgiving and strengthened relationships (Ephesians 5:18-21), as well as effectiveness in sharing one's faith (Acts 2:4, Acts 4:8, Acts 4:31) and in addressing evil (Acts 13:9).

How are we to be filled by the Spirit? We are filled by the Spirit as we seek the Spirit's influence in our lives. We can seek the Spirit's influence by praying for God to pour out more of his Spirit's presence upon us (Luke 11:13, Acts 4:31, Colossians 1:9), and by actively setting our minds on the things of the Spirit (Romans 8:6, Galatians 5:25), as well as living obedient to Scripture and putting an end to sinful activities in our lives (Colossians 3:5).

Homosexuality

Homosexuality is the desire for, or activity of, having sexual intercourse with someone of the same gender. While homosexuality is only one of the many sins listed in the Bible, within our contemporary culture it is being presented by some as an acceptable alternative lifestyle. This makes homosexuality culturally unique, as few are presenting other sins (e.g., stealing or murder) as acceptable ways to live.

Homosexuality was forbidden by the Old Testament law.
You shall not lie with a male as with a woman; it is an abomination. Leviticus 18:22 (ESV)

If a man lies with a male as with a woman, both of them have committed an abomination; they shall surely be put to death; their blood is upon them. Leviticus 20:13 (ESV)

Homosexuality is listed as contrary to God's law.
Now we know that the law is good, if one uses it lawfully, understanding this, that the law is not laid down for the just but for the lawless and disobedient, for the ungodly and sinners, for the unholy and profane, for those who strike their fathers and mothers, for murderers, the sexually immoral, men who practice homosexuality, enslavers, liars, perjurers, and whatever else is contrary to sound doctrine, in accordance with the gospel of the glory of the blessed God with which I have been entrusted. 1 Timothy 1:8-11 (ESV)

Homosexuality is unnatural, shameful and dishonorable.
For this reason God gave them up to dishonorable passions. For their women exchanged natural relations for those that are contrary to nature; and the men likewise gave up natural relations with women and were consumed with passion for one another, men committing shameless acts with men and receiving in themselves the due penalty for their error. Romans 1:26-27 (ESV)

Homosexuality is listed as one of the practices of those who will not inherit the kingdom of God.
Do not be deceived: neither the sexually immoral, nor idolaters, nor adulterers, nor men who practice homosexuality, nor thieves, nor the greedy, nor drunkards, nor revilers, nor swindlers will inherit the kingdom of God. 1 Corinthians 6:9-10 (ESV)

Homosexual unions were not established by God.
Then the Lord God made a woman from the rib, and he brought her to the man. "At last!" the man exclaimed. "This one is bone from my bone, and flesh from my flesh! She will be called 'woman,' because she was taken from 'man.'" This explains why a man leaves his father and mother and is joined to his wife, and the two are united into one. Now the man and his wife were both naked, but they felt no shame. Genesis 2:22-25 (NLT)

Homosexual unions were not affirmed by Jesus.
But 'God made them male and female' from the beginning of creation. This explains why a man leaves his father and mother and is joined to his wife, and the two are united into one.' Since they are no longer two but one, let no one split apart what God has joined together." Mark 10:6-9 (NLT)

Incarnation

Incarnation refers to the *in-fleshing* of the Son of God, the second member of the Trinity. Advent is the four-week season of preparation leading up to the celebration of God's incarnation, being born in the flesh to a virgin named Mary in the city of Bethlehem (Luke 1:34).

Although the term *incarnation* does not appear in the New Testament, a belief in both Jesus Christ's humanity and his deity is foundational to the Christian faith (John 1:14). The apostle Paul explained that "in Christ lives all the fullness of God in a human body" (Colossians 2:9, NLT). This means that the man known as Jesus of Nazareth existed eternally, before being born in time and taking on human form.

While understanding how God, the infinite and eternal Creator and Sustainer of all things, can dwell within human flesh is beyond our mind's ability to fully grasp, Scripture is clear that it is through the incarnation that God initiated, carried out and will complete his work of redemption in the world. Further, while we are unable to fully grasp the realities of the incarnation, we can grasp some of the realities of the incarnation. All aspects of salvation begin with and depend upon the incarnation of God.

Through the incarnation, God revealed himself bodily.
Without question, this is the great mystery of our faith: Christ was revealed in a human body and vindicated by the Spirit. He was seen by angels and announced to the nations. He was believed in throughout the world and taken to heaven in glory. 1 Timothy 3:16 (NLT)

Through the incarnation, God revealed his glory.
So the Word became human and made his home among us. He was full of unfailing love and faithfulness. And we have seen his glory, the glory of the Father's one and only Son. John 1:14 (NLT)

Through the incarnation, God sympathized with our weaknesses and remained sinless.
For we do not have a high priest who is unable to sympathize with our weaknesses, but one who in every respect has been tempted as we are, yet without sin. Hebrews 4:15 (ESV)

Through the incarnation, God destroyed the dividing wall of hostility that separates us from him and one another.
For he himself is our peace, who has made the two groups one and has destroyed the barrier, the dividing wall of hostility, by setting aside in his flesh the law with its commands and regulations. Ephesians 2:14-15 (NIV)

Through the incarnation, God reconciled us to himself and joined us to one another.
His purpose was to create in himself one new humanity out of the two, thus making peace, and in one body to reconcile both of them to God through the cross, by which he put to death their hostility. Ephesians 2:15-16 (NIV)

Through the incarnation, God fulfilled the requirements of the law, in order that we might be free to walk according to the Spirit.
For God has done what the law, weakened by the flesh, could not do. By sending his own Son in the likeness of sinful flesh and for sin, he condemned sin in the flesh, in order that the righteous requirement of the law might be fulfilled in us, who walk not according to the flesh but according to the Spirit. Romans 8:3-4 (ESV)

Through the incarnation, God will return bodily to the earth.
"Men of Galilee, why do you stand looking into heaven? This Jesus, who was taken up from you into heaven, will come in the same way as you saw him go into heaven." Acts 1:11 (ESV)

Israel and the Church

Israel is first mentioned in the Bible when God changed Jacob's name to Israel (Genesis 32:28). Thus, the "children of Israel" are quite literally the descendants of Jacob. This new name of "Israel" was affirmed again when God confirmed his covenant with Jacob (Genesis 35:9-12), emphasizing elements of the covenant that God had originally made with Abraham, Jacob's grandfather (Genesis 15, 17). While Israel certainly received special favor as God's covenant people, God's purposes for selecting Israel were primarily for special service. Remember, that God does not play favorites (Romans 2:11).

Some of the specific purposes for which God made a covenant with Israel include blessing all the nations of the world through Israel's descendants (Genesis 22:18, Genesis 26:4), and having Israel serve as a light to other nations by living according to God's law (Exodus 19:4-6, Isaiah 42:6, 49:6). Thus, the nation of Israel has played a central role in redemptive history but is not itself the focus of redemption. The focus of redemption is providing the Savior, Jesus Christ, as the Messiah by which all people, both Jew and Gentile alike can be saved. While Jesus Christ was born in fulfillment of promises made to Israel, it is only through trusting in his sinless life, sacrificial death and victorious resurrection that anyone is saved (Acts 4:12).

As a part of their covenant with God, Israel received a Promised Land (Deuteronomy 6:10-19). Unfortunately, Israel's failure to live in accordance with the commands given to them by God brought judgement on them, which included eventual exile from the Promised Land (Deuteronomy 29). Although many Israelites would later resettle in the Promised Land, the former glory of the nation was never regained. However, in accordance with God's promises to Israel, Jesus was born in Bethlehem and "will reign over the house of Jacob forever" (Luke 1:32-33). Israel's law and prophets foretold of his coming and that salvation is "from the Jews." (Luke 24:27, John 4:22)

At the same time, Jesus also spoke of building the Church (Matthew 16:18), and sadly many of the leaders of Israel rejected Jesus as God's Messiah. Jesus even told stories of destroying the tenants of the vineyard and giving it to others (Luke 20:9-18). What does this mean for Israel, as God's chosen people? Does this mean that Israel is not included in the Church? This is the very question that Paul asks and answers in Romans 11. He writes, "I ask, then, has God rejected his people?" And Paul's answer is, "By no means!" (Romans 11:1)

Although the nation of Israel often rebelled against God, he always preserved a faithful remnant (1 Kings 19:18). This faithful remnant included David, Joash, Isaiah, and Daniel, as well as Sarah, Deborah, and Hannah. During Jesus' time, the remnant included people like Simeon and Anna (Luke 2:25-38), as well as the Apostles. This means that not all who were descended from Jacob (i.e., Israel), were truly a part of Israel (Romans 9:6), and today any who reject Jesus are not a part of true Israel. For example, many of the scribes and Pharisees of Jesus' day, though they were physically Jewish, were not truly a part of Israel because they rejected Jesus (Romans 2:28-29, Galatians 3:29). On the day of Pentecost, it was only those who were a part of true Israel that formed the nucleus of the Church, with which Gentiles were soon included (Acts 2).

To explain what has transpired in the blending of true Israel and Gentiles into one people within the Church, Paul uses the analogy of grafting branches into an olive tree (Romans 11:17-21). The olive tree represents the work of God in history to save humanity from sin, and Paul compared unbelieving Israel to branches that have been broken off, while Gentiles who are trusting in Jesus are branches that have been grafted into the olive tree. It is important to note that Paul does not say that God cut down the old olive tree of Israel to plant the new olive tree of the Church. That is replacement theology, or Supersessionism, as those who hold to this teaching believe God replaced Israel, or that Israel was superseded, by the Church.

But Scripture teaches that God did not begin a new work in Jesus, but rather that he is fulfilling the historic work he had started when he first called Abraham to himself. It is also important to note that God did not plant a second olive tree, that of the Church, alongside the old tree of Israel, and then graft branches from the old tree Israel into the new tree of the Church. This is a "Traditional Dispensational" perspective. Instead, God continued to grow and tend the same original olive tree that has existed throughout all time. This means Jesus is the *fulfillment* of the old covenant (Romans 3:21, Romans 10:4, Galatians 3:24). True Israelites and Gentiles make up one people of God within the Church. Consequently, only those who are trusting in Jesus are accurately described as the "Israel of God" (Galatians 6:16).

At the same time, Paul also sees a time in the future when "all Israel" will be saved (Romans 11:26), and he has every confidence that God is able to graft back into the olive tree those "natural" branches (i.e., ethnic Israel) that were previously broken off because of unfaithfulness (Romans 11:23-24). While writing that "all" Israel will be saved need not be stretched to mean that every individual descended from Jacob will be saved, it does seem that a future restoration of the nation of Israel is coming, which will involve their being re-grafted into the olive tree, the one people of God in the Church, through faith in the Messiah.

Concerning the importance of unity between Gentiles and Israelites who are trusting in Jesus, we must be careful not to contradict the olive tree metaphor by saying that one's ethnicity continues to define one's person. Paul drives this home saying in fact that there is neither Jew nor gentile (Galatians 3:28). While it is true that I am still a Gentile and true Israelites will continue to be ethnically Israelite, we are one in Christ. This means that the defining element, not only of our bond but also of our lives, is Jesus. As members of the Church, our ethnicity is not the defining element of our lives, whether Gentile or Jew.

Jesus Christ

Jesus Christ is both a name and a title. It is a combination of the first name of the man "Jesus," who was born in Bethlehem (Matthew 2:1) and raised in Nazareth (Matthew 2:23), and the ancient Greek title for "anointed" one, which is translated as "Christ."

The name "Jesus" was a common name among Hebrews in the first century world. In fact, several other men in the New Testament have the name Jesus, including the criminal Barabbas (Matthew 27:16) and Justus (Colossians 4:11). But no one else is called by the name Jesus Christ.

In the New Testament, "anointed one" is translated as "Christ." In the Old Testament to be "anointed" was to be set apart by God for a special function. Priests were anointed with oil for service in the temple (Exodus 29:1-9), kings were anointed with oil for leadership (1 Samuel 10:1, 2 Samuel 2:4) and even prophets were sometimes anointed with oil for ministry (1 Kings 19:16).

For Jesus to be called the "anointed" one means that Jesus was set apart for the special service of bearing the sin of the world through his death (Acts 2:38, Romans 5:1). The writer of the book of Hebrews even relates Jesus' anointing to that of the Old Testament priests (Hebrews 1:9).

Ultimately, being called the "Christ" is an indication that the New Testament authors believed that Jesus of Nazareth fulfilled the Old Testament prophecy foretelling of God providing a Messiah, one who would redeem humanity from sin and death (Acts 5:42).

Jesus Christ was recognized first by his disciples.
Now when Jesus came into the district of Caesarea Philippi, he asked his disciples, "Who do people say that the Son of Man is?" And they said, "Some say John the Baptist, others say Elijah, and others Jeremiah or one of the prophets." He said to them, "But who do you say that I am?" Simon

Peter replied, "You are the Christ, the Son of the living God." And Jesus answered him, "Blessed are you, Simon Bar-Jonah! For flesh and blood has not revealed this to you, but my Father who is in heaven. Matthew 16:13-17 (ESV)

Jesus Christ was anointed with the Holy Spirit.
And you know that God anointed Jesus of Nazareth with the Holy Spirit and with power. Then Jesus went around doing good and healing all who were oppressed by the devil, for God was with him. Acts 10:38 (NLT)

Jesus Christ was proclaimed as the means to forgiveness.
Let all the house of Israel therefore know for certain that God has made him both Lord and Christ, this Jesus whom you crucified." Now when they heard this they were cut to the heart, and said to Peter and the rest of the apostles, "Brothers, what shall we do?" And Peter said to them, "Repent and be baptized every one of you in the name of Jesus Christ for the forgiveness of your sins, and you will receive the gift of the Holy Spirit. For the promise is for you and for your children and for all who are far off, everyone whom the Lord our God calls to himself." Acts 2:36-39 (ESV)

Jesus Christ provides righteousness to all who believe.
But now a righteousness from God, apart from law, has been made known, to which the Law and the Prophets testify. This righteousness from God comes through faith in Jesus Christ to all who believe. Romans 3:21-22 (NIV)

Jesus Christ's Deity

A belief in Jesus Christ's deity is essential to the Christian faith. By Jesus Christ's "deity" we mean that God, the Creator and Ruler of the universe, became a man, being born to a virgin named Mary (Luke 1:34) in the city of Bethlehem (Matthew 2:6) and being known in history as Jesus of Nazareth (Matthew 2:26). As the apostle Paul wrote, "For in Christ lives all the fullness of God in a human body" (Colossians 2:9, NLT). This means that the man known as Jesus of Nazareth existed eternally as the second person of the Trinity, (i.e., God the Son) before being born in time and taking on human form.

Jesus Christ's deity is demonstrated in his being with God the Father in the beginning.
In the beginning was the Word, and the Word was with God, and the Word was God. He was with God in the beginning. The Word became flesh and made his dwelling among us. John 1:1-2 (NIV)

Jesus Christ's deity is evident in his creative role.
Through him all things were made; without him nothing was made that has been made. John 1:3 (NIV)

Jesus Christ's deity is affirmed in his life-giving power.
In him was life, and that life was the light of men. John 1:4 (NIV)

Jesus Christ's deity was declared by Jesus himself.
I and the Father are one. John 10:30-31 (NIV)

Anyone who has seen me has seen the Father. John 14:9 (NIV)

Jesus Christ's deity was declared by Paul.
Theirs are the patriarchs, and from them is traced the human ancestry of Christ, who is God over all. Romans 9:5 (NIV)

Jesus Christ's deity means God's fullness dwells in Jesus.
For in Him all the fullness of Deity dwells in bodily form. Colossians 2:9 (NASB)

Jesus Christ's deity is affirmed in his role as a mediator.
For there is one God, and one mediator also between God and men, the man Christ Jesus. 1 Timothy 2:5 (NASB)

Jesus Christ's deity means he physically represents God.
He is the image of the invisible God, the firstborn of all creation. For by him all things were created, in heaven and on earth, visible and invisible, whether thrones or dominions or rulers or authorities—all things were created through him and for him. For in him all the fullness of God was pleased to dwell, and through him to reconcile to himself all things, whether on earth or in heaven, making peace by the blood of his cross. Colossians 1:15-16, 19-20 (NIV)

Jesus Christ's Humanity

A belief in Jesus Christ's humanity is essential to the Christian faith. By humanity we mean that Jesus has a human body, human emotions, human mind and human will, and that this in no way compromises his also being fully God.

The Advent season is the annual celebration of God coming to earth in the flesh, being born as a baby to a virgin named Mary. God being born in the flesh is called the *incarnation*, which means the *in-fleshing* of God.

Jesus is human in every respect, except sinfulness (Hebrews 2:17, 4:15), having come in the flesh to offer his body as a sinless sacrifice for our sinfulness (Hebrews 10:5). God took on human flesh in order to save humans from their sin—specifically being saved from the death brought by sin's impact on human bodies, minds, emotions and wills. He became man in full so that he might save us in full.

Jesus Christ's humanity is demonstrated in his birth.
This is how Jesus the Messiah was born. His mother, Mary, was engaged to be married to Joseph. But before the marriage took place, while she was still a virgin, she became pregnant through the power of the Holy Spirit. Matthew 1:18 (NLT)

Jesus Christ's humanity is seen in his temptation.
Then Jesus was led by the Spirit into the wilderness to be tempted there by the devil. For forty days and forty nights he fasted and became very hungry. Matthew 4:1-2 (NLT)

Jesus Christ's humanity is seen in his testing.
This High Priest of ours understands our weaknesses, for he faced all of the same testings we do, yet he did not sin. Hebrews 4:15 (NLT)

Jesus Christ's humanity is seen in his weeping for others.
"Where have you put him?" he asked them. They told him, "Lord, come and see." Then Jesus wept. The people who were standing nearby said, "See how much he loved him!" But some said, "This man healed a blind man. Couldn't he have kept Lazarus from dying?" John 11:34-37 (NLT)

Jesus Christ's humanity is demonstrated in his suffering.
"Father, if you are willing, please take this cup of suffering away from me. Yet I want your will to be done, not mine." Then an angel from heaven appeared and strengthened him. He prayed more fervently, and he was in such agony of spirit that his sweat fell to the ground like great drops of blood. Luke 22:42-44 (NLT)

Jesus Christ's humanity is demonstrated in his dying.
By this time it was about noon, and darkness fell across the whole land until three o'clock. The light from the sun was gone. And suddenly, the curtain in the sanctuary of the Temple was torn down the middle. Then Jesus shouted, "Father, I entrust my spirit into your hands!" And with those words he breathed his last. Luke 23:44-46 (NLT)

Jesus Christ's humanity is seen in his bodily resurrection.
Look at my hands. Look at my feet. You can see that it's really me. Touch me and make sure that I am not a ghost, because ghosts don't have bodies, as you see that I do." As he spoke, he showed them his hands and his feet. Luke 24:39-40 (NLT)

Jesus Christ's humanity is seen in his bodily ascension.
After saying this, he was taken up into a cloud while they were watching, and they could no longer see him. Acts 1:9 (NLT)

Jesus Christ's Resurrection

The bodily resurrection of Jesus Christ is the central claim of the Christian faith. All that Christians believe depends upon this historic event. The Apostle Paul admitted that if Jesus Christ has not been raised from the dead, then the Christian faith is pointless (1 Corinthians 15:4).

Through the resurrection Jesus overcame death, the penalty of human sinfulness (1 Corinthians 15:17-21), provided for our new birth through faith (Ephesians 2:1-6; 1 Peter 1:3), ensured the forgiveness of our sin (Romans 4:25), secured the power needed for our earthly life (Romans 6:1-4), and guaranteed our life eternal (1 Corinthians 1:15:20; 2 Corinthians 4:4).

Jesus told of his coming resurrection.
From that time Jesus began to show his disciples that he must go to Jerusalem and suffer many things from the elders and chief priests and scribes, and be killed, and on the third day be raised. Matthew 16:21 (ESV)

For as Jonah was in the belly of the huge fish three days and three nights, so the Son of Man will be in the heart of the earth three days and three nights. Matthew 12:40 (HCSB)

Jesus' enemies took precautions against his body being stolen.
The next day, that is, after the day of Preparation, the chief priests and the Pharisees gathered before Pilate and said, "Sir, we remember how that impostor said, while he was still alive, 'After three days I will rise.' Therefore order the tomb to be made secure until the third day, lest his disciples go and steal him away and tell the people, 'He has risen from the dead,' and the last fraud will be worse than the first." Pilate said to them, "You have a guard of soldiers. Go, make it as secure as you can." So they went and made the tomb secure by sealing the stone and setting a guard. Matthew 27:62-66 (ESV)

Jesus' resurrection was understood as a fulfillment of Old Testament prophecy.

And with great power the apostles were giving their testimony to the resurrection of the Lord Jesus, and great grace was upon them all. Acts 4:33 (ESV)

God raised Him up, ending the pains of death, because it was not possible for Him to be held by it. For David says of Him: "I saw the Lord ever before me; because He is at my right hand, I will not be shaken. Therefore my heart was glad, and my tongue rejoiced. Moreover, my flesh will rest in hope, because You will not leave me in Hades or allow Your Holy One to see decay. You have revealed the paths of life to me; You will fill me with gladness in Your presence." Acts 2:24-28 (HCSB)

Since He raised Him from the dead, never to return to decay, He has spoken in this way, I will grant you the faithful covenant blessings made to David. Therefore He also says in another passage, You will not allow Your Holy One to see decay. For David, after serving his own generation in God's plan, fell asleep, was buried with his fathers, and decayed. But the One God raised up did not decay. Acts 13:34-37 (HCSB)

Jesus' resurrection was witnessed by angels and people.

And they found the stone rolled away from the tomb, but when they went in they did not find the body of the Lord Jesus. While they were perplexed about this, behold, two men stood by them in dazzling apparel. And as they were frightened and bowed their faces to the ground, the men said to them, "Why do you seek the living among the dead? He is not here, but has risen. Remember how he told you, while he was still in Galilee." Luke 24:2-6 (ESV)

Then he said to Thomas, "Put your finger here, and see my hands; and put out your hand, and place it in my side. Do not disbelieve, but believe." Thomas answered him, "My Lord and my God!" John 20:27-28 (ESV)

Afterward he appeared to the eleven themselves as they were reclining at table, and he rebuked them for their unbelief and hardness of heart, because they had not believed those who saw him after he had risen. Mark 16:14 (ESV)

Then he appeared to more than five hundred brothers at one time, most of whom are still alive, though some have fallen asleep. 1 Corinthians 15:6 (ESV)

Jesus taught that his resurrection is to be understood as a fulfillment of Old Testament prophecy.
He said to them, "How unwise and slow you are to believe in your hearts all that the prophets have spoken! Didn't the Messiah have to suffer these things and enter into His glory?" Then beginning with Moses and all the Prophets, He interpreted for them the things concerning Himself in all the Scriptures. Luke 24:25-27 (HCSB)

Jesus' resurrection will be shared by all Christians.
For if we have been united with him in a death like his, we shall certainly be united with him in a resurrection like his. Romans 6:5 (ESV)

According to his great mercy, he has caused us to be born again to a living hope through the resurrection of Jesus Christ from the dead, to an inheritance that is imperishable, undefiled, and unfading, kept in heaven for you. 1 Peter 1:3-4 (ESV)

Why should we believe Jesus was raised?

It is true that we are saved by faith, but it is also true that our faith is reasonable. For example, it is reasonable to believe that Jesus was raised because Jesus said he would rise (Matthew 16:21). While some have suggested that Jesus' followers simply invented Jesus' teachings of his coming resurrection, this is improbable as Jesus' teachings were far too detailed and far too complex to pass as ancient fiction writing. For example, Jesus told the Pharisees that he would raise the Temple in Jerusalem in three days, when in fact he was subtly alluding to the resurrection of his body from the grave (John 2:19-22). Jesus also compared his resurrection to Jonah's experience of being three nights in the belly of a great fish (Matthew 12:40). Yet, these types of literary allusions are uncommon in ancient fiction writing.

In our modern novels, details are added to increase believability. We expect details about things like the heaviness of footsteps in the hallway when reading fiction. That is what makes fiction believable for us, but that was never the case in the ancient world. Jesus' allusions to his coming resurrection are far too detailed and complex for his followers to "make up." Instead, Jesus' teachings, and all the gospel accounts, read like ancient eye-witness testimony.

Finally, it is improbable that Jesus' followers made up his teachings about his resurrection, because women were included in the resurrection account. In the first century, women possessed little credibility. They were not allowed to testify in judicial proceedings, as it was thought they were not smart enough to offer accurate reports and too emotional to offer objective evidence. Yet, in the gospels, women are reported as the first to see Jesus raised (Matthew 28:1-10). If the disciples were fabricating a story about the resurrection, they would have never included women if they wanted to bolster its credibility.

It is also reasonable to believe that Jesus was raised because the tomb was empty (Luke 24:1-13). Considering that Jesus' resurrection was first proclaimed in Jerusalem, the same city in which he was crucified and buried, and that Jesus was buried in the tomb of Joseph of Arimathea, who was himself a member of the Jewish Sanhedrin (Mark 15:42-47), the resurrection story would not have lasted for a single hour if the emptiness of the tomb had not been established.

Of course, the most popular explanation for the empty tomb is that the disciples stole the body. However, Jesus' enemies took precautions to ensure that the body wasn't stolen (Matthew 27:62-66). Moreover, the disciples were filled with fear, not courage, proven by their deserting Jesus at his arrest (Matthew 26:56). One of the disciples was so panicked by the possibility of being arrested with Jesus, that when a soldier grabbed him by the cloak, he shed his clothes and ran away naked (Mark 14:51-52). Yet, strangely some propose that these fear filled men snuck up on trained and armed soldiers, rolled a massive stone away, and stole the body, all while the soldiers slept. This is hard to believe.

It is also hard to believe that the disciples stole the body from the tomb, because of how much they suffered in the years to come. If the disciples stole the body, then that means they later suffered and died for what they *knew* to be a hoax. Lots of people suffer and die for what they *believe* to be true, but no one, in their right mind, would suffer and die for what they *knew* to be a lie.

Realizing the weakness in the argument that the disciples stole the body, in just the last 200 years some have proposed that Jesus was simply unconscious when laid in the tomb. Known as the "swoon" theory, it is proposed that Jesus awoke in the tomb, rolled away the stone by himself, snuck past the armed guard, or overpowered them, and vanished from history, after a few meetings with his disciples in which he convinced them he was in fact raised from the dead.

This theory has surfaced in recent history most probably because anyone who had witnessed a crucifixion would quickly dismiss Jesus' swooning as a possibility. For Jesus to have escaped from the tomb on his own means that he would have rolled away a giant stone all by himself, while in complete darkness, and after having been severely beaten, hung on a cross for six hours, with nails driven through his feet and hands, and stabbed in the side with a spear. This theory is weak based upon all that Jesus had suffered.

It is also weak because the Roman Centurions were professional executioners. They had lots of experience putting people to death. Remember, that after six hours of hanging on the cross, to hasten the death of the two criminals that hung on either side of Jesus, the Centurions broke their legs. But, when they came to Jesus they recognized that he was already dead. However, being professional executioners, they made sure he was dead by piercing his side with a spear (John 19:31-34). The "swoon" theory his little merit considering the expertise of the Romans at crucifixion.

Another reason to believe that Jesus was raised is that the Apostles were dramatically changed after the resurrection, from hopeless and fearful to hope filled and faithful, and the best explanation is that they had seen the risen Christ (Acts 4:13). Even after being imprisoned, beaten, and forbidden to speak in the name of Jesus, the Apostles ignored the warnings (Acts 5:29-42).

Further, it was not simply those who had been closest to Jesus who were dramatically changed, but also his enemies. People like Saul (Acts 7-9). Later known as the Apostle Paul, Saul was a Jewish leader committed to wiping out the followers of Jesus. In Acts 7, Saul stands in authority as Stephen is stoned to death. However, in Acts 9, Jesus appears to Saul and he is forever changed and goes on to write much of the New Testament and suffer greatly as he preaches about the resurrection of Jesus.

Another reason to believe that Jesus is raised is the sheer number of people who saw him. Paul wrote that over 500 saw Jesus raised, of which many were still alive at the time of his writing (1 Corinthians 15:5-6). Paul was saying, "if you don't believe me, talk to the many who saw him."

A final reason to believe is that the resurrection is a fitting climax to Jesus' miraculous life and the best explanation for the existence of the Church. Resurrection is a fitting climax to one who was born to a virgin and turned water into wine. Jesus walked on water. He healed the sick, cast out demons, stilled a storm, and raised the dead. We should not be surprised that death did not have the last word on Jesus' life. In fact, after Jesus was raised from the grave, he met with two men, explaining to them how the resurrection was the fitting climax to his life (Luke 24:26-27).

Resurrection is also the best explanation for the existence of the Church. Despite the sinfulness of the people in the Church, it has continued to grow. While there are a lot of religions that have grown over the last two millennia, the difference is that Christianity grows solely because Jesus is alive. Many make the mistake of thinking that Christianity is primarily a set of teachings, but Christianity is not primarily a set of teachings. Yes, Christianity teaches what it believes, but the beliefs are founded upon relationship with someone who is living—Jesus. Christianity grows as Jesus, who has been raised from the grave, reveals himself to individuals. If Jesus was not revealing himself to people, then the movement would have died out in a single generation. It would die out because everything that Christianity teaches hinges on Jesus being alive and active. In other words, Jesus' resurrection does not hinge on the teachings of the Church, the teachings of the Church hinge on the reality of the resurrection. Frankly, much of what the people in the Church do undermines the Church's growth. But make no mistake. We do not believe what we believe because the Bible records it. We believe what we believe because Jesus is alive.

What benefit is the resurrection to the believing?

The benefits of the resurrection are quite literally infinite, as the resurrection provides everything we need for life in this world, as well as life eternal.

The resurrection provides us with eternal life.
Jesus said to her, "I am the resurrection and the life. The one who believes in Me, even if he dies, will live." John 11:25 (HCSB)

Praise the God and Father of our Lord Jesus Christ. According to His great mercy, He has given us a new birth into a living hope through the resurrection of Jesus Christ from the dead and into an inheritance that is imperishable, uncorrupted, and unfading, kept in heaven for you.
1 Peter 1:3-4 (HCSB)

We do not want you to be uninformed, brothers, concerning those who are asleep, so that you will not grieve like the rest, who have no hope. Since we believe that Jesus died and rose again, in the same way God will bring with Him those who have fallen asleep through Jesus.
1 Thessalonians 4:13-14 (HCSB)

The resurrection displays the riches of God's grace.
Together with Christ Jesus He also raised us up and seated us in the heavens, so that in the coming ages He might display the immeasurable riches of His grace through His kindness to us in Christ Jesus. For you are saved by grace through faith, and this is not from yourselves; it is God's gift—not from works, so that no one can boast. Ephesians 2:6-9 (HCSB)

For they themselves report what kind of reception we had from you: how you turned to God from idols to serve the living and true God and to wait for His Son from heaven, whom He raised from the dead—Jesus, who rescues us from the coming wrath. 1 Thessalonians 1:9-10 (HCSB)

The resurrection ensures the forgiveness of sin.
But the One God raised up did not decay. Therefore, let it be known to you, brothers, that through this man forgiveness of sins is being proclaimed to you, and everyone who believes in Him is justified from everything that you could not be justified from through the law of Moses.
Acts 13:37-39 (HCSB)

And if Christ has not been raised, your faith is worthless; you are still in your sins. 1 Corinthians 15:17 (HCSB)

He was delivered up for our trespasses and raised for our justification. Romans 4:25 (HCSB)

The resurrection provides us with a new way of life.
Therefore we were buried with Him by baptism into death, in order that, just as Christ was raised from the dead by the glory of the Father, so we too may walk in a new way of life. Romans 6:4 (HCSB)

For in light of the fact that He died, He died to sin once for all; but in light of the fact that He lives, He lives to God. So, you too consider yourselves dead to sin but alive to God in Christ Jesus. Romans 6:10-11 (HCSB)

The resurrection ensures our fruitfulness.
Therefore, my brothers, you also were put to death in relation to the law through the crucified body of the Messiah, so that you may belong to another—to Him who was raised from the dead—that we may bear fruit for God. Romans 7:4 (HCSB)

The resurrection provides healing, in this life or the next.
Let it be known to all of you and to all the people of Israel, that by the name of Jesus Christ the Nazarene—whom you crucified and whom God raised from the dead—by Him this man is standing here before you healthy. Acts 4:10 (HCSB)

And if the Spirit of Him who raised Jesus from the dead lives in you, then He who raised Christ from the dead will also bring your mortal bodies to life through His Spirit who lives in you. Romans 8:11 (HCSB)

So it is with the resurrection of the dead: Sown in corruption, raised in incorruption; sown in dishonor, raised in glory; sown in weakness, raised in power; sown a natural body, raised a spiritual body. If there is a natural body, there is also a spiritual body. So it is written: The first man Adam became a living being; the last Adam became a life-giving Spirit. However, the spiritual is not first, but the natural, then the spiritual. The first man was from the earth and made of dust; the second man is from heaven. Like the man made of dust, so are those who are made of dust; like the heavenly man, so are those who are heavenly. And just as we have borne the image of the man made of dust, we will also bear the image of the heavenly man. 1 Corinthians 15:42-49 (HCSB)

The resurrection joins us to Jesus.
For if we have been joined with Him in the likeness of His death, we will certainly also be in the likeness of His resurrection. Romans 6:5 (HCSB)

The resurrection makes possible Jesus' intercession.
Who is the one who condemns? Christ Jesus is the One who died, but even more, has been raised; He also is at the right hand of God and intercedes for us. Romans 8:34 (HCSB)

Therefore, He is always able to save those who come to God through Him, since He always lives to intercede for them. Hebrews 7:24-25 (HCSB)

Jesus' resurrection ensures our future resurrection.
But now Christ has been raised from the dead, the firstfruits of those who have fallen asleep. For since death came through a man, the resurrection of the dead also comes through a man. For as in Adam all die, so also in Christ all will be made alive. But each in his own order: Christ, the firstfruits; afterward, at His coming, those who belong to Christ. 1 Corinthians 15:20-23 (HCSB)

Since we believe that Jesus died and rose again, in the same way God will bring with Him those who have fallen asleep through Jesus.
1 Thessalonians 4:14 (HCSB)

Now concerning the resurrection of the dead, haven't you read what was spoken to you by God: I am the God of Abraham and the God of Isaac and the God of Jacob? He is not the God of the dead, but of the living." Matthew 22:31-32 (HCSB)

The resurrection destroys death.
When this corruptible is clothed with incorruptibility, and this mortal is clothed with immortality, then the saying that is written will take place: Death has been swallowed up in victory. Death, where is your victory? Death, where is your sting? Now the sting of death is sin, and the power of sin is the law. But thanks be to God, who gives us the victory through our Lord Jesus Christ!1 Corinthians 15:54-57 (HCSB)

For they cannot die anymore, because they are like angels and are sons of God, since they are sons of the resurrection. Luke 20:36 (HCSB)

The resurrection gives us purpose in life.
Why are we in danger every hour? I affirm by the pride in you that I have in Christ Jesus our Lord: I die every day! If I fought wild animals in Ephesus with only human hope, what good did that do me? If the dead are not raised, Let us eat and drink, for tomorrow we die.
1 Corinthians 15:30-32 (HCSB)

And He died for all so that those who live should no longer live for themselves, but for the One who died for them and was raised.
2 Corinthians 5:15 (HCSB)

The resurrection provides hope in difficult times.
For we don't want you to be unaware, brothers, of our affliction that took place in Asia: we were completely overwhelmed—beyond our strength—so that we even despaired of life. Indeed, we personally had a death sentence

within ourselves, so that we would not trust in ourselves but in God who raises the dead. 2 Corinthians 1:8-9 (HCSB)

The resurrection proves that judgment is coming.

"Therefore, having overlooked the times of ignorance, God now commands all people everywhere to repent, because He has set a day when He is going to judge the world in righteousness by the Man He has appointed. He has provided proof of this to everyone by raising Him from the dead." Acts 17:30-31 (HCSB)

Do not be amazed at this, because a time is coming when all who are in the graves will hear His voice and come out—those who have done good things, to the resurrection of life, but those who have done wicked things, to the resurrection of judgment. John 5:28-29 (HCSB)

Then I saw a great white throne and One seated on it. Earth and heaven fled from His presence, and no place was found for them. I also saw the dead, the great and the small, standing before the throne, and books were opened. Another book was opened, which is the book of life, and the dead were judged according to their works by what was written in the books. Revelation 20:11-12 (HCSB)

Jesus Christ's Return

The return of Jesus Christ is a central teaching of the New Testament. Often referred to as the "Second Coming of Christ" or "the Day of the Lord," Jesus taught that his return is certain and will be surprising to many (Matthew 24:1-51).

The Greek term used in the New Testament to describe Jesus' coming again is *Parousia*, which means "arrival" or "presence" (Matthew 24:3), and the earliest Christians lived with an expectancy, looking forward to Jesus' return (1 Thessalonians 4:16-18, James 5:7-8), which fueled their pursuit of holiness (1 Peter 1:13-16, 2 Peter 3:10-12) and their efforts in evangelism (Matthew 24:14).

Jesus Christ's return is certain.

Then the sign of the Son of Man will appear in the sky, and then all the peoples of the earth will mourn; and they will see the Son of Man coming on the clouds of heaven with power and great glory. He will send out His angels with a loud trumpet, and they will gather His elect from the four winds, from one end of the sky to the other. Matthew 24:30-31 (HCSB)

Jesus Christ's return will be preceded by signs.

Then Jesus replied to them: "Watch out that no one deceives you. For many will come in My name, saying, 'I am the Messiah,' and they will deceive many. You are going to hear of wars and rumors of wars. See that you are not alarmed, because these things must take place, but the end is not yet. For nation will rise up against nation, and kingdom against kingdom. There will be famines and earthquakes in various places. All these events are the beginning of birth pains. Matthew 24:4-8 (HCSB)

Jesus Christ's return will be surprising.

So you also must be ready, because the Son of Man will come at an hour when you do not expect him. Matthew 24:44 (NIV)

Jesus Christ's return will be bodily and visible.
"Men of Galilee," they said, "why do you stand here looking into the sky? This same Jesus, who has been taken from you into heaven, will come back in the same way you have seen him go into heaven." Acts 1:11 (NIV)

Jesus Christ's return will be personal.
For the Lord himself will come down from heaven, with a loud command, with the voice of the archangel and with the trumpet call of God, and the dead in Christ will rise first. After that, we who are still alive and are left will be caught up together with them in the clouds to meet the Lord in the air. 1 Thessalonians 4:16-17 (NIV)

Jesus Christ's return will bring salvation to the waiting.
Christ was sacrificed once to take away the sins of many people; and he will appear a second time, not to bear sin, but to bring salvation to those who are waiting for him. Hebrews 9:28 (NIV)

Jesus Christ's return calls for our patience.
Be patient, then, brothers, until the Lord's coming. See how the farmer waits for the land to yield its valuable crop and how patient he is for the autumn and spring rains. You too, be patient and stand firm, because the Lord's coming is near. James 5:7-8 (NIV)

Jesus Christ's return is to be eagerly awaited.
He who testifies to these things says, "Yes, I am coming soon." Amen. Come, Lord Jesus. Revelation 22:20 (NIV)

Jesus Christ's return will bring judgment.
"See, the Lord is coming with thousands upon thousands of his holy ones to judge everyone, and to convict all the ungodly of all the ungodly acts they have done in the ungodly way, and of all the harsh words ungodly sinners have spoken against him." Jude 14-15 (NIV)

Jesus Christ, Son of God

The title "Son of God" indicates Jesus' divine relationship with God the Father and God the Spirit, as the second member of the Trinity. However, the title was not first used to refer to Jesus. The nation of Israel was called the firstborn son of God (Exodus 4:22-23, Jeremiah 31:20, Hosea 11:1). God also refers to himself as Israel's father (Jeremiah 31:9, Malachi 1:6), and Israel refers to God as Father (Isaiah 63:16; 64:8, Jeremiah 3:4).

Ultimately however, Jesus' claim to divine sonship is unlike any other. The angels attested to Jesus' divine sonship (Luke 1:32-35), and at his baptism God the Father proclaimed his sonship and God the Spirit descended upon him, (Matthew 3:16-17). The proclamation of sonship was also repeated at Jesus' transfiguration (Luke 9:35).

Further, Jesus described God as "my" father (Matthew 10:32, Luke 2:49), and claimed that he is "one" with the Father (John 10:30). In commissioning his disciples, Jesus directed them to baptize in the name of Father, Son and Holy Spirit (Matthew 28:19-20). Even Satan, when tempting Jesus, twice challenged Jesus' claim to divine sonship (Matthew 4:3-6, Luke 4:3-9).

Jesus followers also acknowledged his divine sonship. John the Baptist testified about him saying, "This is the Son of God" (John 1:34). At the crucifixion a centurion exclaimed, "Surely, he was the Son of God (Mark 15:39), and both Nathaniel (John 1:49) and Peter (Matthew 16:15-16) declared Jesus the Son of God. Paul also clearly acknowledged Jesus' divinity (Romans 1:4), as does the writer of Hebrews (Hebrews 1:1-4).

Finally, the reason John gives for writing his gospel is so that we might believe that Jesus is the Son of God (John 20:30-31), and the promise to any who will acknowledge Jesus' divine sonship is eternal life (1 John 4:15).

Jesus Christ, Son of Man

The title "Son of Man" describes Jesus' unique role as a human within salvation history. It is commonly thought that Jesus built his use of the phrase "Son of Man" upon the message in this Old Testament prophecy of Daniel.

> I continued watching in the night visions, and saw One like a son of man coming with clouds of heaven. He approached the Ancient of Days and was escorted before Him. He was given authority to rule, and glory, and a kingdom; so that those of every people, nation, and language should serve Him. His dominion is an everlasting dominion that will not pass away, and His kingdom is one that will not be destroyed. Daniel 7:13-14 (HCSB)

No other title so clearly attests to his position of authority and purposes as God's Savior. Throughout the gospels, Jesus affirms his authority and God's purposes for him as the Son of Man to execute judgment (Matthew 16:27), as well as forgive sins (Mark 2:10), determine the meaning and application of the Law (Mark 2:28), and to give his life as a ransom for many (Mark 10:45).

While the title "Son of God" refers to Jesus' deity, the title "Son of Man" is a reference to Jesus' humanity. For example, Jesus was born of a woman, but he was conceived of the Holy Spirit (Matthew 1:20), by God's power. Jesus died by crucifixion, just as any man would die while being crucified. However, he was raised from the grave three days after his death (John 2:22), by God's power.

Through the dual titles of "Son of Man" and "Son of God" we gain a complete understanding of Jesus as the "God Man," the man who came to pay the human debt of sin, a price that only God could afford to pay.

Judgment by God

God's judgment against humanity is in response to our sinfulness. Both the Old Testament and New Testament have examples of God's judgment against both nations and individuals, because of sin, and Scripture urges preparation for a final and eternal judgment.

Sometimes referred to as God's "wrath," judgment by God can only be escaped through faith in Jesus Christ (John 3:18, 1 Thessalonians 1:10). However, even those who escape God's wrath, through faith in Jesus Christ, will be judged for their works (i.e., actions/attitudes), which will result in both rewards and/or loss in heaven (1 Corinthians 3:12-15).

God's judgment is determined by his character.
Then the Lord passed in front of him and proclaimed: Yahweh—Yahweh is a compassionate and gracious God, slow to anger and rich in faithful love and truth, maintaining faithful love to a thousand generations, forgiving wrongdoing, rebellion, and sin. But He will not leave the guilty unpunished, bringing the consequences of the fathers' wrongdoing on the children and grandchildren to the third and fourth generation. Exodus 34:6-7 (HCSB)

God's judgment is impartial and based upon our works.
He will repay each one according to his works: eternal life to those who by persistence in doing good seek glory, honor, and immortality; but wrath and indignation to those who are self-seeking and disobey the truth but are obeying unrighteousness. There is no favoritism with God. Romans 2:6-8, 11 (HCSB)

Judgment by God of our actions is certain.
For God will bring every act to judgment, including every hidden thing, whether good or evil. Ecclesiastes 12:14 (HCSB)

Nothing in all creation is hidden from God's sight. Everything is uncovered and laid bare before the eyes of him to whom we must give account. Hebrews 4:13 (NIV)

Judgment by God will result in some receiving eternal life and some receiving eternal punishment.
"Then He will answer them, 'Truly I say to you, to the extent that you did not do it to one of the least of these, you did not do it to Me.'" "These will go away into eternal punishment, but the righteous into eternal life." Matthew 25:45-46 (NASB)

The Lord knows how to rescue the godly from trials and to keep the unrighteous under punishment until the day of judgment, especially those who follow the polluting desires of the flesh and despise authority. 2 Peter 2:9-10 (HCSB)

Christians will not be condemned in judgment but may suffer loss and/or receive rewards in judgment.
If any man builds on this foundation using gold, silver, costly stones, wood, hay or straw, his work will be shown for what it is, because the Day will bring it to light. It will be revealed with fire, and the fire will test the quality of each man's work. If what he has built survives, he will receive his reward. If it is burned up, he will suffer loss; he himself will be saved, but only as one escaping through the flames. 1 Corinthians 3:12-15 (NIV)

For we must all appear before the tribunal of Christ, so that each may be repaid for what he has done in the body, whether good or worthless. 2 Corinthians 5:10 (HCSB)

Judgment by God will include saints judging others.
Do you not know that the saints will judge the world? And if you are to judge the world, are you not competent to judge trivial cases? Do you not know that we will judge angels? How much more the things of this life! 1 Corinthians 6:2-3 (NIV)

Judgment of Others

Many Christians are unsure about whether it is biblically permissible to judge others, and in some cases a misunderstanding of Jesus' teaching contributes to their silence (Matthew 7:1). While we should never pass judgment on other's motives because we don't know what is in their heart, it is clear from Scripture that passing judgment is a Christian responsibility. The challenge is to offer God's judgments on a particular situation rather than our own.

We are to judge whether people are receptive to truth.

Don't give what is holy to dogs or toss your pearls before pigs, or they will trample them with their feet, turn, and tear you to pieces. Matthew 7:6 (HCSB)

Beware of false prophets who come to you in sheep's clothing but inwardly are ravaging wolves. You'll recognize them by their fruit. Matthew 7:15-16 (HCSB)

Paul encouraged the judgment of other Christians.

For I, on my part, though absent in body but present in spirit, have already judged him who has so committed this, as though I were present. 1 Corinthians 5:3 (NASB)

But now I am writing you not to associate with anyone who claims to be a believer who is sexually immoral or greedy, an idolater or verbally abusive, a drunkard or a swindler. Do not even eat with such a person. For what business is it of mine to judge outsiders? Don't you judge those who are inside? But God judges outsiders. Put away the evil person from among yourselves. 1 Corinthians 5:11-13 (HCSB)

Let two or three prophets speak, and let the others pass judgment. 1 Corinthians 14:29 (NIV)

Or don't you know that the saints will judge the world? And if the world is judged by you, are you unworthy to judge the smallest cases? Don't you know that we will judge angels—not to mention ordinary matters? 1 Corinthians 6:2-3 (HCSB)

Judging rightly means judging according to Scripture.
There is one lawgiver and judge who is able to save and to destroy. But who are you to judge your neighbor? James 4:12 (HCSB)

Do not judge, so that you won't be judged. Matthew 7:1 (HCSB)

Stop judging according to outward appearances; rather judge according to righteous judgment. John 7:24 (HCSB)

Therefore, any one of you who judges is without excuse. For when you judge another, you condemn yourself, since you, the judge, do the same things. We know that God's judgment on those who do such things is based on the truth. Romans 2:1-2 (HCSB)

Judging rightly means judging as you want to be judged.
For with the judgment you use, you will be judged, and with the measure you use, it will be measured to you. Matthew 7:2 (HCSB)

Hypocrite! First take the log out of your eye, and then you will see clearly to take the speck out of your brother's eye. Matthew 7:5 (HCSB)

Judging rightly means understanding that some actions are a matter of personal conviction.
Therefore, don't let anyone judge you in regard to food and drink or in the matter of a festival or a new moon or a Sabbath day. These are a shadow of what was to come; the substance is the Messiah. Colossians 2:16-17 (HCSB)

Law

The Law was given by God to Moses (Exodus 19-20). It is a revelation of God's perfect character (Psalm 19:7), and keeping the Law was a part of the old covenant (agreement) that God made with Israel. To maintain their covenant with God, the Israelites had to follow the civil law (national government law), ceremonial law (feasts and sacrifices for worship within the Temple), and moral law (Ten Commandments). Failing to follow the law brought God's punishment upon the Israelites (Leviticus 26).

The bad news is that no one is able to follow the whole Law (Romans 7:9). In fact, it is through the Law that we see our need for the forgiveness of our sin (Galatians 3:24-25). The good news is that all the requirements of the Law were fulfilled by Jesus Christ (Romans 8:3-4; Hebrews 4:15), who is God (Colossians 1:15). All who trust in Jesus' death on the cross for the forgiveness of sin come under the new covenant (agreement) of grace, which is outlined in the New Testament (Romans 3:21-24).

Today, the Old Testament is only fully understood in light of the New Testament, and understanding the Old Testament law, particularly the sacrificial system prescribed by the law, helps us understand the significance of Jesus' moral perfection and sacrificial death on our behalf.

While it's true that the ceremonial and sacrificial laws are no longer applicable to those under the new covenant of grace (Acts 15:5-11), these laws continue to help us understand the righteous character God expects in his people (Romans 7:12). The responsibility of Christians when considering the Old Testament law is to: 1) identify that part of God's character revealed in a particular Old Testament law, 2) celebrate Jesus Christ's fulfillment of that law on their behalf, and 3) then rely upon the Holy Spirit's power to emulate the character of God as revealed in the life of Jesus Christ (Galatians 5:18).

Lent

Lent is the 40-day season of preparation that precedes Easter on the church calendar. Many churches follow the Christian calendar in their worship services. Following the Christian calendar throughout the year in worship provides unity and direction to services by highlighting the central message of Jesus Christ's birth, life, death and resurrection.

The Christian calendar is divided into two primary cycles, or seasons. The first cycle is Advent—Christmas—Epiphany, which begins each year at the end of November and runs through January. The second cycle is Lent—Easter—Pentecost, which begins each year in early February or March and runs through late March or April.

The dates of the second cycle (Lent—Easter—Pentecost) vary year to year because the date for Easter is based upon the lunar calendar, rather than the solar calendar. Easter is always the Sunday immediately following the first full moon after the vernal (spring) equinox.

The portions of the annual worship calendar that fall outside these two cycles are simply referred to as "Ordinary Time," because they are not associated with any particular feast. The months of May, June, July, August, September and October make up the largest portion of Ordinary Time.

Both of the primary cycles in the Christian calendar begin with a season of preparation. Advent is the season of preparation that precedes Christmas—Epiphany and Lent is the season of preparation that precedes the Easter—Pentecost celebration.

The word Lent comes for the Anglo-Saxon word that means "spring." At first, Lent was simply the season of special preparation for new converts, who were making themselves ready for baptism on Easter morning. In preparation, new converts would be taught the gospel message, the Lord's Prayer and spend time fasting and praying.

Eventually though, Lent became a season of repentance that the church as whole observed. Beginning in the fourth century, the Lenten season became the 40 days prior to Easter Sunday (not counting the six Sunday's during the Lenten season itself), dedicated to reprioritizing one's relationship with God and yielding once again to his work in our lives. For this reason, the Lenten season has historically been marked by activities classically associated with repentance, namely fasting and prayer.

Fasting is abstaining from food and/or drink, and many within the Scripture are reported to have fasted including Moses, David, Paul and Jesus. While Jesus was fasting, he was tempted by Satan to turn stones into bread in order to feed himself. In reply to Satan's temptation Jesus said, "Man does not live on bread alone, but on every word that comes from the mouth of God" (Matthew 4:4). In fasting, we acknowledge that we have a need that is greater than food, a need satisfied only by God's Word.

Lent always begins on a Wednesday, and most churches will offer a special Ash Wednesday worship service. Ash Wednesday services include Scripture readings, quiet moments for reflection, communion, and an invitation to take the traditional mark of repentance—ashes on the forehead.

Ashes are the traditional symbol of our mortality, the death that has come to all humanity as a result of sin and are cited throughout the Bible as the mark taken by those who are repentant (Esther 4:1,3, Isaiah 58:5, Daniel 9:3, Matthew 11:21, Luke 10:13). Ashes are thus a public recognition of the consequences of sin, as well as a reminder of our need for God's redemption provided through Jesus Christ.

While nothing we can do, whether attending a worship service, praying, or even fasting, can save us, these types of activities can open us to the Holy Spirit's work in our lives, and ready us to celebrate God's victory over death on Easter morning.

Marriage

Marriage is the legal and spiritual union of a man and woman for life. Designed and instituted by God at creation and affirmed by Jesus, marriage involves: "leaving father and mother" (public declaration/social dimension), "cleaving" to one another (covenant/legal commitment), and "becoming one flesh" (spiritual union through sexual relationship) (Genesis 2:18-24, Matthew 19:4-6).

Marriage was designed by God as a monogamous, lifelong, heterosexual union, that promotes holiness, as well as represents symbolically the loving relationship between God and his people (Isaiah 54:5, Jeremiah 3:20, Ezekiel 16:8, Hosea 2:14-23, Ephesians 5:21-33).

When a man and woman are united in marriage, they are to provide a living example of Christ's love for the Church, his spiritual bride (Ephesians 5:21-33). This means that as spouses create a loving environment for each other, we will clearly see the attributes of God's patience, kindness and selflessness played out in a concrete manner. It also means that as spouses fail to demonstrate Christ's selfless and sacrificial love toward one another, the testimony of God's selfless and sacrificial love through Jesus Christ's death on the cross is weakened.

For this reason, God directs believers to marry only other believers (2 Corinthians 6:14) and the Church is to support marriages, equipping spouses to demonstrate the character of Christ within marriage.

Marriage was instituted by God at creation.
For this reason a man will leave his father and mother and be united to his wife, and they will become one flesh. Genesis 2:24 (NIV)

Marriage is a picture of God's love for his people.
Then the LORD said to me, "Go again, love a woman who is loved by her husband, yet an adulteress, even as the LORD loves the sons of Israel, though they turn to other gods and love raisin cakes." Hosea 3:1 (NASB)

Marriage of believers is to be only with other believers.
Do not be yoked together with unbelievers. For what do righteousness and wickedness have in common? Or what fellowship can light have with darkness? 2 Corinthians 6:14 (NIV)

Marriage is defined as a lifelong, heterosexual union.
He answered, "Have you not read that he who created them from the beginning made them male and female, and said, 'Therefore a man shall leave his father and his mother and hold fast to his wife, and the two shall become one flesh'? So they are no longer two but one flesh. What therefore God has joined together, let not man separate." Matthew 19:4-6 (ESV)

Marriage is a picture of Christ's union with the Church.
"For this reason a man will leave his father and mother and be united to his wife, and the two will become one flesh." This is a profound mystery— but I am talking about Christ and the church. Ephesians 5:31-32 (NIV)

Marriage is a help for those struggling with immorality.
But since there is so much immorality, each man should have his own wife, and each woman her own husband. The husband should fulfill his marital duty to his wife, and likewise the wife to her husband. 1 Corinthians 7:2-3 (NIV)

Heterosexual Marriage as the Biblical Design

Heterosexual life-long monogamy within marriage is identified in Scripture as God's design for human sexuality (Genesis 2:24, Leviticus 18:1-24, Matthew 19:8, John 8:11, 1 Corinthians 6:12-20, Ephesians 5:10), and homosexual behavior is forbidden (Leviticus 18:22, Leviticus 20:13, Romans 1:26-27, 1 Corinthians 6:9, 1 Timothy 1:10). Further, for 99% of the Church's history, homosexual behavior has been considered sinful. Yet, some today are teaching that homosexual behavior is biblically permissible.

While it is true that church tradition is not infallible, when we begin approving what virtually every Christian who has ever lived would consider sinful, it ought to give us pause. And while it is also true that homosexuality is only one of many sins listed in the Bible, it is a culturally unique sin, in that few, if any, behaviors historically considered sinful among Christians (e.g., stealing, lying, murder) are now being labeled as biblically permissible.

Within this debate there are generally two sides. Those who argue for the biblical permissibility of homosexual behavior are labeled as "Side A." This side is also often described as "affirming." Those supporting heterosexual life-long monogamy within marriage are described as "Side B." This side is also often referred to as "non-affirming." Below is a point counterpoint in support of the historic biblical design of marriage (i.e., Side B).

Perhaps one of the most common arguments among "Side A" proponents is that Jesus never explicitly condemned homosexual behavior. The point is that if refraining from homosexual behavior is what Jesus expected, then he would have most certainly addressed it. However, this type of argument from silence is weak in that Side A proponents must also admit that Jesus never explicitly condemned rape or bestiality, but we would certainly not assume he was in favor of these types of sexual behaviors. Even more to the point, "Side A" proponents must admit that time and time again Jesus expressed a conservative sexual ethic. For example, he condemned adultery, even raising the bar by noting that lusting in one's heart is contravening the seventh commandment (Matthew 5:28, John 4:17, John 8:1-11). He also condemned divorce (Matthew 19:8, Mark 10:6), describing it as outside God's designed intent, which he points out was demonstrated in Eden as heterosexual life-long monogamy within marriage.

Especially notable in Jesus' condemnation of divorce is his reference to Genesis 1:27, which describes God's design in making humanity distinctly male and female (Matthew 19:4, Mark 10:6). This is noteworthy in that there was no need for Jesus to mention maleness and femaleness in teaching on divorce, unless he was meaning to communicate that a male-female pairing is in fact God's design for marriage. Interestingly, the Hebrew word *kenegdo*, which is used in describing Eve's "suitability" for Adam (Genesis 2:18), is a compound word that means "as opposite him." In short, Eve was suitable to be Adam's helper because she was "as" Adam in her humanity, but "opposite him" in her sexuality, which is a reality that homosexual unions would not fulfill.

A second common claim of "Side A" proponents is to say that when the Bible does condemn homosexual behavior it has in mind specific non-consensual homosexual relationships (e.g., pederasty, prostitution, and/or rape), not mutually loving consensual homosexual monogamy. For example, "Side A" proponents will point out that what was sought by the citizens of Sodom was a criminal sex act, namely rape, and that a loving consensual homosexual relationship was not in view and thus not condemned (Genesis 19:4-5). Along this line, many "Side A" proponents go on to argue that biblical writers had no concept of mutually loving consensual and committed life-long same-sex relationships.

However, the ancient world did in fact conceive of consensual and non-exploitative same sex relationships. For example, Aristophanes' speech in Plato's *Symposium*, tells of Zeus splitting the original human beings in half, creating both heterosexual and homosexual humans, each of which were seeking to be reunited to their lost halves—that is heterosexuals seeking the opposite sex and homosexuals seeking the same sex. Although Zeus' actions are mythical, the content of the myth illustrates how ancient Greek culture recognized that some people are inherently attracted to the same sex and looking for a consensual and non-exploitative relationship with the opposite sex. Admittedly, while it is true that pederasty was the most common form of same-sex relationship in the ancient world. It wasn't the only type of same-sex relationship. There are many examples of both male and female same-sex relationships that are established among peers, consensual and mutually loving (*People to Be Loved*, Sprinkle 61-64).

More importantly, in Romans 1:26-27 Paul describes homosexual behaviors as unnatural, and they are not described as exploitative or non-consensual in that passage. In fact, the men are described as being "inflamed with lust for one another," a description that communicates mutuality. Further, if Paul wanted to describe rape, or prostitution, or pederasty, there were specific Greek terms available to describe such, which Paul didn't use. In other words, Paul both knew of consensual homosexual relationships possessing mutuality and he prohibited them.

Further, when explicit prohibitions against homosexual behavior are given in Scripture they are given without any qualifications. In other words, no comments or specifications are given that might limit the prohibition to only exploitative or non-consensual same-sex relationships. There is never any mention in these passages about criminal acts such as rape or pederasty. When homosexual activity is condemned in Scripture it is broadly condemned, without any qualifications. In fact, when the penalty for these acts are given all participants are to be put to death (Leviticus 20:13), which seems to assume consensual participation by all parties. Both parties are deemed guilty and thus both must bear the punishment.

A third argument that "Side A" proponents also offer is that the trajectory of biblical ethics is toward a loving acceptance and inclusivity of all people, rather than an exclusivity based upon lifestyle, noting how the gospel tears down barriers to fellowship with God and one another. For example, "Side A" proponents will note that Paul celebrated that through Christ "There is neither Jew nor Gentile, neither slave nor free, nor is there male and female, for you are all one in Christ Jesus" (Galatians 3:28).

It's true that the gospel removed barriers that previously existed between Jew and Gentile, as well as slave and free, and male and female, barriers that were a part of the Old Testament civil (national governmental law) and ceremonial (feasts and sacrifices for worship within the Temple) laws. While it is true that the New Testament is inclusive in a way that the Old Testament was not, Paul's point is not that the gospel eradicated all together ethnicity, or all socio-economic distinctions, or gender. Paul's point in Galatians 3:28 is that we are all "one" through faith in Jesus, while at the same time having ethnic (Jew/Gentile), socio-economic (slave/free) and gender (male/female) differences, which were historically a barrier to fellowship, but are now no longer a barrier to unity.

More to the point, at no point do any New Testament writers suggest that the Old Testament moral law no longer applies (e.g., Ten Commandments). In other words, if the unity, or "oneness" provided in Christ did away with what formerly divided (e.g., ethnicity, economics, gender), it in no way canceled the moral code in the Old Testament. The converse is true. Paul provides lists of immoral behaviors that are not to be a part of the people of God, and in these lists he explicitly names homosexual behaviors (1 Corinthians 6:9-10, 1 Timothy 1:8-11).

Recognizing this reality, some "Side A" advocates will suggest the prohibition against homosexuality (Leviticus 18:22) be handled as the prohibition against eating shellfish is now handled (Leviticus 11:9-12), namely that it should be set aside. Yet, this again confuses Old Testament civil and ceremonial laws with the moral law. In the book of Acts 15:5-11 we learn that it is the civil and ceremonial laws that are no longer binding. Further, while Jesus himself taught that the food laws are no longer in force (Mark 7:15), the prohibitions against homosexuality are re-stated in the New Testament. If Christians were to use this type of logic regarding morality, they would be "free" to set aside potentially all ethics, and it is impossible to read the New Testament in this way. Further, a close reading of Leviticus 18-20 reveals that there are nearly a dozen other behaviors prohibited in this section of Scripture that no one is advocating that we set aside (e.g., incest, child sacrifice, bestiality, theft).

Finally, "Side A" proponents will often invite us to agree to disagree on the matter, positioning the disagreement on homosexuality much like other Christian disagreements (e.g., divorce, remarriage, tongues). However, until very recently, there had been complete unanimity about homosexuality in the church across all centuries, cultures, and denominations. This makes the disagreement about homosexuality categorically different from issues such as divorce, remarriage, and tongues, of which there have been long standing disagreements for many hundreds of years.

In closing, Christians are not expected to be morally perfect. However, Christians are called to flee from sin and pursue righteousness—with victories and defeats along the way—which means that unrepentant homosexuals, along with unrepentant thieves, drunkards, idolaters, adulterers, revilers, swindlers, and lovers of money, will not inherit the kingdom of God (1 Corinthians 6:9-10, Galatians 5:19-21).

Mercy

Mercy is kindness shown toward others through demonstrations of compassion and benevolence. To be kind toward those who deserve punishment, to forgive those deserving condemnation, or to end someone's suffering are each acts of mercy.

Throughout the Bible, God is described as merciful, showing kindness and compassion toward those who deserve condemnation as sinners (2 Corinthians 1:3). In fact, a major theme in the Bible is God's offer of mercy to those who deserve otherwise (Isaiah 63:7, Ephesians 2:4-5).

A secondary theme in the Bible is the call upon those who have received God's mercy to extend mercy to others (Matthew 5:7). While we do not have the power to forgive sin for God, we are to show compassion and extend forgiveness toward those who have sinned against us, as well as care for the needs of others, rather than letting them suffer (James 2:13).

Mercy is found as we turn to God in confession of sin.
David answered Gad, "I have great anxiety. Please, let us fall into the Lord's hands because His mercies are great, but don't let me fall into human hands." 2 Samuel 24:14 (HCSB)

The one who conceals his sins will not prosper, but whoever confesses and renounces them will find mercy. Proverbs 28:14 (HCSB)

Mercy is what God desires to show his people.
But when He heard this, He said, "Those who are well don't need a doctor, but the sick do. Go and learn what this means: I desire mercy and not sacrifice. For I didn't come to call the righteous, but sinners." Matthew 9:12-13 (HCSB)

Showing mercy to others opens us to God's blessings.
The merciful are blessed for they will be shown mercy. Matthew 5:7 (HCSB)

Mercy is a means to loving our neighbor.
Which of these three do you think proved to be a neighbor to the man who fell into the hands of the robbers?" "The one who showed mercy to him," he said. Then Jesus told him, "Go and do the same." Luke 10:36-37 (HCSB)

Mercy from God provides our salvation.
So then it does not depend on human will or effort but on God who shows mercy. For the Scripture tells Pharaoh: "I raised you up for this reason so that I may display My power in you and that My name may be proclaimed in all the earth." So then, He shows mercy to those He wants to, and He hardens those He wants to harden. Romans 9:16-18 (HCSB)

But God, who is rich in mercy, because of His great love that He had for us, made us alive with the Messiah even though we were dead in trespasses. You are saved by grace! Ephesians 2:4-5 (HCSB)

Praise the God and Father of our Lord Jesus Christ. According to His great mercy, He has given us a new birth into a living hope through the resurrection of Jesus Christ from the dead and into an inheritance that is imperishable, uncorrupted, and unfading, kept in heaven for you. 1 Peter 1:3-4 (HCSB)

For we do not have a high priest who is unable to sympathize with our weaknesses, but One who has been tested in every way as we are, yet without sin. Therefore let us approach the throne of grace with boldness, so that we may receive mercy and find grace to help us at the proper time. Hebrews 4:15-16 (HCSB)

Once you were not a people, but now you are God's people; you had not received mercy, but now you have received mercy. 1 Peter 2:10 (HCSB)

Miracles

Miracles are events that occur without any natural, or scientific, explanation, the result of God's direct intervention in the world. Although all created order is itself a "miracle" by this definition, the direct result of God's creative initiative, miracles are events that occur despite, or outside of, the natural order that God has ordained.

The Bible is full of miracles. There is recorded in Scripture the story of a talking serpent (Genesis 3:1) and donkey (Numbers 22:28), as well as a large sea creature that carries Jonah in his stomach for three days, only to spit him up on a beach (Jonah 1:17; 2:10), and numerous healings. Of course, the greatest of all biblical miracles is the birth (John 1:1-5), life (Matthew 13:55), death and resurrection of Jesus Christ (John 2:22; 21:14). To believe the Bible requires believing in miracles.

Miracles brought deliverance for the Jews from Egypt.
"So I will stretch out My hand and strike Egypt with all My miracles which I shall do in the midst of it; and after that he will let you go. Exodus 3:20 (NASB)

Miracles were worked by Jesus.
Then He took the five loaves and the two fish, and looking up to heaven, He blessed and broke the loaves. He kept giving them to His disciples to set before the people. He also divided the two fish among them all. Everyone ate and was filled. Then they picked up 12 baskets full of pieces of bread and fish. Now those who ate the loaves were 5,000 men. Mark 6:41-44 (HCSB)

Then the news about Him spread throughout Syria. So they brought to Him all those who were afflicted, those suffering from various diseases and intense pains, the demon-possessed, the epileptics, and the paralytics. And He healed them. Matthew 4:24 (HCSB)

Sometimes, miracles could not occur because of unbelief.
And He did not do many miracles there because of their unbelief. Matthew 13:58 (HCSB)

Miracles were offered as evidence of Jesus' deity.
Believe me when I say that I am in the Father and the Father is in me; or at least believe on the evidence of the miracles themselves. John 14:11 (NIV)

Miracle working was an expectation for Jesus' followers.
I tell you the truth, anyone who has faith in me will do what I have been doing. He will do even greater things than these, because I am going to the Father. John 14:12 (NIV)

Miracles alone are not proof of a relationship with Jesus.
On that day many will say to Me, 'Lord, Lord, didn't we prophesy in Your name, drive out demons in Your name, and do many miracles in Your name?' Matthew 7:22 (HCSB)

Miracles were extraordinary through Paul in Ephesus.
God did extraordinary miracles through Paul, so that even handkerchiefs and aprons that had touched him were taken to the sick, and their illnesses were cured and the evil spirits left them. Acts 19:11-12 (NIV)

Miracle working is a gift given to some by the Holy Spirit.
Now you are the body of Christ, and each one of you is a part of it. And in the church God has appointed first of all apostles, second prophets, third teachers, then workers of miracles, also those having gifts of healing, those able to help others, those with gifts of administration, and those speaking in different kinds of tongues. 1 Corinthians 12:27-28 (NIV)

Modesty

Modesty is utilizing God's gifts for his glory and the good of all. Immodestly is utilizing God's gifts for personal glory and selfish gain. God's gifts may include wealth, beauty, physical strength, intellect, and/or relational skills. Humility is a synonym for modesty, while arrogance is a synonym for immodesty, as we draw attention away from God as the giver of every good gift and work to gain attention and selfish advantage through the gifts he has given us. For example, a businessman who is immodest may brag about their achievements or abilities in order to gain increased influence, while a businessman who is modest will share their achievements or abilities in order to tell of God's goodness and to find their place on a team.

While modesty is a virtue that most are eager to cultivate, it can be difficult to give specific examples of modesty for a couple of reasons. First, it is difficult to give examples because they are ultimately matters of the heart. In other words, two people can say or do the exact same thing, but for very different reasons. For example, two businessmen may talk about their achievements and abilities, saying the exact same words but mean in their hearts to accomplish two very different goals, one wanting to gain attention and influence, while the other wanting to tell of God's goodness and strengthen the team. The same is true in clothing choices. It is virtually impossible to know why someone else has selected to wear certain types of clothing. For example, it's easy to imagine two women wearing the exact same dress at the same time and in the same place, but for entirely different reasons. For one woman, the dress may reflect a posture of humility, in that she could have afforded to wear a much more expensive dress, but instead chose to not flaunt her wealth. While for the other woman, that same dress may reflect a heart's posture of immodesty, as it is the most expensive dress she owns, and she is hoping to gain attention and influence by intentionally flaunting the dress.

Modesty and immodesty can be difficult to identify for a second reason. While there are certainly biblical guidelines in matters of speech and dress, the guidelines are broad enough to leave room for cultural expression. For this reason, what was immodest in the Jewish or Greek cultures of the first century may or may not be immodest in twenty-first century America. For example, Paul encouraged "women to dress modestly, with decency and propriety," but then defined modesty, decency and propriety in ways that today are not considered immodest, namely wearing "braided hair," "gold or pearls." While both Paul and Peter were clear on the goal, believers are to adorn their lives with "good deeds," their description of indecency and impropriety no longer holds (1 Timothy 2:9-10, 1 Peter 3:3-4). To make matters even more difficult, expressions of modesty and immodesty can vary during the same time period and from culture to culture. The best example of this might be to compare standards of modesty in America with those in remote parts of Africa, where women wouldn't dare show their knees, but walk around topless without a problem.

So, what are we do? First, let's reserve judgement, admitting that we don't know what is in another person's heart. Let's do our best to spur one another on to love and good deeds. Second, let's do our best to live as salt and light in a "warped and crooked generation" (Philippians 2:15). For example, an American woman living in remote Africa might cover her knees and her breasts, thus upholding her own standards and embracing the standards of the African culture.

Finally, let's pay close attention to our speech, clothing, and spending habits, making sure that our goal is to bring God glory and bless all, rather than simply gain greater influence and power. Our goal in all matters is to set an example of godliness (1 Timothy 4:12), humbling ourselves by acting in such a way as not to draw attention to ourselves, but rather to give attention to Jesus.

Money

Sixteen of the thirty-eight parables told by Jesus concerned money and possessions. One of out every ten verses in the Gospels deals with money. The Bible gives disproportionate attention to money because there is a fundamental connection between our spiritual wellbeing and how we handle our wealth. We cannot divorce our faith and our finances, any more than we can separate our sexuality and our spirituality, or our willingness to forgive others and our desire to be forgiven by God. Our faith and our finances are necessarily and inseparably linked.

Money is a means for storing up treasure in heaven.
"Do not store up for yourselves treasures on earth, where moth and rust destroy, and where thieves break in and steal. "But store up for yourselves treasures in heaven, where neither moth nor rust destroys, and where thieves do not break in or steal; for where your treasure is, there your heart will be also. "No one can serve two masters; for either he will hate the one and love the other, or he will be devoted to one and despise the other. You cannot serve God and wealth. Matthew 6:19-21, 24 (NASB)

Money can make it hard for the rich to get into heaven.
Truly, I say to you, only with difficulty will a rich person enter the kingdom of heaven. Again I tell you, it is easier for a camel to go through the eye of a needle than for a rich person to enter the kingdom of God. Matthew 19:23-25 (ESV)

Money is an opportunity to give, even out of our poverty.
Calling His disciples to Him, He said to them, "Truly I say to you, this poor widow put in more than all the contributors to the treasury; for they all put in out of their surplus, but she, out of her poverty, put in all she owned, all she had to live on." Mark 12:43-44 (NASB)

Money can choke out the seed of God's Word in our lives.
"The seed which fell among the thorns, these are the ones who have heard, and as they go on their way they are choked with worries and riches and pleasures of this life, and bring no fruit to maturity. "But the seed in the good soil, these are the ones who have heard the word in an honest and good heart, and hold it fast, and bear fruit with perseverance. Luke 8:14-15 (NASB)

Money is a means for testing the sincerity of our love.
But just as you excel in everything—in faith, in speech, in knowledge, in complete earnestness and in your love for us—see that you also excel in this grace of giving. I am not commanding you, but I want to test the sincerity of your love by comparing it with the earnestness of others. For you know the grace of our Lord Jesus Christ, that though he was rich, yet for your sakes he became poor, so that you through his poverty might become rich. 2 Corinthians 8:7-9 (NIV)

Money can lead us into temptation and destroy our faith.
But those who desire to be rich fall into temptation, into a snare, into many senseless and harmful desires that plunge people into ruin and destruction. For the love of money is a root of all kinds of evils. It is through this craving that some have wandered away from the faith and pierced themselves with many pangs. 1 Timothy 6:9-10 (ESV)

Money is an opportunity to be rich in good deeds.
Command those who are rich in this present world not to be arrogant nor to put their hope in wealth, which is so uncertain, but to put their hope in God, who richly provides us with everything for our enjoyment. Command them to do good, to be rich in good deeds, and to be generous and willing to share. In this way they will lay up treasure for themselves as a firm foundation for the coming age, so that they may take hold of the life that is truly life. 1 Timothy 6:17-19 (NIV)

Money is to be given generously and cheerfully.
The point is this: whoever sows sparingly will also reap sparingly, and whoever sows bountifully will also reap bountifully. Each one must give as he has decided in his heart, not reluctantly or under compulsion, for God loves a cheerful giver. 2 Corinthians 9:6-7 (ESV)

Money is to be used to support the local church.
Who serves as a soldier at his own expense? Who plants a vineyard without eating any of its fruit? Or who tends a flock without getting some of the milk? Do I say these things on human authority? Does not the Law say the same? For it is written in the Law of Moses, "You shall not muzzle an ox when it treads out the grain." Is it for oxen that God is concerned? Does he not speak entirely for our sake? It was written for our sake, because the plowman should plow in hope and the thresher thresh in hope of sharing in the crop. If we have sown spiritual things among you, is it too much if we reap material things from you? If others share this rightful claim on you, do not we even more? 1 Corinthians 9:7-12 (ESV)

Anyone who receives instruction in the word must share all good things with his instructor. Galatians 6:6 (ESV)

Money is to be given away regularly and proportionally.
On the first day of every week, each one of you should set aside a sum of money in keeping with his income, saving it up, so that when I come no collections will have to be made.
1 Corinthians 16:2 (ESV)

Money handled well can provide assurance of salvation.
And Zacchaeus stood and said to the Lord, "Behold, Lord, the half of my goods I give to the poor. And if I have defrauded anyone of anything, I restore it fourfold." And Jesus said to him, "Today salvation has come to this house, since he also is a son of Abraham. For the Son of Man came to seek and to save the lost." Luke 19:8-10 (ESV)

Names of God

God has revealed himself in the Bible using dozens of different names. The names of God are like titles that capture his character, as well as his purposes for his people. The list below is not exhaustive but is a sampling of some of the names from the Old Testament. By sharing his names, God invites us into a relationship with him, granting us special access and intimacy with him.

Elohim - A general term for God, this name denotes that God is the Creator and Sustainer of all things. In our modern translations the Hebrew word *Elohim* is translated simply as "God." In Genesis 1:1 we read, *"In the beginning God (Elohim) created the heavens and the earth.." (NIV).*

El Roeh - The God who sees me (Genesis 16:13). God is not caught off guard by our location in life. He knows that many of us have been driven to foolish and sinful decisions by the behavior of others, which is not an excuse. It is only to say that God knows why we are where we are, and he sees us. Seeing us in our sinful condition is a necessary precursor to God caring for us.

El Shaddai - God almighty, or all sufficient one (Genesis 17:1). God is able to do whatever he purposes. Nothing thwarts his will. Nothing is too difficult for him. God almighty is able to deliver us from every evil and save us completely.

Adonai - Translated as "Lord" in English Bibles, Adonai is always used in the plural form and denotes that God is owner and master of all things (Exodus 4:10).

Yahweh-Rophe - "The Lord heals" (Exodus 15:22-26). This denotes God's care of us spiritually, emotionally and physically.

Yahweh - Translated as "LORD" in English Bibles, or "Jehovah." This is the name of God first revealed to Moses (Exodus 3:14) and is a form of the verb meaning "to be." This name literally means "I AM," and denotes God's eternality. The spelling of the name is a transliteration of four consonant letters in the Hebrew language, YHWH.

Yahweh-Yireh (Jehovah-Jireh) - "The Lord will provide" (Genesis 22:14). This denotes God providing what is needed for life.

Yahweh-Nissi - "The Lord is Our Banner" (Exodus 17:15). While this is a strange name in our modern context, this name denotes God's protection and deliverance for his people.

Yahweh-M'Kaddesh - "The Lord Sanctifies" (Leviticus 20:7-8). This name denotes God's work to set apart his people for lives of holiness.

Yahweh-Shalom - "The Lord Our Peace" (Judges 6:24). This name denotes God's completed work to provide peace with him, oneself and others.

Yahweh-Tsidkenu - "The Lord Our Righteousness" (Jeremiah 23:6). This name denotes God's provision of righteousness.

Yahweh-Rohi - "The Lord Our Shepherd" (Psalm 23:1). This name denotes God's work to guide and care for his people.

Yahweh-Shammah - "The Lord is There" (Ezek. 48:35). This name denotes God's presence will be with his people.

Yahweh-Sabbaoth - "The Lord of hosts" (1 Samuel 17:45). This name designates God as a warrior, who leads a vast army of angels, as well as calls upon his people to defend his glory.

Obedience

Obedience to God's commands is an essential quality of our relationship with God. God has revealed his character, purposes and plans in Scripture, and our obedience is the expected and appropriate response to his revelation. Obedience to God's commands brings God's reward and produces joy in our lives, while disobedience brings God's judgment and produces loss in our lives. Although we are incapable of perfect obedience to all of God's commands, Jesus Christ died that we might receive forgiveness for our disobedience, and he was raised from the grave so that we might live increasingly obedient. Obedience is a response of gratitude to God's grace.

Obedience was modeled by Jesus.
Then Jesus replied, "I assure you: The Son is not able to do anything on His own, but only what He sees the Father doing. For whatever the Father does, the Son also does these things in the same way.
Matthew 5:19 (HCSB)

For just as through one man's disobedience the many were made sinners, so also through the one man's obedience the many will be made righteous.
Romans 5:19 (HCSB)

He humbled Himself by becoming obedient to the point of death—even to death on a cross. Philippians 2:8 (HCSB)

Though He was God's Son, He learned obedience through what He suffered. Hebrews 5:8 (HCSB)

Obedience to Jesus is an indication of our love for Jesus.
Whoever has my commands and obeys them, he is the one who loves me. He who loves me will be loved by my Father, and I too will love him and show myself to him." John 14:21 (NIV)

Jesus replied, "If anyone loves me, he will obey my teaching. My Father will love him, and we will come to him and make our home with him. He who does not love me will not obey my teaching. These words you hear are not my own; they belong to the Father who sent me. John 14:23-24 (NIV)

Obedience to Jesus assures us we remain in his love.
If you obey my commands, you will remain in my love, just as I have obeyed my Father's commands and remain in his love. John 15:10 (NIV)

Obedience to Jesus means loving one another.
*And this is love: that we walk in obedience to his commands. As you have heard from the beginning, his command is that you walk in love.
2 John 1:6 (NIV)*

Obedience is required in order to escape punishment.
*He will punish those who do not know God and do not obey the gospel of our Lord Jesus. They will be punished with everlasting destruction and shut out from the presence of the Lord and from the majesty of his power.
2 Thessalonians 1:8-9 (NIV)*

Obedience to Scripture is a requirement for fellowship.
As for you, brothers, do not grow weary in doing good. If anyone does not obey what we say in this letter, take note of that person, and have nothing to do with him, that he may be ashamed. Do not regard him as an enemy, but warn him as a brother. 2 Thessalonians 3:13-15 (ESV)

Original Sin and Imputed Righteousness

The "original" sin, or first sin committed, was Adam's sin of disobedience in the Garden of Eden (Genesis 3). This original sin of Adam is the cause of physical and spiritual death today, as humanity was separated from God's presence, which was available to Adam and Eve in the Garden of Eden, as well as being cut off from the life-giving fruit of the Tree of Life. Today, all humanity is stained by Adam's original sin, and that stain, along with its deadly consequences, are passed to all humanity at the time of biological birth. The idea that Adam's sin, thousands of years ago, has affected our relationship with God today is often perceived as irrational and/or unjust. It seems unfair to many that we suffer because of Adam's disobedience, but this is actually to our advantage.

The imputation (i.e., imparting) of the stain of sin through Adam to all people is actually to our benefit in that by God's design the same mechanism of imputation becomes the means by which God provides us with righteousness through faith in Jesus Christ. Unless we are willing to acknowledge our place *in*, or relationship *to*, sinful Adam—that is to acknowledge our connection to Adam and our sinfulness as a result of Adam—we cannot experience God's remedy for sin through Jesus Christ, by which God imputes righteousness to all who believe. The imputation of Adam's sin to all humanity serves as a model, or a paradigm, for the imparting of righteousness to all who believe.

If we refuse to acknowledge our place in Adam's family—that is our association with and spiritual tie to the spiritual father of all humanity—then our only option is to be judged on our own merits, judged apart from the merits of the one Paul described as the "second" Adam (Romans 5:12-17), namely Jesus. In other words, it is impossible to receive the benefits of being *in* righteous Jesus Christ, all-the-while being unwilling to acknowledge the liability of being *in* sinful Adam.

Original sin is the consequence of Adam's disobedience.
The Lord God placed the man in the Garden of Eden to tend and watch over it. But the Lord God warned him, "You may freely eat the fruit of every tree in the garden—except the tree of the knowledge of good and evil. If you eat its fruit, you are sure to die." Genesis 2:15-17 (NLT)

Original sin was taught by the Apostle Paul.
When Adam sinned, sin entered the world. Adam's sin brought death, so death spread to everyone, for everyone sinned. Yes, people sinned even before the law was given. But it was not counted as sin because there was not yet any law to break. Still, everyone died—from the time of Adam to the time of Moses—even those who did not disobey an explicit commandment of God, as Adam did. Now Adam is a symbol, a representation of Christ, who was yet to come. Romans 5:12-14 (NLT)

Imputed righteousness is received by faith in Jesus.
But there is a great difference between Adam's sin and God's gracious gift. For the sin of this one man, Adam, brought death to many. But even greater is God's wonderful grace and his gift of forgiveness to many through this other man, Jesus Christ. And the result of God's gracious gift is very different from the result of that one man's sin. For Adam's sin led to condemnation, but God's free gift leads to our being made right with God, even though we are guilty of many sins. For the sin of this one man, Adam, caused death to rule over many. But even greater is God's wonderful grace and his gift of righteousness, for all who receive it will live in triumph over sin and death through this one man, Jesus Christ. Romans 5:15-17 (NLT)

Peace

Peace is a feeling and/or state of tranquility. It is the absence of hostility and the presence of harmony, whether within relationships or the circumstances of life. Peace is an attribute of God's character, as God is always at peace in himself. Peace is also a blessing given to us through faith in Jesus, and the certain and eternal experience of heaven.

Peace is an attribute of God's character.
The God of peace will soon crush Satan under your feet. The grace of our Lord Jesus be with you. Romans 16:20 (HCSB)

And the prophets' spirits are under the control of the prophets, since God is not a God of disorder but of peace. 1 Corinthians 14:32-33 (HCSB)

Peace is a blessing of God.
The Lord gives his people strength; The Lord blesses his people with peace. Psalm 29:11 (HCSB)

When a man's ways please the Lord, He makes even his enemies to be at peace with him. Proverbs 16:7 (HCSB)

Jesus is our Prince of Peace.
For a child will be born for us, a son will be given to us, and the government will be on His shoulders. He will be named Wonderful Counselor, Mighty God, Eternal Father, Prince of Peace. Isaiah 9:6 (HCSB)

"Peace I leave with you. My peace I give to you. I do not give to you as the world gives. Your heart must not be troubled or fearful. John 14:27 (HCSB)

Peace with God comes through faith in Jesus.
Therefore, since we have been made right in God's sight by faith, we have peace with God because of what Jesus Christ our Lord has done for

us. Because of our faith, Christ has brought us into this place of undeserved privilege where we now stand, and we confidently and joyfully look forward to sharing God's glory. Romans 5:1-2 (NLT)

For God in all his fullness was pleased to live in Christ, and through him God reconciled everything to himself. He made peace with everything in heaven and on earth by means of Christ's blood on the cross. Colossians 1:19-20 (NLT)

Peace comes through prayer.
Don't worry about anything; instead, pray about everything. Tell God what you need, and thank him for all he has done. Then you will experience God's peace, which exceeds anything we can understand. His peace will guard your hearts and minds as you live in Christ Jesus. Philippians 4:6-7 (NLT)

Peace comes as we fix our thoughts on God.
You will keep in perfect peace all who trust in you, all whose thoughts are fixed on you! Trust in the Lord always, for the Lord God is the eternal Rock. Isaiah 26:3-4 (NLT)

Peace in our relationships with others is something for which we are to work.
Turn away from evil and do what is good; seek peace and pursue it. Psalm 34:14 (HCSB)

Work at living in peace with everyone, and work at living a holy life, for those who are not holy will not see the Lord. Hebrews 12:14 (NLT)

Pentecost

Pentecost means fiftieth and is the Old Testament festival that comes fifty days after Passover. Often referred to as the Feast of Weeks (Exodus 34:22, Deuteronomy 16:10), this festival came seven full weeks after Passover and was a celebration of God's provision in the wheat harvest season (Leviticus 23:17-20, Deuteronomy 16:9-10).

Pentecost was one of the three annual Hebrew pilgrimage festivals, which meant that everyone who was physically able was to travel to Jerusalem for this celebration. Some estimate that during the first century, the population of Jerusalem would triple at Pentecost, as people pressed into the city.

For Christians, Pentecost is the birthday of the Church. It is the anniversary of the coming of the Holy Spirit upon the first disciples, which marks the beginning of the Church age. Before Jesus ascended, he gave instructions to his first disciples to wait in Jerusalem for "power from on high" (Luke 24:29). Jesus warned his disciples that he would be leaving them, but that he would also send the "Helper", the Holy Spirit (John 16:7, Acts 1:8).

On the day of Pentecost, as Jerusalem was filled with thousands who had arrived to celebrate the festival, the Holy Spirit descended upon the first disciples while they were gathered in the Upper Room (Acts 2:1-41). The coming of the Holy Spirit was powerful, as the disciples "began to speak in other tongues" (Acts 2:2-4), enabling those who had gathered in the city from foreign lands to hear and understand the gospel in their native language (Acts 2:5-13), which led to many being born again (Acts 2:14-41).

Most of the questions that people ask about Pentecost have to do with the "tongues" that appeared as "fire" (Acts 2:3-4), languages that they would not have otherwise been able to speak, as they had not studied these languages. This supernatural power to speak in foreign languages was a fulfillment of Jesus' promise that the Holy Spirit would provide the disciples with power needed for witnessing (Acts 1:8), and the result was some 3000 people believed in Jesus as Savior that day (Acts 2:40). Tongues also signaled the beginning of a new age—the Church age, the age in which God is reuniting all nations, languages, and tribes of people to himself through faith in Jesus Christ (Revelation 5:9).

As the population of the earth increased, the people of Babel built a tower to reach "to the heavens" (Genesis 11:4). This Tower was a ziggurat, which had a very particular purpose. Ziggurats were tall, solid-brick towers, housing a single set of winding stairs, which were believed to serve as a gateway through which the gods could descend. Ancient priests climbed to the top of these towers to care for the gods through ritualistic offerings. In this way it was thought that the deity's favor would be earned, and the expectation was that the deity would then descend the stairway and meet the needs of their worshippers.

The ancients thought that if they met the god's needs through sacrifice, then the gods were obligated to do their bidding. But this type of relationship, one based upon mutual benefit, is idolatry and God would have none of it. God calls his people into a relationship based upon submission and obedience to him (Genesis 11:1-9).

Pentecost signaled the reversal of God's judgment at Babel, as tongues are a sign of the new day that has come, the day in which all nations, languages and tribes are enabled by God to live in submission to him through the power provided by the Holy Spirit's presence (Romans 8:3-4). Luke, the author of the book of Acts, even takes great pains to offer a list of the different people groups that were present in Jerusalem at Pentecost, in order to emphasize God's work to begin gathering all the people that were formerly scattered at Babel (Acts 2::9-13). Through the gift of the Holy Spirit at Pentecost, all people can be united through faith in Jesus Christ within the Church (Romans 8:3-4).

Polygamy

Polygamy is the practice of being married to more than one woman at the same time, and several prominent Israelites practiced polygamy including Abraham, Jacob, Moses, David and Solomon. In the ancient world, polygamy provided an opportunity for increased numbers of children, which were helpful in working herds and land. In fact, in the ancient world the most common reason for taking a second wife was that the first wife was barren. Kings also often practiced polygamy in an effort to make alliances with other nations. Taking a wife from a foreign nation was the standard ancient way of formalizing political alliances.

While some would suggest that the Old Testament laws governing the practice of polygamy imply God's support of the practice, this conclusion is often based upon a fundamental misunderstanding of God's purposes for Scripture. God never intended that Scripture should provide guidelines for constructing a perfect society. For this same reason, no one in their right mind believes that the Old Testament legal regulations governing slavery ought to be interpreted as God's approval of human enslavement.

Scripture's primary aim is to reveal God's holy character and saving purposes, both of which are most fully seen in the life, death and resurrection of Jesus Christ. To this end, the laws of the Old Testament were given as a means for revealing God's character, as well as preserving the Israelite community, through whom Jesus Christ, the Messiah, would come into the world. A pertinent example of this type of legislative goal is seen in the prohibition against Israelite kings taking many wives. Israelite kings were not to be polygamists as marrying many wives, especially from foreign lands, would certainly lead the king's heart away from God, which would then undermine the stability of God's covenant community and threaten God's plans to provide a Messiah through Israel (Deuteronomy 17:17).

For this reason, although polygamy did provide protection for some women in the ancient world (e.g., allowing barren women to remain married, rather than being cast aside and left destitute), it was handled within Scripture much like other regrettable practices were handled (e.g., divorce and slavery). In short, the practice of polygamy was regulated by Old Testament law with an eye toward protecting women who might be taken advantage of in polygamous relationships, which could undermine the strength of the Israelite community and potentially jeopardize God's work through Israel to bring the Messiah.

In fact, it should be noted that virtually all the laws regulating polygamy had the effect of protecting the women in polygamous marriages (Exodus 21:10, Deuteronomy 21:15-17, Deuteronomy 25:5-10). Considering the laws governing polygamy in the Old Testament, perhaps one of the best conclusions to draw is that God is concerned about those who might be victimized by common social practices, and that he is eager for his people to care for the weak and vulnerable within society.

Although polygamy was common in the ancient world, the design of one man and one woman being married for life is clearly outlined throughout Scripture. For example, God gave only one woman to Adam in marriage in the Garden of Eden (Genesis 2:18-24) and Jesus affirmed God's design as evidenced at creation when questioned about divorce (Matthew 19:4-6). Paul also described marriage between one man and one woman as symbolically representing the loving relationship between God and his people (Ephesians 5:21-33, Revelation 19:6-9), and elders, who serve as leaders of the church and as examples to Christian families, are notably to be one-woman men (1 Timothy 3:2-12).

Prayer

Prayer is talking with God. It involves both speaking and listening and is both a private as well as a community activity. Common elements of prayer include petition, intercession, adoration, thanksgiving, confession and silence, as we listen for God's voice. The primary aims in prayer are knowing, partnering with God in the work of redemption and honoring God.

Prayer was a regular part of Jesus' life and ministry.
The news about Him spread even more, and large crowds would come together to hear Him and to be healed of their sicknesses. Yet He often withdrew to deserted places and prayed. Luke 5:15-16 (HCSB)

Prayer is an activity of the Holy Spirit.
In the same way the Spirit also joins to help in our weakness, because we do not know what to pray for as we should, but the Spirit Himself intercedes for us with unspoken groanings. Romans 8:26 (HCSB)

Prayer is a means to experiencing God's healing.
If my people who are called by my name humble themselves, and pray and seek my face and turn from their wicked ways, then I will hear from heaven and will forgive their sin and heal their land. 2 Chronicles 7:14 (ESV)

Prayer is to be offered in Jesus' name and for his glory.
Whatever you ask in My name, I will do it so that the Father may be glorified in the Son. If you ask Me anything in My name, I will do it. John 14:13-14 (HCSB)

Prayer is made effective by agreement with one another.
"If two of you agree on earth about anything that they may ask, it shall be done for them by My Father who is in heaven. "For where two or three have gathered together in My name, I am there in their midst." Matthew 18:19-20 (NASB)

Prayer was taught by Jesus to his disciples.
He was praying in a certain place, and when He finished, one of His disciples said to Him, "Lord, teach us to pray, just as John also taught his disciples." Luke 11:1 (HCSB)

Prayer requires faith and perseverance.
All the things you pray and ask for—believe that you have received them, and you will have them. Mark 11:24 (HCSB)

He then told them a parable on the need for them to pray always and not become discouraged. Luke 18:1 (HCSB)

Prayer is God's will and to be a continual part of life.
Rejoice always! Pray constantly. Give thanks in everything, for this is God's will for you in Christ Jesus. 1 Thessalonians 5:16-18 (HCSB)

Prayer is a means for enlightenment.
I pray that the perception of your mind may be enlightened so you may know what is the hope of His calling, what are the glorious riches of His inheritance among the saints, and what is the immeasurable greatness of His power to us who believe, according to the working of His vast strength. Ephesians 1:18-19 (HSCB)

Prayer is a means for strengthening.
That according to the riches of his glory he may grant you to be strengthened with power through his Spirit in your inner being. Ephesians 3:16 (ESV)

Prayer of a righteous man is powerful and effective.
The urgent request of a righteous person is very powerful in its effect. James 5:16 (HSCB)

Why pray in Jesus' name?

There are few practices as universal among Christians as praying in Jesus' name. In fact, it is such a common practice that it is often adopted without question. Many do it without ever even understanding why we are to pray in Jesus' name. Still others wield Jesus' name in prayer like it is the spiritual equivalent of 'Abracadabra," the magic word recited at the end of an incantation (Acts 19:13-17).

Praying in Jesus' name invokes his person, position, and power. To pray in Jesus' name is to call upon him as the only means to the Father (John 14:6), as the sole mediator between God and man (1 Timothy 2:5, Hebrews 4:14-16, Hebrews 7:25, Hebrews 13:15), and as the only person who possess the name by which we must be saved (Acts 4:12). For this reason, to pray in Jesus' name assumes that we are praying for what he would want us to receive (James 4:2), and for the purpose of bringing glory to his Father (Matthew 6:9-10).

Jesus gave us his name for the purpose of prayer.
Until now you have asked for nothing in My name. Ask and you will receive, so that your joy may be complete. John 16:24 (HCSB)

If you ask Me anything in My name, I will do it. John 14:14 (HCSB)

Praying in Jesus' name invokes his presence and power.
Again, I assure you: If two of you on earth agree about any matter that you pray for, it will be done for you by My Father in heaven. For where two or three are gathered together in My name, I am there among them." Matthew 18:19-20 (HCSB)

Praying in Jesus' name brings answers and joy.
Until now you have asked for nothing in My name. Ask and you will receive, so that your joy may be complete. John 16:24 (HCSB)

Praying in Jesus' name gives us access to the Father.
I assure you: Anything you ask the Father in My name, He will give you. John 16:23 (HCSB)

In that day you will ask in My name. I am not telling you that I will make requests to the Father on your behalf. For the Father Himself loves you, because you have loved Me and have believed that I came from God. John 16:26-27 (HCSB)

Whatever you ask in My name, I will do it so that the Father may be glorified in the Son. John 14:13 (HCSB)

Praying in Jesus' name celebrates Jesus' love for us and demonstrates faith in him as God.
In that day you will ask in My name. I am not telling you that I will make requests to the Father on your behalf. For the Father Himself loves you, because you have loved Me and have believed that I came from God. John 16:26-27 (HCSB)

Praying in Jesus' name is a means to bearing fruit.
You did not choose Me, but I chose you. I appointed you that you should go out and produce fruit and that your fruit should remain, so that whatever you ask the Father in My name, He will give you. John 15:16 (HCSB)

Why might our prayers go unanswered?

We know that God's people are to pray without ceasing and for all people (1 Thessalonians 5:17, 1 Timothy 2:1). We also know that God always hears the prayers of his people, despite their unrighteousness and because of the righteousness of Jesus (John 14:13-14, 1 Timothy 2:5, Revelation 5:8). However, in some cases God's people may not receive what they requested in prayer.

Our prayers may go unanswered if we lack faith.
But when you ask him, be sure that your faith is in God alone. Do not waver, for a person with divided loyalty is as unsettled as a wave of the sea that is blown and tossed by the wind. Such people should not expect to receive anything from the Lord. James 1:6-7 (NLT)

Because of their unbelief, he couldn't do any miracles among them except to place his hands on a few sick people and heal them. And he was amazed at their unbelief. Mark 6:5-6 (NLT)

Our prayers may go unanswered if we are disobedient.
If our hearts do not condemn us, we have confidence before God and receive from him anything we ask, because we keep his commands and do what pleases him. 1 John 3:21-22 (NIV)

If you remain in me and my words remain in you, ask whatever you wish, and it will be done for you. John 15:7 (NIV)

Our prayers may go unanswered if we have wrong motives.
You ask and don't receive because you ask with wrong motives, so that you may spend it on your evil desires. James 4:3 (HCSB)

Our prayers may go unanswered if we mistreat others.
Husbands, in the same way be considerate as you live with your wives, and treat them with respect as the weaker partner and as heirs with you of the

gracious gift of life, so that nothing will hinder your prayers. 1 Peter 3:7 (NIV)

Our prayers may go unanswered if God is testing us.
It was there at Marah that the Lord set before them the following decree as a standard to test their faithfulness to him. He said, "If you will listen carefully to the voice of the Lord your God and do what is right in his sight, obeying his commands and keeping all his decrees, then I will not make you suffer any of the diseases I sent on the Egyptians; for I am the Lord who heals you." Exodus 15:25-26 (NLT)

But he knows the way that I take; when he has tested me, I will come forth as gold. Job 23:10 (NIV)

Three times I pleaded with the Lord about this, that it should leave me. But he said to me, "My grace is sufficient for you, for my power is made perfect in weakness." Therefore I will boast all the more gladly of my weaknesses, so that the power of Christ may rest upon me. 2 Corinthians 12:8-9 (ESV)

Our prayers may go unanswered because of opposition from our spiritual enemy.
Then he said, "Don't be afraid, Daniel. Since the first day you began to pray for understanding and to humble yourself before your God, your request has been heard in heaven. I have come in answer to your prayer. But for twenty-one days the spirit prince of the kingdom of Persia blocked my way. Then Michael, one of the archangels, came to help me, and I left him there with the spirit prince of the kingdom of Persia." Daniel 10:12-13 (NLT)

Prayer and Laying on Hands

While the laying on of hands may appear to be little more than placing a hand on someone's shoulder during prayer, it has a strong biblical history and is meant to communicate the power and presence of God.

Laying on hands was something Jesus did in healing and prayer.
When the sun was setting, the people brought to Jesus all who had various kinds of sickness, and laying his hands on each one, he healed them. Luke 4:40 (NIV)

One day some parents brought their children to Jesus so he could lay his hands on them and pray for them. But the disciples scolded the parents for bothering him. Matthew 19:13 (NLT)

Laying on hands accompanied Paul's personal healing.
Then Ananias went to the house and entered it. Placing his hands on Saul, he said, "Brother Saul, the Lord—Jesus, who appeared to you on the road as you were coming here—has sent me so that you may see again and be filled with the Holy Spirit." Acts 9:17 (NIV)

Laying on hands was something Paul did for others.
His father was sick in bed, suffering from fever and dysentery. Paul went in to see him and, after prayer, placed his hands on him and healed him. Acts 28:8 (NIV)

As it happened, Publius's father was ill with fever and dysentery. Paul went in and prayed for him, and laying his hands on him, he healed him. Acts 28:18 (NLT)

Laying on hands accompanied ordination.
They presented these men to the apostles, who prayed and laid their hands on them. Acts 6:6 (NIV)

So after they had fasted and prayed, they placed their hands on them and sent them off. Acts 13:3 (NIV)

Do not neglect the spiritual gift you received through the prophecy spoken over you when the elders of the church laid their hands on you. 1 Timothy 4:14 (NLT)

Do not be hasty in the laying on of hands, and do not share in the sins of others. Keep yourself pure. 1 Timothy 5:22 (NIV)

Laying on hands was considered an elementary teaching.
Therefore let us leave the elementary doctrine of Christ and go on to maturity, not laying again a foundation of repentance from dead works and of faith toward God, and of instruction about washings, the laying on of hands, the resurrection of the dead, and eternal judgment. Hebrews 6:1-2 (ESV)

What does it mean to pray in the Spirit?

The charge to "pray in the Spirit" comes at the end of the description of God's armor (Ephesians 6:10-17). God's armor is designed to help us stand against the devil's schemes. We take our stand against the devil in prayer. Is prayer all that Christians are to be doing? Certainly not. But prayer is a primary means by which we experience Jesus' victory over evil.

Notice that it is not just any kind of prayer we are to be offering. Paul wrote that we are to be praying "in the Spirit." Praying in the Spirit is also something Jude assumes that believers will be doing (Jude 20). But what does it mean to pray in the Spirit? To pray in the Spirit involves partnering with the Spirit in spiritual warfare. The context of Paul's encouragement to "pray in the Spirit" is important. It comes at the end of a charge to be prepared for spiritual warfare. And Jude's charge to do the same is given in the context of "contending" for the faith. Just as Jesus was led into the wilderness by the Spirit where he faced the enemy (Matthew 4:1-11), the Spirit will lead us into battle as well. To pray in the Spirit is to follow the Spirit's leading into battle.

To pray in the Spirit is to utilize the armor of God in prayer. Again, the context of the admonition to "pray in the Spirit" is important. Clearly, we are to utilize the armor of God as we carry it into battle during prayer. For example, to pray in the Spirit we must wear the "belt of truth" in prayer (Ephesians 6:14). Whether it is confessing our sin or confessing our hopes and dreams and deepest longings, praying in the Spirit means opening ourselves completely and unreservedly to God by telling the truth. As we are truth tellers, our prayers are more effective (James 1:6).

To pray in the Spirit, we must wear the "breastplate of righteousness" (Ephesians 6:14). This will involve celebrating the righteousness of God provided to us through faith in Christ (Romans 3:21-26). To pray in the Spirit, we must have our feet "fitted with the readiness that comes from the gospel of peace" (Ephesians 6:15), which means praying for God to send laborers into the harvest field (Luke 10:2), embolden our witness (Acts 4:29) and save lost people (John 1:13). This means that the first step in effectively sharing our faith is not talking to lost people, or even preparing to answer the questions of lost people. The first step in effectively sharing our faith is asking the Lord of the harvest to bring in the harvest (Luke 10:2).

To pray in the Spirit, we must raise the "shield of faith" in prayer (Ephesians 6:16), which means we must stand in prayer on God's good character and purposes. This will involve quoting Scripture that tells of God's goodness and his good purposes for his people during our prayer. As we declare the goodness of God's character and celebrate his good purposes our faith is strengthened, and it is faith that moves mountains (Mark 11:23).

To pray in the Spirit, we must wear the "helmet of salvation" (Ephesians 6:17), which involves recounting God's work of salvation in our lives and in history. Repeatedly God's people are told to remember God's works of salvation. Remembering involves retelling and to pray in the Spirit we must retell of God's victory over the enemy in days past. At a most practical level, this will include recounting God's feats of deliverance for the Israelites and his provision for the Church.

To pray in the Spirit, we must wield the "sword of the Spirit" in prayer (Ephesians 6:17). Specifically, this will involve addressing lies that have been believed, as well as rebuking and casting out the enemy. Our enemy the devil is the father of lies (John 8:44), and renouncing lies believed and announcing the truth of God's Word is critical to spiritual warfare.

Finally, to pray in the Spirit is to appeal to the Spirit's power for victory. To pray in the Spirit is to acknowledge our powerlessness to accomplish any good work, and to wait in faith upon God's deliverance (John 15:5). The Spirit is the only means by which we are effective in prayer (Zechariah 4:6).

Prayer in the New Testament

They prayed together.
They all joined together constantly in prayer, along with the women and Mary the mother of Jesus, and with his brothers. Acts 1:14 (NIV)

They devoted themselves to the apostles' teaching and to the fellowship, to the breaking of bread and to the prayers. Acts 2:42 (ESV)

They prayed for faithfulness and with perseverance.
We constantly pray for you, that our God may count you worthy of his calling, and that by his power he may fulfill every good purpose of yours and every act prompted by your faith. 2 Thessalonians 1:11 (NIV)

They prayed for God's direction in selecting leaders.
"Lord, you know everyone's heart. Show us which of these two you have chosen. Acts 1:24 (NIV)

They presented these men to the apostles, who prayed and laid their hands on them. Acts 6:5-6 (NIV)

So after they had fasted and prayed, they placed their hands on them and sent them off. Acts 13:3 (NIV)

Paul and Barnabas appointed Elders for them in each church and, with prayer and fasting, committed them to the Lord, in whom they had put their trust. Acts 14:23 (NIV)

They prayed for boldness, healing and miraculous signs.
"Now, Lord, consider their threats and enable your servants to speak your word with great boldness. Stretch out your hand to heal and perform miraculous signs and wonders through the name of your holy servant Jesus." Acts 4:29-30 (NIV)

They prayed as a ministry priority.
Brothers, choose seven men from among you who are known to be full of the Spirit and wisdom. We will turn this responsibility over to them and will give our attention to prayer and the ministry of the word. Acts 6:3-4 (NIV)

They prayed during persecution.
While they were stoning him, Stephen prayed, "Lord Jesus, receive my spirit." Acts 7:59 (NIV)

So Peter was kept in prison, but the church was earnestly praying to God for him. Acts 12:5 (NIV)

They prayed for healing.
Peter sent them all out of the room; then he got down on his knees and prayed. Turning toward the dead woman, he said, "Tabitha, get up." She opened her eyes, and seeing Peter she sat up. Acts 9:40 (NIV)

His father was sick in bed, suffering from fever and dysentery. Paul went in to see him and, after prayer, placed his hands on him and healed him. Acts 28:8 (NIV)

They prayed for strengthening through the Holy Spirit.
I pray that out of his glorious riches he may strengthen you with power through his Spirit in your inner being. Ephesians 3:16 (NIV)

They prayed for the salvation of unbelievers.
Brothers, my heart's desire and prayer to God for the Israelites is that they may be saved. Romans 10:1 (NIV)

They prayed for spiritual enlightenment.
I pray also that the eyes of your heart may be enlightened in order that you may know the hope to which he has called you, the riches of his glorious inheritance in the saints, and his incomparably great power for us who believe. Ephesians 1:18-19 (NIV)

They prayed in joy and with confidence in Christ.
I thank my God every time I remember you. In all my prayers for all of you, I always pray with joy because of your partnership in the gospel from the first day until now, being confident of this, that he who began a good work in you will carry it on to completion until the day of Christ Jesus. Philippians 1:3-6 (NIV)

They prayed for love and discernment.
And this is my prayer: that your love may abound more and more in knowledge and depth of insight, so that you may be able to discern what is best and may be pure and blameless until the day of Christ, filled with the fruit of righteousness that comes through Jesus Christ—to the glory and praise of God. Philippians 1:9-11 (NIV)

They prayed to be filled with knowledge.
For this reason, since the day we heard about you, we have not stopped praying for you and asking God to fill you with the knowledge of his will through all spiritual wisdom and understanding. Colossians 1:9 (NIV)

They prayed with devotion.
Night and day we pray most earnestly that we may see you again and supply what is lacking in your faith.
1 Thessalonians 3:10 (NIV)

They prayed for others to be active in sharing their faith.
I pray that you may be active in sharing your faith, so that you will have a full understanding of every good thing we have in Christ. Philemon 1:6 (NIV)

They prayed for good health and for success.
I pray that you may enjoy good health and that all may go well with you, even as your soul is getting along well. 3 John 1:2 (NIV)

The Prayer of a Righteous Man

The Apostle James wrote, "The prayer of a righteous man is powerful and effective" (James 5:16). Why are some peoples' prayers more powerful and more effective than other people? The answer is because of their righteousness. In short, how we live affects whether we receive answers to our prayers. Too many Christians mistakenly believe that because we are saved by grace, apart from anything that we do, that our obedience once we are saved does not matter. Obedience matters to God, especially when it comes to answered prayer.

Why is this the case? While our Heavenly Father is eager to "give good gifts" to his children (Matthew 7:9-11), he will not reward disobedience. This is not to say that the prayers of the disobedient are never answered. Even disobedient children may receive their requests from time to time. But the most powerful and most effective in prayer are those who are obedient to Jesus' teachings. Jesus said:

> If you remain in me and my words remain in you, ask whatever you wish, and it will be given you. John 15:7 (NIV)

While obedience does not obligate God to answer our prayers, it places us in a position to better understand his will and ways. Look at what Jesus says about the connections between our obedience and answered prayer.

> If you remain in me and my words remain in you, ask whatever you wish, and it will be given you. This is to my Father's glory, that you bear much fruit, showing yourselves to be my disciples. John 15:7-8 (NIV)

Jesus answers the prayers of those who are remaining in his word (i.e., his teachings), because these are the people whose lives bring the Father glory by showing themselves to be followers of Jesus. Answered prayer is for our good, but it is ultimately and always meant for God's glory. God our Father is not as eager to answer the prayer of disobedient children, because it would be bad for the children and bring dishonor to him. In his first letter to the church John writes:

> Dear friends, if our hearts do not condemn us, we have confidence before God and receive from him anything we ask, because we obey his commands and do what pleases him. And this is his command: to believe in the name of his Son, Jesus Christ, and to love one another as he commanded us. 1 John 3:21-23 (NIV)

Unfortunately, some learn of the importance of obedience in the effectiveness of prayer and immediately feel that perfection is required in life. But we do not have to be perfect in order to receive answers to prayer. The righteous person is not a sinless person, but rather a person who acknowledges their sin and is turning from their sin. In fact, James directs us to confess our sinfulness and to pray (James 5:16). This means that we must both affirm the importance of obedience and accept the reality of our sinfulness if we are to pray with power and effectiveness.

Problem of Evil

The problem of evil is best summarized in the question: "If God is good and all powerful, then why does he continue to allow evil?" This question is a "problem" in that many draw the conclusion that God is either:

- Good, but cannot stop evil, and thus not all powerful.
- Able to stop evil, but unwilling, and thus not good.

Neither of these conclusions is biblical, as Scripture teaches us that in God's goodness and power he has already overcome the Evil One and provided for all those who have faith in Jesus Christ the strength needed to endure.

God's goodness and his power over evil is demonstrated by Jesus' suffering in our place and for our redemption.
But he was pierced for our transgressions, he was crushed for our iniquities; the punishment that brought us peace was upon him, and by his wounds we are healed. Isaiah 53:5 (NIV)

God's goodness and his power over evil is demonstrated in God's plan to end suffering once and for all.
And I heard a loud voice from the throne saying, "Behold, the dwelling place of God is with man. He will dwell with them, and they will be his people, and God himself will be with them as their God. He will wipe away every tear from their eyes, and death shall be no more, neither shall there be mourning, nor crying, nor pain anymore, for the former things have passed away." Revelation 21:3-4 (ESV)

God's goodness and his power over evil is demonstrated by the strength God provides to those with faith in Jesus.
For I can do everything through Christ, who gives me strength. Philippians 4:13 (NLT)

But he said to me, "My grace is sufficient for you, for my power is made perfect in weakness." Therefore I will boast all the more gladly about my weaknesses, so that Christ's power may rest on me. 2 Corinthians 12:9 (NIV)

God's goodness and his power over evil is demonstrated in the Spirit's care of Christians when we suffer.
I consider that our present sufferings are not worth comparing with the glory that will be revealed in us. In the same way, the Spirit helps us in our weakness. We do not know what we ought to pray for, but the Spirit himself intercedes for us with groans that words cannot express. And we know that in all things God works for the good of those who love him, who have been called according to his purpose. What, then, shall we say in response to this? If God is for us, who can be against us? He who did not spare his own Son, but gave him up for us all—how will he not also, along with him, graciously give us all things? Romans 8:18, 26, 28, 31, 32 (NIV)

God's goodness and his power over evil is provided through the Spirit, who is at work within Christians.
But the Holy Spirit produces this kind of fruit in our lives: love, joy, peace, patience, kindness, goodness, faithfulness, gentleness, and self-control. Galatians 5:22-23 (NLT)

God's goodness and his power over evil is demonstrated in the joy given to Christians in the midst of suffering.
You became imitators of us and of the Lord, for you welcomed the message in the midst of severe suffering with the joy given by the Holy Spirit. 1 Thessalonians 1:6 (NIV)

God's goodness and his power over evil is demonstrated in God's instruction to overcome the forces of evil.
Finally, be strong in the Lord and in his mighty power. Put on the full armor of God, so that you can take your stand against the devil's schemes. Ephesians 6:10-11 (NIV)

Puritans

Puritans wanted to further "purify" religious practice in worship services and doctrine, removing what they viewed as continued Catholic influences upon the Protestant church. Most specifically, Puritans took aim at the Church of England, working to remove worship liturgy, hierarchical leadership, priestly vestments, and praying to saints, basically anything that smacked of Catholicity. The word "Puritan" was initially used as a term of derision by those who criticized their desire for reform, but it quickly became a badge of honor.

Puritan influence spanned the sixteenth century through the eighteenth century, as well as spread across several continents, and was tremendously influential in colonial America. The Pilgrims that founded the Massachusetts Bay Colony were Puritans, and Harvard College (1639) was founded by Puritans. Roger Williams, founder of the Rhode Island colony, was also a Puritan.

Generally, Puritans were Calvinistic in their theology, emphasizing the total depravity of humanity and the sovereignty of God in the work of salvation. They held a high view of Scripture, and believed that every individual Christian was a priest, gifted and called by God to minister. They emphasized individual, as well as ecclesiastical, responsibility, which politically made them separatistic, not wanting the government to meddle in church matters.

While having a passion for Scripture and holiness, Puritanism also had a harsh underbelly. H.L. Mencken, a twentieth century American journalist, described the posture of Puritanism as "the haunting fear that someone, somewhere, may be happy." In the American colonies, Puritan leaders used the Old Testament law as a guide for legal and social order. In their zeal for purity, Puritans, or at the very least the culture that Puritanism created, led to abusive outcomes, and in some cases even violent realities.

Some of the most egregious outcomes included the Salem Witch Trials, which were a direct result of a Puritanical fear of all things Satanic. The famed "Scarlet Letter" (1850), written by Nathaniel Hawthorne is based upon Puritanical punishments. The protagonist in the "Scarlett Letter," Hester Prynne, is publicly shamed by her Puritan neighbors for her sin of adultery, imprisoned and made to wear a red letter "A" for the rest of her life. In the American colonies and in large part because of Puritan influence, virtually all sin was subject to public shaming and punishment, and the Puritans made famous the use of devices of punishment, such as the "stockade" and the "cleft stick."

Racism

Race is a socio-cultural construct, which is to say people elevated certain physical attributes and discriminated against one another based upon those prejudices. While the Bible never speaks against racism directly, there are many vice lists in the New Testament which clearly identify racism as contrary to the character and purposes of God. Paul lists "discord, jealousy, fits of rage, selfish ambition, dissensions, factions and envy" as works of the flesh (Galatians 5:19-21), all of which are involved in racist attitudes and actions. Racism at its core is sinful in its prideful posture, exalting one people group over another, while denigrating or altogether denying the image-bearing capacity of certain groups (Genesis 1:26-27).

Scripture teaches that all people are made in the image of God (Genesis 1:26-27), and that the Kingdom of God will include "every nation, tribe, people and language" (Revelation 7:9-10). As a result, all people are inherently valuable and equally valued in God's sight, and those who are trusting in Christ for salvation are "one" (Galatians 3:28). As a result, the church is to include all peoples. The multi-racial reality of the gospel was clearly seen in Jesus' efforts to make his ministry inclusive of Samaritans (Luke 10:25-37, John 4:7-10), as well as the Canaanite woman (Matthew 15:21-28). This reality was also demonstrated in the early church where the Spirit was poured out on peoples from many nations (Acts 2:8-12), and the prophets and teachers in Antioch were of different races (Acts 13:1). Paul later explained that reconciliation between people groups is a direct result of the gospel's ministry (Ephesians 2:11-13). Admittedly, not everything was perfect in the early church. They had racial issues to address as well. For example, Paul famously confronted Peter in Antioch for drawing back from fellowship with Gentiles, which was little more than a posture of racism on Peter's part, albeit expressed through Jewish ethnic food laws (Galatians 2:11-13).

Racism has often undermined unity within the American Church too. This began with slavery, but sadly did not end with the passage of the Thirteenth Amendment. Racism is any attitude or system of oppression based upon racial makeup (e.g., skin color). When racism is present division always results. Even after the Civil War, many of our political, economic, social, and religious institutions functioned with racist laws, ideologies, policies, and practices, which persisted for decades. Examples include: 1) Jim Crow laws; 2) policies by local school boards designed to thwart desegregation and the U.S. Supreme Court's pronouncement that "separate is inherently unequal;" and 3) the practice of systematically excluding black Americans in some of America's most prominent institutions of higher education, religious organizations, social clubs, and even local facilities such as parks and local sports teams. Although discrimination based on race is illegal in America, the effects of these laws, policies and practices are still too often felt today by many Americans of color. Examples include, among other things, housing and zoning policies, lending practices, the availability of quality education, and aspects of the criminal justice system.

Much of the progress on issues of race has allowed society to see that racism is often more subtle and, in some cases, is even embedded within the normal day to day operations of cultural institutions. This leads to a "racialized society." A racialized society is one that affords different economic, political, social, and even psychological rewards along racial lines. Often referred to as "systemic" racism, statistical evidence for racialization within American society is overwhelming and is seen in black-white inequalities in health, income, college graduation rates, home ownership, and incarceration rates. As a result, and often without realizing it, people of good faith can sustain a racialized society in the ordinary activities of life.

Scripture denounces racism and racialization in all forms, naming it as a sin, and calls God's people to lament the damage done by racism. Scripture calls us to repent of all racist beliefs, postures and/or practices, and to embrace Christ's teaching to love our neighbor as ourselves (Matthew 22:37-40) and live in unity with one another (Galatians 3:28, Colossians 3:14). Finally, God's people are to pursue justice by addressing racism and working to strengthen unity within the church and the broader community, living as ambassadors of healing, justice, and reconciliation (Micah 6:8, 2 Corinthians 5:18-20).

Biblically, we know that God does not show favoritism (Deuteronomy 10:17, Acts 10:34-35, Romans 2:11, Ephesians 6:9) and that we are not to discriminate against anyone for any reason (James 2:1-4). Unfortunately, some have confused God's "choosing" Israel and requiring them to live separated from other nations as an affirmation of racism. However, God's selection of Israel was based not upon any physical attribute or cultural heritage of a people group, but was rather the calling of a singular man, Abram, through whom God decided to bless all peoples of the world (Genesis 12:3, Genesis 18:18). God's purposes in keeping Israel separate from other nations was not an affirmation of Israel's racial superiority but was rather a means to blessing all peoples through Israel (Romans 9:3-5). Unfortunately, Israel failed to keep the Law of God and their sin created hostility with other nations. If the Law had been kept by Israel, a law which included loving God and all their neighbors (Deuteronomy 6:5, Leviticus 19:18, 33-34), then Israel would have maintained communion with God as well as a good standing with all other people groups.

Through the Gospel the dividing wall of hostility that grew between Jews and Gentiles was destroyed (Ephesians 2:14), creating one new humanity (Ephesians 2:15-16). This means that all forms of racism are affronts to the work of Christ on the cross, and antithetical to the gospel. As a result, Christians have been given a ministry of reconciliation (2 Corinthians 5:18-20) that includes exposing the evil deeds of darkness and calling all people to embrace the multiethnic reality of Heaven (Ephesians 5:11, Revelation 5:9-10, 22:1-5).

Remarriage

Remarriage is the legal and spiritual union of an individual, or a couple, who was formerly married. The New Testament clearly allows for remarriage after the death of a spouse (1 Corinthians 7:39) and for the purpose of being reconciled to one from whom you were previously divorced (1 Corinthians 7:11). However, beyond these two specific situations there is much debate concerning the biblical permissibility of remarriage.

Given the range of opinion within the Christian community regarding the permissibility of divorce, specifically in situations involving adultery, abandonment, and/or abuse (Matthew 5:32, 19:9; 1 Corinthians 7:15), there is predictably much debate concerning the permissibility of remarriage. Therefore, when considering remarriage, it is wisest to exercise caution because remarriage causes some to commit adultery. Jesus said:

> But I say to you that everyone who divorces his wife, except on the ground of sexual immorality, makes her commit adultery, and whoever marries a divorced woman commits adultery. Matthew 5:32 (ESV)

> And I say to you: whoever divorces his wife, except for sexual immorality, and marries another, commits adultery. Matthew 19:9 (ESV)

Prohibited in the seventh commandment, adultery is committed by having sexual intercourse with someone other than one's spouse. Remarriage causes some to commit adultery because divorce, although legally severing a marriage, does not break the marital bond from a biblical and spiritual perspective.

The marital bond is the spiritual union established through sexual intimacy as "two become one flesh" (Genesis

2:24, Matthew 19:5, Mark 10:8). The marital bond is broken only as sexual immorality occurs within a marriage, which means that it is entirely possible to be legally divorced from one's spouse while still spiritually united to that spouse. Therefore, those remarrying commit adultery, unless the marital bond was previously broken by a spouse's "sexual immorality."

It is also wisest to exercise caution when considering remarriage because remarriage can prevent reconciliation between a divorced couple. The Apostle Paul wrote:

> To the married I give this command (not I, but the Lord): A wife must not separate from her husband. But if she does, she must remain unmarried or else be reconciled to her husband. And a husband must not divorce his wife. 1 Corinthians 7:10-11 (NIV)

Scripture places a high priority on forgiveness and reconciliation (Matthew 6:14-15, 2 Corinthians 5:18). For this reason, those who are divorced are directed to remain unmarried or to be reconciled (i.e., remarried) to their spouse. If one does decide to remarry, then believers should remarry only other believers (1 Corinthians 7:39, 2 Corinthians 6:14-15), and once remarried they should not divorce (1 Corinthians 7:27).

Repentance

Repentance is a godly sorrow for personal sin that leads to an active forsaking of sinful attitudes and actions and a cultivation of godly attitudes and actions in an effort to honor God with one's life.

Repentance is God's expectation for humanity.
If a man does not repent, He will sharpen His sword; He has bent His bow and made it ready. Psalm 7:12 (NASB)

Repentance brings salvation.
For thus the Lord GOD, the Holy One of Israel, has said, "In repentance and rest you will be saved, In quietness and trust is your strength." But you were not willing. Isaiah 30:15 (NASB)

Repentance has specific actions that are verifiable.
"Therefore bear fruit in keeping with repentance; and do not suppose that you can say to yourselves, 'We have Abraham for our father'; for I say to you that from these stones God is able to raise up children to Abraham. Matthew 3:8-9 (NASB)

Repentance is the reason Jesus came.
And Jesus answered and said to them, "It is not those who are well who need a physician, but those who are sick. "I have not come to call the righteous but sinners to repentance." Luke 5:31-32 (NASB)

Repentance is a gift from Jesus.
He is the one whom God exalted to His right hand as a Prince and a Savior, to grant repentance to Israel, and forgiveness of sins. Acts 5:31 (NASB)

When they heard this, they quieted down and glorified God, saying, "Well then, God has granted to the Gentiles also the repentance that leads to life." Acts 11:18 (NASB)

Repentance was the message of the early church.
First to those in Damascus, then to those in Jerusalem and in all Judea, and to the Gentiles also, I preached that they should repent and turn to God and prove their repentance by their deeds. Acts 26:20 (NIV)

Repentance is brought by God's kindness.
Or do you show contempt for the riches of his kindness, tolerance and patience, not realizing that God's kindness leads you toward repentance? Romans 2:4 (NIV)

Repentance is a result of godly sorrow and produces fruit.
*As it is, I rejoice, not because you were grieved, but because you were grieved into repenting. For you felt a godly grief, so that you suffered no loss through us. For godly grief produces a repentance that leads to salvation without regret, whereas worldly grief produces death. For see what earnestness this godly grief has produced in you, but also what eagerness to clear yourselves, what indignation, what fear, what longing, what zeal, what punishment! At every point you have proved yourselves innocent in the matter.
2 Corinthians 7:9-11 (ESV)*

Repentance brings escape from the devil's trap.
God may perhaps grant them repentance leading to a knowledge of the truth, and they may come to their senses and escape from the snare of the devil, after being captured by him to do his will. 2 Timothy 2:25-26 (ESV)

Repentance is what God wants in everyone's life.
The Lord is not slow in keeping his promise, as some understand slowness. He is patient with you, not wanting anyone to perish, but everyone to come to repentance. 2 Peter 3:9 (NIV)

Resurrected Bodies

Jesus was raised from the dead, and the work of the gospel ultimately culminates with all those who have faith in Jesus receiving resurrected bodies (1 Corinthians 15:20-23).

The need for resurrection is created by the presence of sin, which makes death a certain and powerful enemy. In other words, death is made deadly through sin (Romans 6:23, 1 Corinthians 15:56). In fact, if the need for the resurrection of our bodies does not seem urgent to us, then we may not be facing death honestly. We may be buying into a false hope that death can somehow be avoided. Death is certain for all of humanity and with every moment that passes we move closer to experiencing its sting. Of course, the good news of the gospel is that for those who have faith in Jesus, the hope of bodily resurrection is even more certain and even more powerful than death (Romans 10:9-13, Revelation 20:6). Paul describes that death is "swallowed up" through the resurrection of Jesus Christ, the sting of death removed and victory over death won through the resurrection of Christ (1 Corinthians 15:55).

What will it be like to live in a raised body? We know what it is like to live embodied on earth, but Scripture describes the experience of living in resurrected bodies as categorically different than our experience here on earth. For example, we know that our raised bodies will be "imperishable," which means that all the experiences that go along with death, including disease, decay and suffering will not be experienced in our resurrected bodies (1 Corinthians 15:42-44). While our resurrected bodies will have physical attributes, that are not described as "flesh and blood," but rather as "spiritual" bodies (1 Corinthians 15:44), after the resurrection we will have a body perfectly suited for living in heaven.

Some of the implications of living in a spiritual body are that it will not need food or sleep for sustaining one's physical strength, and we will not be as physically limited by time and space in the same way that we are limited physically on earth. While we will be able to eat and move, much like we do now, it appears that our "spiritual" bodies will not require food and movement will not be as limited.

We get a glimpse of what our resurrection experience will be like when we recall Jesus' post-resurrection appearances to his disciples (Philippians 3:21). Jesus still had visible wounds from the crucifixion after he was raised, but the wounds were not a cause of continued suffering for him (Luke 24:37-43). Instead, Jesus displayed his crucifixion wounds more like badges of faithfulness might be displayed, a demonstration of his person and work in salvation (John 20:19-29). And while his disciples could physically touch his body, he was also able to travel effortlessly through time and space, appearing and disappearing at will (Luke 24:31). He could also go through walls and doors, as well as eat and drink and sit and talk with others (John 20:19). It appears that all of the physical limitations brought by sin that keep us from being able to fully experience and serve God on earth will be overcome, freeing us to praise and serve and glorify God for eternity.

The reality of the resurrection is a source of great hope for Christians, especially if we are facing difficult physical challenges (1 Thessalonians 4:13-18, Revelation 21:4). Whatever we face in this life, there is hope because Jesus was raised and we will be raised just as he was raised. The reality of the resurrection is also a source of motivation in service. The promise of the resurrection gives us purpose in life and motivates us to "work enthusiastically" for the Lord (1 Corinthians 15:58). In fact, the best preparation for receiving our resurrected bodies is to begin using our earthly body now to honor God. If our hope is to spend an eternity bringing glory to God in a raised body, then there is no better time than now to begin living completely and totally for his glory.

Rewards in Heaven

The Apostle Paul wrote that the life of every Christian will be inspected, or judged, by God for how they build upon their foundation of faith in Jesus Christ, and that each person will either receive a reward or suffer loss based upon the quality of their workmanship.

> For no one can lay any foundation other than the one already laid, which is Jesus Christ. If anyone builds on this foundation using gold, silver, costly stones, wood, hay or straw, their work will be shown for what it is, because the Day will bring it to light. It will be revealed with fire, and the fire will test the quality of each person's work. If what has been built survives, the builder will receive a reward. If it is burned up, the builder will suffer loss but yet will be saved—even though only as one escaping through the flames.
> 1 Corinthians 3:11-15 (NIV)

But why are rewards necessary? God's desire is to reward us in heaven for lives faithfully lived on earth (Matthew 25:14-30, Romans 8:17). This means that we have important questions to ask ourselves about how we are living. What will the judgement show about how we have spent our time, talents, and our treasures? Are we building upon the foundation of faith we have in Jesus Christ with gold, silver, costly stones, wood, hay or with straw?

This "Day," which is capitalized in the passage above, is a specific day. It's the Day of Judgment for Christians. However, it is not a judgment about who gets into heaven and who does not, but rather a judgement for the purpose of rewarding Christians for their faithfulness. Paul describes the judgment as an experience of being tried by fire. Picture in your mind's eye how different materials are affected differently by fire. Gold, silver and costly jewels are refined by fire. Diamonds, for example, are actually made over time through constant pressure and heat. The value of precious metals and jewels is seen clearly when tried by fire, while wood, hay and straw are each consumed by fire, and their value is diminished.

There are many Christians who hate the notion of judgement all together. If God really loved us, then wouldn't he reward everyone? Wouldn't he simply let us do what we want and love us as we are? Of course, God does love us just as we are, and God does allow us to do as we want. But he also loves us too much to let us live without accountability. In other words, he loves us too much to not encourage us to live well. After all, we intuitively know that good fathers both love unconditionally and provide accountability.

How can we "build with care" and what might it look like to use the highest quality materials in our lives so that we receive a reward? It is interesting to note that Jesus talked about rewards more than anyone else in the New Testament. So this notion of working for rewards is not something that Paul invented. Jesus promised reward for those who:

- Endured persecution (Matthew 5:12)
- Loved their enemies (Matthew 5:46)
- Gave financially, prayed, and fasted in secret (Matthew 6:4-18)
- Welcomed a prophet (Matthew 10:41)
- Cared for followers of Jesus (Matthew 10:42)
- Showed others care in Jesus' name (Mark 9:41)

This is just a short list of what it might look like to build with care, but any and every act of faithfulness will receive God's reward.

Sabbath

"Sabbath" means "day of rest" and to keep it holy means to "set it apart" from other days for a special purpose. God set the seventh day apart (Genesis 2:1-3), and God's people are to do the same. The fourth commandment reads:

> "Remember the Sabbath day, to keep it holy. Six days you shall labor, and do all your work, but the seventh day is a Sabbath to the Lord your God. On it you shall not do any work, you, or your son, or your daughter, your male servant, or your female servant, or your livestock, or the sojourner who is within your gates. For in six days the Lord made heaven and earth, the sea, and all that is in them, and rested on the seventh day. Therefore the Lord blessed the Sabbath day and made it holy. Exodus 20:8-11 (ESV)

Violating the Sabbath law was a serious offense (Exodus 31:14), and the prophets tied Israel's fate directly to Sabbath obedience (Jeremiah 17:19-27, Ezekiel 20:12).

While Jesus kept the Sabbath, he was clear that God made the Sabbath for man, not man for the Sabbath (Mark 2:27). His point was that merciless applications of Sabbath law that prohibited men from doing good to each other were perversions of God's intention for a holy day of rest. As God, Jesus has the authority to interpret Sabbath law (Mark 2:28), and he often did so in a fashion contrary to common interpretations of his day (Matthew 12:1-8, Matthew 12:10, Mark 1:21-26).

Although there is debate about how to observe the fourth commandment, a day of rest from work and worship is the most common application. A day dedicated to rest and worship honors God's rule and reign, which is the original intent of the law.

Salvation

Salvation is the work of God's grace to deliver us from sin through faith in the life, death and resurrection of Jesus Christ. Salvation includes deliverance from the penalty of sin and its certain consequences of death, deliverance from the power of sin over us in this present life, as well as ultimately deliverance from the very presence of sin as we enter the kingdom of heaven. In this way, salvation includes not only deliverance from sin, but also delivery to a new reality of freedom from sin and life eternal.

Salvation comes by grace through faith, not by works.
For it is by grace you have been saved, through faith—and this not from yourselves, it is the gift of God—not by works, so that no one can boast. Ephesians 2:8-9 (NIV)

Salvation comes through faith in Jesus Christ.
He then brought them out and asked, "Sirs, what must I do to be saved?" They replied, "Believe in the Lord Jesus, and you will be saved—you and your household." Acts 16:30-31 (NIV)

Salvation comes only through faith in Jesus Christ.
"Salvation is found in no one else, for there is no other name under heaven given to men by which we must be saved." Acts 4:12 (NIV)

Salvation comes as we call upon the name of the Lord.
If you confess with your mouth that Jesus is Lord and believe in your heart that God raised him from the dead, you will be saved. For with the heart one believes and is justified, and with the mouth one confesses and is saved. Romans 10:9-10 (ESV)

Salvation is made available through Christ's blood.
Much more then, having now been justified by His blood, we shall be saved from wrath through Him. For if when we were enemies we were reconciled

to God through the death of His Son, much more, having been reconciled, we shall be saved by His life. Romans 5:9-10 (NKJV)

Salvation comes through the message of the cross.
For the message of the cross is foolishness to those who are perishing, but to us who are being saved it is the power of God. 1 Corinthians 1:18 (NIV)

Salvation cannot be inherited but must be received by each person individually.
Therefore bear fruit in keeping with repentance; and do not suppose that you can say to yourselves, 'We have Abraham for our father'; for I say to you that from these stones God is able to raise up children to Abraham. Matthew 3:8-9 (NASB)

Salvation results in our receiving God's Holy Spirit.
In Him you also trusted, after you heard the word of truth, the gospel of your salvation; in whom also, having believed, you were sealed with the Holy Spirit of promise, who is the guarantee of our inheritance until the redemption of the purchased possession, to the praise of His glory. Ephesians 1:13-14 (NKJV)

Salvation and God's Sovereignty

Sovereignty is the power to act freely, and God is sovereign in salvation, saving all those whom he freely chooses to save. God's sovereignty in salvation is good news because it means no one is beyond salvation. No one is too sinful to be saved. Anyone can be saved, as salvation is a work of God, apart from anything we do (Ephesians 2:8-9).

God's sovereignty in salvation is also good news because it means that we are completely secure. In that God chose freely to save us, apart from anything we have done, are doing or will do, our salvation depends solely upon the will and power of God. God has laid hold of us. We have not laid hold of God, nor are we holding on to God (John 6:39, John 10:28-29).

God's sovereignty in salvation is also good news because it provides a clear understanding of the urgency in prayer. Prayer is not simply hoping for good things to happen. Prayer is a conversation with the One who possesses all power and authority. Prayer is a response to the invitation of God to join in his saving work (Luke 10:2, Romans 10:1).

Finally, God's sovereignty in salvation is also good news because it provides freedom in evangelism. God's sovereignty in salvation demonstrates clearly that others coming to faith does not depend upon our ability. Our call is simply to communicate the gospel. God's role is to convince minds and transform hearts.

At a practical level, God's sovereignty in salvation explains why some reject the gospel. Those without the Spirit of God at work in their lives will not accept the things that come from God (1 Corinthians 2:14). The difference between the saved and the unsaved is that God has provided understanding to the saved. This should humble the church. Realizing that we were saved only because God cared enough to pursue us and not because we are deserving, then our hearts are broken and we urgently share the Gospel.

God's revelation is revealed by Jesus to those he chooses.
"All things have been committed to me by my Father. No one knows who the Son is except the Father, and no one knows who the Father is except the Son and those to whom the Son chooses to reveal him." Luke 10:22 (NIV)

God's decision brings new birth to those who believe.
Yet to all who received him, to those who believed in his name, he gave the right to become children of God—children born not of natural descent, nor of human decision or a husband's will, but born of God. John 1:12-13 (NIV)

God draws to Jesus those he wills.
No one can come to me unless the Father who sent me draws him, and I will raise him up at the last day. John 6:44 (NIV)

"This is why I told you that no one can come to me unless the Father has enabled him." John 6:65 (NIV)

God foreknew those he will glorify.
For those God foreknew he also predestined to be conformed to the likeness of his Son, that he might be the firstborn among many brothers. And those he predestined, he also called; those he called, he also justified; those he justified, he also glorified. Romans 8:29-30 (NIV)

God predestined us to be adopted as sons through Jesus.
He chose us in him before the foundation of the world, that we should be holy and blameless before him. In love he predestined us for adoption as sons through Jesus Christ, according to the purpose of his will. Ephesians 1:4-5 (ESV)

God must reveal himself to us if we are to be saved.
The natural person does not accept the things of the Spirit of God, for they are folly to him, and he is not able to understand them because they are spiritually discerned. 1 Corinthians 2:14 (ESV)

Salvation and Our Assurance

Assurance of our salvation is both objective and subjective. Objectively, assurance is available based upon God's purposes to save all whom he has predestined (John 6:37, John 10:28-29). In this respect, our assurance is separate from our feelings, as well as our behavior, and rests solely on the power of God to deliver from death all whom he has determined to save (Romans 8:28-30). Those whom God predestined, he also "seals" for salvation (Ephesians 1:13-14, 2 Corinthians 5:5). God, having begun this work himself, also finishes the work of salvation himself (Philippians 1:6, Hebrews 12:2, 1 John 5:11-13).

While our objective assurance is based upon God's purposes to save, apart from anything we have done, are doing, or will do, his power to save does not work apart from our acting in faith. God's salvation always evidences itself through a personal expression of faith in those being saved and thus always produces some form of obedience, however small it may be (James 2:17-26, 1 John 2:19).

Subjectively, assurance of salvation is a measure of one's feelings of confidence in right standing before God. All who are presently trusting in Jesus' death for the forgiveness of sin have a Scriptural basis for having feelings of confidence in their justification (Colossians 1:23, Hebrews 3:14, Hebrews 6:12). Further, all who are born again receive the testimony of the Holy Spirit speaking to their heart (Romans 8:15-16, 1 John 4:13, 1 John 5:9-10). Finally, all who evidence the work of the Holy Spirit in their lives; including dependence upon Jesus and connection to his people (John 15:4-7, 1 John 2:23-24, 1 John 4:6), as well as obedience to God's commands (James 2:17-18, 1 John 2:4-10, 1 John 3:14-17), may possess feelings of assurance.

While having feelings of assurance is appropriate and comforting for those who are born again, it is possible to inappropriately possess feelings of assurance and we are cautioned that some who feel confident will not enter the kingdom of heaven (Matthew 7:21).

Scripture also teaches that some who are born again may lack feelings of assurance. We may lack feelings of assurance because of psychological damage, which creates an inability to feel confident in God's love (Romans 8:39). We may also lack feelings of assurance due to suffering, whether physical suffering due to illness or spiritual suffering due to attack by the enemy. For this reason, James writes that we are to count suffering as a joy, allowing the experience of suffering to produce in us maturity (James 1:1-8).

Finally, disobedience may undermine our feelings of assurance. While perfection is neither expected nor required in the Christian life (Philippians 3:12, 1 John 1:8-10, 1 John 2:1), those who fall into sin may lack feelings of assurance of their salvation because of the work of sin in their lives, which causes us to have disbelieving hearts (Galatians 5:16-18, Hebrews 3:12-13, 1 Peter 2:11).

Objectively, assurance is a result of God's will and work to save.
All that the Father gives me will come to me, and whoever comes to me I will never cast out. John 6:37 (ESV)

I give them eternal life, and they will never perish, and no one will snatch them out of my hand. John 10:28 (ESV)

And we know that for those who love God all things work together for good, for those who are called according to his purpose. For those whom he foreknew he also predestined to be conformed to the image of his Son, in order that he might be the firstborn among many brothers. And those whom he predestined he also called, and those whom he called he also justified, and those whom he justified he also glorified. Romans 8:28-30 (ESV)

In him you also, when you heard the word of truth, the gospel of your salvation, and believed in him, were sealed with the promised Holy Spirit, who is the guarantee of our inheritance until we acquire possession of it, to the praise of his glory. Ephesians 1:13-14 (ESV)

He who has prepared us for this very thing is God, who has given us the Spirit as a guarantee. 2 Corinthians 5:5 (ESV)

And I am sure of this, that he who began a good work in you will bring it to completion at the day of Jesus Christ. Philippians 1:6 (ESV)

Subjectively, assurance comes by believing God's promises and keeping God's commands.
If we confess our sins, he is faithful and just and will forgive us our sins and purify us from all unrighteousness. 1 John 1:9 (NIV)

And by this we know that we have come to know him, if we keep his commandments. 1 John 2:3 (ESV)

Subjectively, assurance comes as we produce works of faith.
What good is it, my brothers, if a man claims to have faith but has no deeds? Can such faith save him? James 2:14 (NIV)

Subjectively, assurance comes by a testimony in our heart.
Anyone who believes in the Son of God has this testimony in his heart. 1 John 5:10 (NIV)

Subjectively, assurance comes through the Spirit's presence.
Because you are sons, God sent the Spirit of his Son into our hearts, the Spirit who calls out, "Abba, Father." So you are no longer a slave, but a son; and since you are a son, God has made you also an heir. Galatians 4:6-7 (NIV)

Salvation and Our Perseverance

All who are born again are kept by God's power. Although the saved are kept by God's power, it is also true that the saved are called to exert their effort in persevering to live out the faith.

Perseverance in faith is promised by Jesus.
For this is the will of my Father, that everyone who looks on the Son and believes in him should have eternal life, and I will raise him up on the last day. John 6:40 (ESV)

I give them eternal life, and they will never perish, and no one will snatch them out of my hand. My Father, who has given them to me, is greater than all, and no one is able to snatch them out of the Father's hand. John 10:28-29 (ESV)

Perseverance in the faith is guaranteed by the Holy Spirit.
In him you also, when you heard the word of truth, the gospel of your salvation, and believed in him, were sealed with the promised Holy Spirit, who is the guarantee of our inheritance until we acquire possession of it, to the praise of his glory. Ephesians 1:13-14 (ESV)

Perseverance in the faith is secured by God's power.
According to his great mercy, he has caused us to be born again to a living hope through the resurrection of Jesus Christ from the dead, to an inheritance that is imperishable, undefiled, and unfading, kept in heaven for you, who by God's power are being guarded through faith for a salvation ready to be revealed in the last time. 1 Peter 1:3-5 (ESV)

And I am sure of this, that he who began a good work in you will bring it to completion at the day of Jesus Christ. Philippians 1:6 (ESV)

Perseverance will require standing firm until the end.
All men will hate you because of me, but he who stands firm to the end will be saved. Matthew 10:22 (NIV)

Perseverance will require holding firm to the Gospel.
By this gospel you are saved, if you hold firmly to the word I preached to you. Otherwise, you have believed in vain. 1 Corinthians 15:2 (NIV)

If indeed you continue in the faith, stable and steadfast, not shifting from the hope of the gospel that you heard, which has been proclaimed in all creation under heaven, and of which I, Paul, became a minister. Colossians 1:23 (ESV)

We have come to share in Christ if we hold firmly till the end the confidence we had at first. Hebrews 3:14 (NIV)

Perseverance will involve helping others turn from sin.
My brothers, if one of you should wander from the truth and someone should bring him back, remember this: Whoever turns a sinner from the error of his way will save him from death and cover over a multitude of sins. James 5:19-20 (NIV)

Perseverance will involve exalting even in tribulations.
And not only this, but we also exult in our tribulations, knowing that tribulation brings about perseverance; and perseverance, proven character; and proven character, hope; and hope does not disappoint, because the love of God has been poured out within our hearts through the Holy Spirit who was given to us. Romans 5:3-5 (NASB)

Perseverance will mean working out our faith.
So then, my beloved, just as you have always obeyed, not as in my presence only, but now much more in my absence, work out your salvation with fear and trembling; for it is God who is at work in you, both to will and to work for His good pleasure. Philippians 2:12-13 (NASB)

Salvation and Our Security

All who are born again are kept by God's power. This teaching is often referred to as "once saved, always saved," or described as "eternal security."

Security in salvation comes by Jesus' promise and power.
All that the Father gives me will come to me, and whoever comes to me I will never cast out." John 6:37 (ESV)

My Father, who has given them to me, is greater than all; no one can snatch them out of my Father's hand. John 10:29 (NIV)

Security in salvation comes by the Holy Spirit's presence.
In Him, you also, after listening to the message of truth, the gospel of your salvation--having also believed, you were sealed in Him with the Holy Spirit of promise, who is given as a pledge of our inheritance, with a view to the redemption of God's own possession, to the praise of His glory. Ephesians 1:13-14 (NASB)

Now He who prepared us for this very purpose is God, who gave to us the Spirit as a pledge. 2 Corinthians 5:5 (NASB)

Security in salvation comes from God's will to save.
Those God foreknew he also predestined to be conformed to the likeness of his Son, that he might be the firstborn among many brothers. And those he predestined, he also called; those he called, he also justified; those he justified, he also glorified. Romans 8:29-30 (NIV)

Security in salvation is demonstrated by remaining.
They went out from us, but they were not really of us; for if they had been of us, they would have remained with us; but they went out, so that it would be shown that they all are not of us. 1 John 2:19 (NASB)

What happens in the process of salvation?

An order to the process of salvation is outlined by Paul in the book of Romans. He wrote:

> *For those whom he foreknew he also predestined to be conformed to the image of his Son, in order that he might be the firstborn among many brothers. And those whom he predestined he also called, and those whom he called he also justified, and those whom he justified he also glorified. Romans 8:29-30 (ESV)*

Below are some of the more common steps in the process that are most often identified by Reformed theologians.

1. Election: God's choice to predestine some for salvation, by his foreknowledge and good pleasure. (Romans 8:29, 9:11-13, Ephesians 1:4-6)
2. Regeneration: God's work to give life to spiritually dead people. (John 3:3-8, James 1:18, 1 Peter 1:3)
3. Conversion: Man's expression of faith in Jesus and demonstration of repentance. (Romans 10:9-10, Matthew 3:8-9, Acts 26:20)
4. Justification: God's act of declaring those converted as forgiven of sin and righteous. (Romans 3:23-28, Romans 5:1, Galatians 2:16)
5. Adoption: God's act of bringing those justified into his family. (John 1:12, Romans 8:14-17)
6. Sanctification: God's work accomplished by the adopted, to increasingly free us from sin and conform us to the character of Christ. (1Thessalonians 4:3)
7. Perseverance: God's work to keep those he adopted from falling away (John 6:39, 10:27-29, 1 Peter 1:5)
8. Glorification: God's final work in salvation to provide resurrected bodies for all his children. (1 Corinthians 15:51-52, Philippians 3:20-21)

Satan

Satan means "adversary." He is also called "the devil" (Matthew 4:1), "Beelzebul" (Matthew 10:25), and "the prince of the power of the air" (Ephesians 2:2). He actively opposes God's work of redemption, which includes attacking God's people to undermine their faith.

Satan was seen by Jesus falling from heaven.
"I saw Satan fall like lightning from heaven." Luke 10:18 (NIV)

Satan is a murderer and the father of lies, who destroys.
He was a murderer from the beginning, not holding to the truth, for there is no truth in him. When he lies, he speaks his native language, for he is a liar and the father of lies. John 8:44 (NIV)

The thief comes only to steal and kill and destroy; I have come that they may have life, and have it to the full. John 10:10 (NIV)

And no wonder, for Satan himself masquerades as an angel of light. 2 Corinthians 11:14 (NIV)

Be self-controlled and alert. Your enemy the devil prowls around like a roaring lion looking for someone to devour. Resist him, standing firm in the faith. 1 Peter 5:8-9 (NIV)

Satan comes to try and steal God's Word when it is sown.
Some people are like seed along the path, where the word is sown. As soon as they hear it, Satan comes and takes away the word that was sown in them. Mark 4:15 (NIV)

Satan's work in the world will be defeated by Jesus.
The God of peace will soon crush Satan under your feet The grace of our Lord Jesus be with you. Romans 16:20 (NASB)

Scripture

Scripture denotes the collection of 66 books making up the Christian Bible. Although made up of many different books, Scripture is considered a singular book, which tells the story of God's historic work to save humans from their sin. As the author of Scripture, it is noteworthy that God wrote the Ten Commandments on Mount Sinai himself, engraving them on stone for Moses (Exodus 31:18). However, God also directed others to record his words so that many could have a record of his person, plans and purposes (Jeremiah 30:2). Ultimately, Scripture was given for God's glory and our benefit.

Scripture was provided by God himself.
And he gave to Moses, when he had finished speaking with him on Mount Sinai, the two tablets of the testimony, tablets of stone, written with the finger of God. Exodus 31:18 (ESV)

The tablets were the work of God, and the writing was the writing of God, engraved on the tablets. Exodus 32:16 (ESV)

The LORD said to Moses, "Cut for yourself two tablets of stone like the first, and I will write on the tablets the words that were on the first tablets, which you broke. Exodus 34:1 (ESV)

Scripture was provided as God directed authors to write.
Then Moses wrote this law and gave it to the priests, the sons of Levi, who carried the ark of the covenant of the LORD, and to all the elders of Israel. Deuteronomy 31:9 (ESV)

And Joshua wrote these words in the Book of the Law of God. And he took a large stone and set it up there under the terebinth that was by the sanctuary of the Lord. Joshua 24:26 (ESV)

And now, go, write it before them on a tablet and inscribe it in a book, that it may be for the time to come as a witness forever. Isaiah 30:8 (ESV)

"Thus says the Lord, the God of Israel: Write in a book all the words that I have spoken to you. Jeremiah 30:2 (ESV)

Above all, you must understand that no prophecy of Scripture came about by the prophet's own interpretation. For prophecy never had its origin in the will of man, but men spoke from God as they were carried along by the Holy Spirit. 2 Peter 1:20-21 (NIV)

And we also thank God continually because, when you received the word of God, which you heard from us, you accepted it not as the word of men, but as it actually is, the word of God, which is at work in you who believe. 1 Thessalonians 2:13 (NIV)

The eyes of everyone in the synagogue were fastened on him, and he began by saying to them, "Today this scripture is fulfilled in your hearing." Luke 4:20-21 (NIV)

And beginning with Moses and all the Prophets, he explained to them what was said in all the Scriptures concerning himself. Luke 24:27 (NIV)

Scripture was provided for God's glory and our good.
All Scripture is God-breathed and is useful for teaching, rebuking, correcting and training in righteousness, so that the man of God may be thoroughly equipped for every good work. 1 Timothy 3:16-17 (NIV)

Scripture's Authority

Scripture's authority is rooted in the claim that its message is from God. Although Scripture was written by humans, the claim of Scripture is that the message has its origin in God's person and purposes. For this reason, Scripture has authority over our lives. We are to believe and obey all of Scripture. To do otherwise is to disbelieve and/or disobey God.

Scripture's authority is shown in its divine authorship.
"For as the rain and the snow come down from heaven, and do not return there without watering the earth and making it bear and sprout, and furnishing seed to the sower and bread to the eater; So will My word be which goes forth from My mouth; It will not return to Me empty, without accomplishing what I desire, and without succeeding in the matter for which I sent it. Isaiah 55:10-11 (NASB)

For no prophecy was ever produced by the will of man, but men spoke from God as they were carried along by the Holy Spirit. 2 Peter 1:21 (ESV)

Scripture's authority is demonstrated in the command to integrate it into every facet of our lives.
And these words that I command you today shall be on your heart. You shall teach them diligently to your children, and shall talk of them when you sit in your house, and when you walk by the way, and when you lie down, and when you rise. You shall bind them as a sign on your hand, and they shall be as frontlets between your eyes. You shall write them on the doorposts of your house and on your gates. Deuteronomy 6:6-9 (ESV)

Do not let this Book of the Law depart from your mouth; meditate on it day and night, so that you may be careful to do everything written in it. Then you will be prosperous and successful. Joshua 1:8 (NIV)

Scripture's authority is demonstrated in its power.
I have stored up your word in my heart, that I might not sin against you. Psalm 119:11 (NIV)

Jesus answered, "It is written: 'Man does not live on bread alone, but on every word that comes from the mouth of God.'" Matthew 4:4 (NIV)

For the word of God is living and active and sharper than any two-edged sword, and piercing as far as the division of soul and spirit, of both joints and marrow, and able to judge the thoughts and intentions of the heart. Hebrews 4:12 (NASB)

Scripture's authority is seen in its fulfillment.
Then beginning with Moses and with all the prophets, He explained to them the things concerning Himself in all the Scriptures. Luke 24:27 (NASB)

The Scripture, foreseeing that God would justify the Gentiles by faith, preached the gospel beforehand to Abraham, saying, "ALL THE NATIONS WILL BE BLESSED IN YOU." Galatians 3:8 (NASB)

Scripture's authority is seen in its usefulness.
All Scripture is God-breathed and is useful for teaching, rebuking, correcting and training in righteousness, so that the man of God may be thoroughly equipped for every good work. 2 Timothy 3:16-17 (NIV)

Scripture's authority is shown in that it is to be preached.
Preach the word; be ready in season and out of season; reprove, rebuke, exhort, with great patience and instruction. 2 Timothy 4:2 (NASB)

Give attention to the public reading of Scripture, to exhortation and teaching. 1 Timothy 4:13 (NASB)

Scripture's Historicity

Scripture's historicity refers to its historic reliability. In fact, if we were to list the top four stories from the Old Testament that are most often called into question as historically accurate the list would probably include:

- Adam and Eve and a talking serpent (Genesis 3:1-7)
- Noah's Ark and the great flood (Genesis 6:14)
- Sodom's and Gomorrah's destruction (Genesis 19:24)
- Jonah's being swallowed by a whale (Jonah 1:17)

While faith is needed to believe these stories took place, none of these stories are recorded with any hint that they should be considered as fable, and Jesus references each of these stories during his ministry as historic events.

- Jesus said, "as it was in the days of Noah, so it will be at the coming of the Son of Man (Matthew 24:37, NIV).
- Jesus said, "Truly I tell you, it will be more bearable for Sodom and Gomorrah on the day of judgment than for that town (Matthew 10:15, NIV).
- Jesus said, "Haven't you read, that at the beginning the Creator 'made them male and female,' and said, 'For this reason a man will leave his father and mother and be united to his wife, and the two will become one flesh'? (Matthew 19:4-6, NIV).
- Jesus said, "For as Jonah was three days and three nights in the belly of a huge fish, so the Son of Man will be three days and three nights in the heart of the earth." (Matthew 12:40, NIV).
- Jesus affirmed his resurrection, his second coming, and his final judgment by referencing some of the most controversial stories of the Old Testament.

Scripture's Inerrancy

Scripture's inerrancy is the belief that the Bible is without error in all that it teaches (Psalm 12:6). While this doctrine is not explicitly stated in Scripture, it is clearly derived. Because the Bible is God's Word (1 Timothy 3:16-17, 2 Peter 1:20-21), and we know that God never lies (Titus 1:2, Hebrews 6:18), we also know that the Bible never lies.

Inerrancy does not mean the Bible tells us everything there is to know, but rather that it is truthful in all that it addresses. We must work hard to understand what it is, and is not, addressing. We must work hard because the Bible was written by ancient authors to ancient audiences. These ancient authors utilized ancient writing standards and methods, which require diligence in study as modern readers. For example, this means that where the Bible makes particular claims, whether scientific (e.g., descriptions of how the natural order works), historic (e.g., descriptions of what took place or how many were involved), or mathematical (e.g., reporting numbers), it might lack modern precision.

None of this compromises the truthfulness of Scripture, but it does make it important that we work hard to understand the ancient author's and audience's context. God spoke through ancient authors, working through their unique personalities, particular writing styles and within their cultural settings, to communicate his message.

Remember, the Bible is not a miracle book in that God spoke through ancient authors to modern audiences. The Bible is a miracle book in that God spoke through ancient authors to ancient audiences, and his message is still speaking today. When there are apparent errors or contradictions within the Bible, we must be diligent in study, admitting that we are finite in our understanding and that collecting more data may change our understanding. Ultimately, to deny inerrancy is to undermine the authority and reliability of Scripture.

Scripture's Sufficiency

Scripture's sufficiency means that the Bible contains all the words God intended for his people to have at each stage of salvation history. In short, the Bible is sufficient for our salvation, as well as our sanctification. While this does not mean that the Bible contains the answers to all possible questions, it does mean that the Bible contains the answers to all the questions God is concerned we are able to answer.

Scripture's sufficiency is seen in God writing Scripture himself, as well as directing others to write.
When the LORD finished speaking to Moses on Mount Sinai, he gave him the two tablets of the Testimony, the tablets of stone inscribed by the finger of God. Exodus 20:18 (NIV)

Then the LORD said to Moses, "Write this as a memorial in a book and recite it in the ears of Joshua, that I will utterly blot out the memory of Amalek from under heaven." Exodus 17:14 (ESV)

And Moses wrote down all the words of the LORD. He rose early in the morning and built an altar at the foot of the mountain, and twelve pillars, according to the twelve tribes of Israel. Exodus 24:4 (ESV)

After Moses finished writing in a book the words of this law from beginning to end, he gave this command to the Levites who carried the ark of the covenant of the LORD. Deuteronomy 31:24-25 (NIV)

And Joshua recorded these things in the Book of the Law of God. Then he took a large stone and set it up there under the oak near the holy place of the LORD. Joshua 24:26 (NIV)

This is the word that came to Jeremiah from the LORD: "This is what the LORD, the God of Israel, says: 'Write in a book all the words I have spoken to you.'" Jeremiah 30:1-2 (NIV)

Scripture's sufficiency is seen in God prohibiting changes to what was written in Scripture.
You shall not add to the word that I command you, nor take from it, that you may keep the commandments of the Lord your God that I command you. Deuteronomy 4:2 (ESV)

I testify to everyone who hears the prophetic words of this book: If anyone adds to them, God will add to him the plagues that are written in this book. And if anyone takes away from the words of this prophetic book, God will take away his share of the tree of life and the holy city, written in this book. Revelation 22:18-19 (HCSB)

Scripture's sufficiency was affirmed by Daniel.
In the first year of his reign, I, Daniel, perceived in the books the number of years that, according to the word of the Lord to Jeremiah the prophet, must pass before the end of the desolations of Jerusalem, namely, seventy years. Daniel 9:2 (ESV)

Scripture's sufficiency was affirmed by Jesus.
And beginning with Moses and all the Prophets, he explained to them what was said in all the Scriptures concerning himself. John 24:27 (NIV)

Scripture's sufficiency is demonstrated in the Spirit's ministry to the apostles.
But when he, the Spirit of truth, comes, he will guide you into all truth. John 16:13 (NIV)

But the Counselor, the Holy Spirit, whom the Father will send in my name, will teach you all things and will remind you of everything I have said to you. John 14:26 (NIV)

Scripture's sufficiency is demonstrated in the apostle's testimony of the Spirit's ministry to them.
However, as it is written: "No eye has seen, no ear has heard, no mind has conceived what God has prepared for those who love him"—but God has revealed it to us by his Spirit. 1 Corinthians 2:9-10 (NIV)

This is what we speak, not in words taught us by human wisdom but in words taught by the Spirit, expressing spiritual truths in spiritual words. 1 Corinthians 2:13 (NIV)

Scripture's sufficiency is affirmed by the early church.
Long ago, at many times and in many ways, God spoke to our fathers by the prophets, but in these last days he has spoken to us by his Son, whom he appointed the heir of all things, through whom also he created the world. Hebrews 1:1-2 (NIV)

If anybody thinks he is a prophet or spiritually gifted, let him acknowledge that what I am writing to you is the Lord's command. 1 Corinthians 14:37 (NIV)

Above all, you must understand that no prophecy of Scripture came about by the prophet's own interpretation. For prophecy never had its origin in the will of man, but men spoke from God as they were carried along by the Holy Spirit. 2 Peter 1:20-21 (NIV)

I want you to recall the words spoken in the past by the holy prophets and the command given by our Lord and Savior through your apostles. 2 Peter 3:2 (NIV)

Scripture's sufficiency is seen in Peter's affirmation that Paul's writings are equal with the other Scripture.
There are some things in them that are hard to understand, which the ignorant and unstable twist to their own destruction, as they do the other Scriptures. 2 Peter 3:16 (ESV)

How can we accurately interpret Scripture?

An accurate interpretation of Scripture always includes prayer. Scripture is God's Word, and it is God who provides understanding (1 Corinthians 2:14). Because God is the author of Scripture, we can be confident that Scripture is a unified and understandable whole, accessible to all who seek the truth in faith (Matthew 7:7), as we study Scripture asking God to teach us by the Holy Spirit (John 16:13).

An accurate interpretation of Scripture also always includes diligent study (2 Timothy 2:15), working hard to avoid imposing our personal presuppositions upon the Scripture. Diligent study includes:

- Reading the passage in context, reviewing the surrounding verses, paragraphs, and chapters, as well as understanding the genre of the book.
- Working to understand the ancient cultural context of the author and audience. God revealed his saving work to ancient audiences through ancient authors.
- Researching the grammar, looking for comparisons, contrasts and identifying basic structures. Noting word usage (i.e., definitions, key words or repeated words or phrases), indications of literal or figurative intent based on the context. If you do not know the original languages, then comparing various English translations can help gain greater understanding.
- Researching complementary passages of Scripture. The best interpreter of Scripture is Scripture. When a passage is difficult to understand we are to use the Scripture that is clearest to interpret passages that are less clear, as well as using explicit passages to interpret the implicit.

Finally, an accurate interpretation includes faith, believing Scripture has a message for us (Hebrews 4:12).

How do we answer Old Testament questions?

There are a lot of strange stories in the Old Testament. Stories of a talking serpent (Genesis 3:1-7), of a cataclysmic flood (Genesis 7:4), of fire from heaven consuming cities (Genesis 19:24), and of a prophet riding in the belly of great fish for three days (Jonah 1:17). Questions about these types of stories are not uncommon, and the best way to begin answering questions about these strange stories is by first pointing out that Jesus handled these Old Testament as true. Wrestling with the events of the Old Testament is much more manageable once we realize that Jesus affirmed them as true.

For example, when teaching about his second coming, Jesus stated, "as it was in the days of Noah, so it will be at the coming of the Son of Man" (Matthew 24:37). And when talking about the final judgment, Jesus said, "Truly I tell you, it will be more bearable for Sodom and Gomorrah on the day of judgment than for that town" (Matthew 10:15). And when asked about the permissibility of divorce, Jesus taught that God's intention for marriage, beginning in the Garden of Eden, was that it would last a lifetime (Matthew 19:6). Jesus also used the Old Testament to explain the importance of his life and death, as well as the truth of his resurrection (Luke 24:27). Jesus said, "For as Jonah was three days and three nights in the belly of a huge fish, so the Son of Man will be three days and three nights in the heart of the earth" (Matthew 12:40).

Jesus' treating the Old Testament as true is of primary importance because Jesus was raised from the dead (1 Corinthians 15:6). Jesus' resurrection proves that he is who he said he was (i.e. God), and that what he taught was true, including his affirmation of the strange stories in the Old Testament. Ultimately, if someone will not accept Jesus' authority as a teacher, as evidenced in his resurrection, then discussing the purposes and meanings of Old Testament passages is exceedingly difficult.

Why are there so many different Bible versions?

The books of the Bible were originally written in Hebrew (Old Testament) and Greek (New Testament), and English translations of these languages have different strengths, depending upon the priorities of the translators.

The following translations are known as "formal" equivalents, meaning the original languages were translated word for word into English. These translations can be stilted and more difficult to read. However, what they lose in readability, they gain in grammatical accuracy. These translations are recommended to those wanting to know what the Bible *says*.

- New American Standard Bible (NASB)
- English Standard Version (ESV)
- Revised Standard Version (RSV)

At the other end of the spectrum are "functional" equivalents, which are translated "thought for thought," which makes them easier to read. While these translations lose some of the exactness of word meaning, they are often preferred by those wanting to know what the Bible *means*.

- New Living Translation (NLT)
- The Message

Between formal and functional translations are those translations that aim at optimizing both accuracy and readability. In some instances, these translations are "word for word," while in other instances "phrase for phrase." Some examples are:

- New International Version (NIV)
- Holman Christian Standard Bible (HCSB)

Service

Jesus came to serve humanity through his death on the cross (Mark 10:45), and everyone who follows Jesus is called to serve others (Luke 14:27).

Service is the reason we were created by God.
For we are God's workmanship, created in Christ Jesus to do good works, which God prepared in advance for us to do. Ephesians 2:10 (NIV)

Service was modeled and commanded by Jesus.
Have this attitude in yourselves which was also in Christ Jesus, who, although He existed in the form of God, did not regard equality with God a thing to be grasped, but emptied Himself, taking the form of a bond-servant, and being made in the likeness of men. Being found in appearance as a man, He humbled Himself by becoming obedient to the point of death, even death on a cross. Philippians 2:5-8 (NASB)

If I then, the Lord and the Teacher, washed your feet, you also ought to wash one another's feet. John 13:14 (NASB)

Service is accomplished through the Holy Spirit.
To each is given the manifestation of the Spirit for the common good. 1 Corinthians 12:7 (ESV)

Service is the reason Christians are to be equipped.
It was he who gave some to be apostles, some to be prophets, some to be evangelists, and some to be pastors and teachers, to prepare God's people for works of service, so that the body of Christ may be built up. Ephesians 4:11-12 (NIV)

Service is what Christians are to offer one another.
You, my brothers, were called to be free. But do not use your freedom to indulge the sinful nature; rather, serve one another in love. Galatians 5:13 (NIV)

Sexuality

Sexuality impacts spiritual wellbeing, and spiritual wellbeing impacts sexuality. For example, Adam and Eve were naked and unashamed at Creation, but spiritual rebellion produced sexual shame (Genesis 2:25, 3:7). Likewise, Sodom and Gomorrah were judged, at least in part, because of the sexual sin (Jude 1:7). On a positive note, circumcision was a sexual symbol of God's lordship over the Israelites' bodies (Genesis 17:1-10, Genesis 22:18). Even the metaphor given for understanding the relationship between Christ and his Church is the sexual "oneness" shared between a man and woman within marriage (Ephesians 5:25-32).

Sexuality is an integral part of our personality.
So God created man in His own image; He created him in the image of God; He created them male and female. Genesis 1:27 (HCSB)

Sexual union is a primer for communion with God.
Therefore, I am going to persuade her, lead her to the wilderness, and speak tenderly to her. In that day—this is the Lord's declaration—you will call Me, "My husband," and no longer call Me, "My Baal." I will take you to be My wife forever. I will take you to be My wife in righteousness, justice, love, and compassion. I will take you to be My wife in faithfulness, and you will know Yahweh. Hosea 2:14, 16, 19, 20 (HCSB)

For this reason a man will leave his father and mother and be joined to his wife, and the two will become one flesh. This mystery is profound, but I am talking about Christ and the church. Ephesians 5:31-32 (HCSB)

Sex was designed by God to join husband and wife.
This explains why a man leaves his father and mother and is joined to his wife, and the two are united into one. Now the man and his wife were both naked, but they felt no shame. Genesis 2:24-25 (NLT)

Do you not know that he who unites himself with a prostitute is one with her in body? For it is said, "The two will become one flesh." But he who unites himself with the Lord is one with him in spirit. 1 Corinthians 6:16-17 (NIV)

Sex is a means to honoring God with our body.
Run from sexual sin! No other sin so clearly affects the body as this one does. For sexual immorality is a sin against your own body. Don't you realize that your body is the temple of the Holy Spirit, who lives in you and was given to you by God? You do not belong to yourself, for God bought you with a high price. So you must honor God with your body.
1 Corinthians 6:18-20 (NLT)

For this is God's will, your sanctification: that you abstain from sexual immorality, so that each of you knows how to control his own body in sanctification and honor, not with lustful desires, like the Gentiles who don't know God. 1 Thessalonians 4:3-5 (HCSB)

Sexual depravity is a result of God's judgment.
This is why God delivered them over to degrading passions. For even their females exchanged natural sexual relations for unnatural ones. The males in the same way also left natural relations with females and were inflamed in their lust for one another. Males committed shameless acts with males and received in their own persons the appropriate penalty of their error. Romans 1:26-27 (HCSB)

Sin

Sin is any attitude or action contrary to the character of God (1 John 3:4), as well as a state of alienation from God (Colossians 1:21). This means that sin is both something we *do*, as well as something we *are*. We sin, committing acts contrary to the character of God, and we are sinners, alienated from God.

Sinfulness is the condition into which all humans are born (Ephesians 2:3). It is our state of being. It is like being right-handed. One is not right-handed because he writes with his right hand. One writes with his right hand because he is right-handed. This is to say right-handedness preceded writing. By the same token, we are not sinners because we sin, we sin because we are sinners. We are by nature sinners and for that reason we sin.

Scripture teaches all are sinful (Romans 3:23-26), and in need of God's forgiveness and reconciliation with God (Romans 5:9-11). Sin cannot be overcome through human effort but is overcome only by faith in Jesus. Through faith in the work of Jesus on our behalf we are forgiven our sin, reconciled to God and empowered for godly living. By God's grace, those trusting in Jesus, can learn to live lives pleasing to God (Ephesians 5:10, Colossians 1:10, Titus 2:11-14).

Sin and death are overcome through the life of Jesus.
Where sin increased, grace abounded all the more, so that, as sin reigned in death, even so grace would reign through righteousness to eternal life through Jesus Christ our Lord. Romans 5:21 (NASB)

This righteousness from God comes through faith in Jesus Christ to all who believe. There is no difference, for all have sinned and fall short of the glory of God, and are justified freely by his grace through the redemption that came by Christ Jesus. Romans 3:22-24 (NIV)

Slavery

Many people ask, "Why isn't slavery expressly condemned in the Bible?" First, it is important to understand that the ancient practice of slavery was vastly different from the modern practice. For example, the Bible condemns stealing people (Exodus 21:16, 1 Timothy 1:10), which was the backbone of the modern slave trade. God's people were prohibited from participating in slave trafficking. For this reason, slavery among God's people was most often the result of prisoners taken in war, financial indebtedness and criminal convictions, all three of which continue to have their modern parallels.

Regarding prisoners of war, while God used Israel to judge the wickedness of other nations through military defeat, and in some instances directed them to take their enemies as slaves, this served to preserve other nations by preventing genocide. In fact, Israel was preserved as a nation in this manner, as God allowed Israel to be taken captive by foreign nations as a consequence of their wickedness (Nehemiah 9:36). Of course, modern nations continue to take political prisoners today.

The most common form of slavery in the ancient world was the result of financial indebtedness. A bad crop meant a family would go without food and debt-slavery was the solution. Ancient peoples would sell themselves into slavery in order to provide for themselves food and lodging. In modern times, many are "enslaved" by financial institutions through credit card debt. However, unlike our modern laws, Israel canceled all debt and released all slaves every seven years (Exodus 21:2, Leviticus 25:13, Deuteronomy 15:12). In fact, a freed debt-slave was to receive gifts from those to whom they owed money (Deuteronomy 15:14). Can you imagine modern banks forgiving debt every seven years?

Finally, criminals could also become slaves because of their conviction. Of course, still today, millions live imprisoned as convicted criminals and earn very poor wages for performing menial tasks in prison.

In wrestling with the reality of slavery in the Bible, we must acknowledge the purpose of the Bible. The Bible was not written to set up social institutions, such as a central banking system, national governance (e.g., monarchy vs. democracy) or education (e.g., homeschool vs. nationalized curriculum).

Imagine how long the Bible would be if its purpose was to outline God's plan for a utopian society. Instead, the Bible was written for the purpose of revealing God to humanity and recording God's saving work in the world, first selecting, and preserving Israel through whom Jesus Christ, the Messiah, was born and secondly spreading the gospel through the Church. For this reason, there are lots of social issues that are left unaddressed or that seem under addressed (e.g., polygamy, divorce, sexuality). Jesus often even avoided offering specific commentary on hot topics of his day (e.g., Roman occupation and taxation), remaining instead focused on the greater goal of offering his life as a ransom for sin (Matthew 20:28).

This means that to the extent slavery is addressed in the Bible, it was to provide legal boundaries for slave masters. These boundaries were aimed at either preserving the Israelite community, so that Messiah could be born, and/or the witness of the Church, so that the gospel could advance. Toward this end, the mistreatment of slaves was strictly prohibited (Exodus 21:20-21), the care of slaves was proscribed (Deuteronomy 23:15-17, Exodus 20:10, Deuteronomy 5:14), and the inclusion of slaves in religious observance required (Genesis 17:13, Exodus 12:44, Leviticus 22:11).

Ultimately, the Bible's primary concern was that God's people, whether slave or master, treat each other with respect so that God's community is strengthened and more people will be saved from their sin (Ephesians 6:5-9, Colossians 4:1, 1 Timothy 6:1-2, Philemon 1:16).

Speaking in Tongues

Speaking in tongues is the biblical term used to describe syllables spoken by, yet unknown to, the speaker (1 Corinthians 12:28). A tongue speaker is defined as one who "utters mysteries" to God (1 Corinthians 14:2-3), and Paul says of those who speak in tongues, "no one understands" them and they speak directly to God (1 Corinthians 14:2). For this reason, speaking in tongues is often described as sounding like gibberish, by both the speaker and the listener, as most unknown languages would sound. But, just because something sounds like gibberish, doesn't mean that it is without meaning and value.

There are two biblically described uses for tongues, private use (e.g., in prayer or when singing) and public use (e.g., when addressing the congregation during worship). When used publicly, Paul said that he would rather have five known words spoken, to 10,000 words spoken in an unknown tongue (1 Corinthians 14:19). Paul's point seems to be that when in public worship it is wisest to focus on speaking known words.

However, the Bible does make some provision for tongues (i.e., unknown words) to be spoken in worship, as long as they are interpreted. If tongues are spoken publicly, an interpretation is required (1 Corinthians 14:27-28). There needs to be an interpretation simply because no one understands an unknown language unless it is interpreted. Just as God gives the gift of tongues to one, he will also give the gift of interpretation to another (1 Corinthians 12:10). So, while the Biblical directive in public worship is to prefer 5 known words to 10,000 unknown words, in some cases unknown words, if interpreted, can add value.

When tongues are used privately in prayer or while singing, those using tongues are to ask God for an interpretation (1 Corinthians 14:13). While no interpretation is required when tongues are spoken in private, those praying or singing in private are to ask for an interpretation so that they can be encouraged.

Tongues is a gift given to some by the Holy Spirit.
And in the church God has appointed first of all apostles, second prophets, third teachers, then workers of miracles, also those having gifts of healing, those able to help others, those with gifts of administration, and those speaking in different kinds of tongues. 1 Corinthians 12:28 (NIV)

Prayer and singing in tongues is unintelligible but profitable.
For if I pray in a tongue, my spirit prays, but my mind is unfruitful. What is the outcome then? I will pray with the spirit and I will pray with the mind also; I will sing with the spirit and I will sing with the mind also.
1 Corinthians 14:14-15 (NASB)

Tongues speakers speak mysteries to God, not to men.
For one who speaks in a tongue does not speak to men but to God; for no one understands, but in his spirit he speaks mysteries.
1 Corinthians 14:2 (NASB)

Tongues speakers edify themselves, while those who speak in known languages edify the church.
One who speaks in a tongue edifies himself; but one who prophesies edifies the church. 1 Corinthians 14:4 (NASB)

Speaking in tongues is not to be forbidden.
Therefore, my brethren, desire earnestly to prophesy, and do not forbid to speak in tongues. 1 Corinthians 14:39 (NASB)

Known languages are preferable to unknown in worship.
I thank God, I speak in tongues more than you all; however, in the church I desire to speak five words with my mind so that I may instruct others also, rather than ten thousand words in a tongue. 1 Corinthians 14:18-19 (NASB)

Why does God use tongues to communicate?

God used tongues initially as a sign that his work of redemption through Jesus Christ is fully underway. Speaking in tongues was first utilized on the day of Pentecost, as Jerusalem was filled with thousands who had arrived to celebrate the festival. The Holy Spirit descended upon the first disciples while they were gathered in the Upper Room together for prayer (Acts 2:1-41). The coming of the Holy Spirit was evidenced as the disciples "began to speak in other tongues," enabling those who had gathered in the city from foreign lands to hear and understand the gospel (Acts 2:2-13), which led to many being born again (Acts 2:14-41).

Tongues not only provide the bridge needed to overcome the language barrier and reach thousands of foreigners with the gospel, but tongues also signaled the beginning of a new age—the Church age, when God is reuniting all nations, languages and tribes of people to himself through faith in Jesus Christ (Revelation 7:9-12). In this way, tongues at Pentecost signaled the reversal of God's judgment at Babel (Genesis 11:1-9). We even find in Acts a list of the different ethnic groups that were present in Jerusalem at the time of Pentecost, apparently emphasizing God's work to begin gathering all the language groups that were formerly scattered at Babel into a singular people who will live to give praise to Jesus Christ (Acts 2:9-13).

God also uses tongues as an ongoing sign that his work of redemption through faith in Jesus Christ is continuing. Although unity among all language groups through faith in Jesus is at the moment incomplete, speaking in tongues with interpretation in church worship today continues to give further evidence of the promise that one day the divide between language groups will be completely overcome. Through faith in Jesus Christ all people and language groups can be united within the Church (Romans 12:4-5, Galatians 3:28).

God also uses tongues to strengthen communication, whether private with him in prayer, or communication during worship through interpretation. For example, many who have the gift describe it as a less encumbered way to pray, because they do not have to fumble for words. Tongues is essentially a gift that enables one to express what is otherwise inexpressible, and for that reason many who have the gift of tongues are also often called to the ministry of intercessory prayer, feeling a desire to pray with and for others.

Some have asked, "If interpreters are present, why not only speak in tongues during worship?" But Paul suggests that we refrain from the public use of tongues almost entirely, because it undermines credibility with non-believers. Paul wrote:

> If the whole church comes together and everyone speaks in tongues, and some who do not understand or some unbelievers come in, will they not say that you are out of your mind? 1 Corinthians 14:23 (NIV)

Many non-Christians already think Christians are crazy. Activities like attending weekly worship services and tithing make many non-believers scratch their head. But tongues often pushes them over the edge, and Paul is saying that we can remove this barrier by simply speaking in known languages as much as possible.

Finally, God also uses tongues as means to exercising faith. Although tongues seem uniquely strange to many, most acts of faith, whether tithing or even praying in English, can seem foolish. Yet, we are to "live by faith," and "not by sight" (2 Corinthians 5:7), and Paul tells us that without the Spirit's help we cannot accept activities of faith (1 Corinthians 2:14). While not everyone will speak in tongues (1 Corinthians 12:29-30), God seems to use tongues in the lives of some because it allows them to exercise faith (i.e., our dependence upon him), which is necessary for pleasing him (Hebrews 11:6).

Spiritual Gifts and Sign Gifts

Spiritual gifts are given at the time of spiritual new birth, while talents are abilities given at the time of biological birth. Much like gifts are brought to a baby shower, the Holy Spirit brings gifts into the life of a Christian at the time of new birth. Paul wrote:

> To each is given the manifestation of the Spirit for the common good. 1 Corinthians 12:7 (ESV)

There are several lists of spiritual gifts in the New Testament (ex. 1 Corinthians 12:7-13, 28-31, 13:1-3). These lists are not thought to be exhaustive but examples of how the Holy Spirit gifts Christians for ministry.

Some spiritual gifts have historically been identified as "sign" gifts, in that they play a unique role in signaling the power of the gospel. The sign gifts are healing, tongues, interpretation of tongues, working of miracles and prophecy. For example,

- Tongues at Pentecost were a sign of the beginning of the new age of the church (Acts 2:29).
- Miracles done through the Apostles were a sign of the Gospel's truth (Acts 2:43, 5:12, 6:8, 14:3).
- Tongues were described as a sign of judgment for non-believers (1 Corinthians 14:22).
- Prophecy a sign of judgment for believers (1 Corinthians 14:22).

While signs are not an end in themselves, the Apostles did pray for signs to confirm the Gospel (Acts 4:30). Although signs confirming the gospel are desirable, we know that the antichrist will have power to work signs too (2 Thessalonians 2:9). The goal of a sign gift is ultimately and only to point to Jesus as Savior.

Spiritual Maturity

Spiritual maturity is a biblical goal for those following Jesus (Hebrews 6:1). Spiritual maturity is indicated by our receptivity to Scripture (Luke 8:14) and is attained through the diligent pursuit of godliness (Philippians 3:12-15). Spiritual maturity is demonstrated through an ability to distinguish between good and evil, and a habit of consistently choosing what is good (Hebrews 5:13-14).

The benefits of spiritual maturity are a greater understanding of God's work of redemption in the world (Hebrews 6:1-3), an increased peacefulness and stability in life (Ephesians 4:14), and a greater freedom from sinful entanglements (John 8:36).

Spiritual maturity can be prevented in our lives.
As for what fell among the thorns, they are those who hear, but as they go on their way they are choked by the cares and riches and pleasures of life, and their fruit does not mature. Luke 8:14 (ESV)

Spiritual maturity is reflected in our thinking.
Brothers, do not be children in your thinking. Be infants in evil, but in your thinking be mature. 1 Corinthians 14:20 (ESV)

Spiritual maturity among believers was Paul's goal.
Him we proclaim, warning everyone and teaching everyone with all wisdom, that we may present everyone mature in Christ. Colossians 1:28 (ESV)

Spiritual maturity is defined by the character of Jesus.
So Christ himself gave the apostles, the prophets, the evangelists, the pastors and teachers, to equip his people for works of service, so that the body of Christ may be built up until we all reach unity in the faith and in the knowledge of the Son of God and become mature, attaining to the whole measure of the fullness of Christ. Ephesians 4:11-13 (NIV)

Spiritual maturity brings stability in our life.
Then we will no longer be infants, tossed back and forth by the waves, and blown here and there by every wind of teaching and by the cunning and craftiness of people in their deceitful scheming. Instead, speaking the truth in love, we will grow to become in every respect the mature body of him who is the head, that is, Christ. Ephesians 4:14-15 (NIV)

Spiritually mature comes through constant training.
Anyone who lives on milk, being still an infant, is not acquainted with the teaching about righteousness. But solid food is for the mature, who by constant use have trained themselves to distinguish good from evil. Hebrews 5:13-14 (NIV)

Spiritual maturity requires teaching and learning.
Therefore let us move beyond the elementary teachings about Christ and be taken forward to maturity, not laying again the foundation of repentance from acts that lead to death, and of faith in God, instruction about cleansing rites, the laying on of hands, the resurrection of the dead, and eternal judgment. And God permitting, we will do so. Hebrews 6:1-3 (NIV)

Spiritually mature is moving toward Christ-likeness.
I press on toward the goal to win the prize for which God has called me heavenward in Christ Jesus. All of us, then, who are mature should take such a view of things. And if on some point you think differently, that too God will make clear to you. Philippians 3:14-15 (NIV)

Spiritual maturity comes by perseverance.
Consider it pure joy, my brothers and sisters, whenever you face trials of many kinds, because you know that the testing of your faith produces perseverance. Let perseverance finish its work so that you may be mature and complete, not lacking anything. James 1:2-4 (NIV)

Spiritual Warfare

Spiritual warfare denotes the spiritual battle going on between God and the Devil. Referred to in Scripture as Satan, which means "adversary," the Devil attacks God's people (John 10:10). For this reason, the Bible tells Christians to be aware of the Devil's schemes, to be prepared for battle by wearing the armor of God (Ephesians 6:11-13), and to actively resist the Devil's work in their lives, as well as in the world (James 4:4-7).

Spiritual warfare takes place on at least two fronts. First, there is the battle of the flesh (Galatians 5:17). While we wrestle against our own evil desires (Romans 7:15-25, James 1:14), Satan is active in this arena by tempting us to sin (Mark 1:13, 1 Corinthians 7:5). Scripture teaches that Christians are to put to death the evil desires that belong to the flesh (Colossians 3:5), as well as run temptation (2 Timothy 2:22), and to renew our mind (Romans 12:1-2, Ephesians 4:22-23), by setting our focus on heavenly things (Colossians 3:2).

Spiritual warfare also takes place externally, on the battlefield often described in Scripture as "the world" (1 John 2:15-17). Here we meet with evil caused by sin that is present within the broader community of humanity (2 Peter 1:4). Satan is active in this arena by influencing the systematic destruction of humanity through injustice and oppression (John 10:10, 2 Corinthians 2:12). Christians are to fight the good fight of faith in the world by resisting injustice, defending the weak, providing for the poor and the sick, as well as working to free those enslaved (Luke 7:22, James 1:27, James 4:4).

There are two common and opposite responses to the topic of spiritual warfare. Some respond with fear and avoidance, while others respond with fascination and fixation. The goal for Christians is to avoid both extremes. Our call is to actively engage in spiritual warfare by being aware of the Devil's schemes, wearing the full armor of God and fighting the good fight of faith (1 Timothy 6:12).

Spiritual warfare was experienced by Jesus.
The tempter came to him and said, "If you are the Son of God, tell these stones to become bread." Matthew 4:3 (NIV)

Spiritual warfare is made possible by divine weapons.
For though we live in the world, we do not wage war as the world does. The weapons we fight with are not the weapons of the world. On the contrary, they have divine power to demolish strongholds. 2 Corinthians 10:3-4 (NIV)

Spiritual warfare includes addressing arguments that are contrary to the knowledge of God.
We demolish arguments and every pretension that sets itself up against the knowledge of God, and we take captive every thought to make it obedient to Christ. 2 Corinthians 10:5 (NIV)

Spiritual warfare was experienced by the early church.
Paul, having become greatly annoyed, turned and said to the spirit, "I command you in the name of Jesus Christ to come out of her." And it came out that very hour. Acts 16:18 (ESV)

Spiritual war is won by Jesus' blood and our testimony.
They overcame him by the blood of the Lamb and by the word of their testimony; they did not love their lives so much as to shrink from death. Revelation 12:11 (NIV)

Spiritual warfare is fought using Jesus' name.
The seventy-two returned with joy and said, "Lord, even the demons submit to us in your name." Luke 10:17 (NIV)

Spiritual war can distract us from rejoicing in salvation
However, do not rejoice that the spirits submit to you, but rejoice that your names are written in heaven." Luke 10:20 (NIV)

Spiritual warfare is to be fought with God's armor.
Put on the whole armor of God, that you may be able to stand against the schemes of the devil. Ephesians 611 (ESV)

Spiritual warfare is fought against spiritual forces of evil.
For our struggle is not against flesh and blood, but against the rulers, against the authorities, against the powers of this dark world and against the spiritual forces of evil in the heavenly realms. Ephesians 6:12 (NIV)

Spiritual warfare involves self-control and suffering.
Be sober-minded; be watchful. Your adversary the devil prowls around like a roaring lion, seeking someone to devour. Resist him, firm in your faith, knowing that the same kinds of suffering are being experienced by your brotherhood throughout the world. 1 Peter 5:8-9 (ESV)

Spiritual warfare is supported by heavenly forces.
And Elisha prayed, "O LORD, open his eyes so he may see." Then the LORD opened the servant's eyes, and he looked and saw the hills full of horses and chariots of fire all around Elisha. 2 Kings 6:17 (NIV)

Then he said to me, "Do not be afraid, Daniel, for from the first day that you set your heart on understanding this and on humbling yourself before your God, your words were heard, and I have come in response to your words. "But the prince of the kingdom of Persia was withstanding me for twenty-one days; then behold, Michael, one of the chief princes, came to help me, for I had been left there with the kings of Persia." Daniel 10:12-13 (NASB)

What does it mean to wear the armor of God?

Wearing the armor of God means firmly standing in faith upon the work of Jesus Christ on our behalf. Paul wrote:

> Stand firm then, with the belt of truth buckled around your waist, with the breastplate of righteousness in place, and with your feet fitted with the readiness that comes from the gospel of peace. In addition to all this, take up the shield of faith, with which you can extinguish all the flaming arrows of the evil one. Take the helmet of salvation and the sword of the Spirit, which is the word of God. Ephesians 6:14-17 (NLT)

We stand firm in our faith as we tell the truth (belt of truth buckled around your waist). Satan is the "father of lies" (John 8:44), while Jesus is "the way, the truth and the life" (John 14:6). To fight and win the battles we face we must seek and tell the truth, which involves both speaking and listening, specifically confessing the truth about our sin to others, as well as listening to other's confessions. Telling the truth sets us free from the bondage of sin (John 8:32, James 5:16).

We stand firm in faith as we depend upon the righteousness provided through Jesus for justification (breastplate of righteousness). If we are depending upon our good behavior for justification before God, then our hope dissolves when we sin. But if we are depending upon Jesus' righteousness for our justification, then our hope is certain (Romans 3:21-24).

We stand firm in faith as we share the gospel (feet fitted with the readiness that comes from the gospel of peace). The Apostle Peter tells Christians to be prepared to give a reason for the hope we have in Christ (1 Peter 3:15), and actively sharing our faith in Jesus actually helps us to win spiritual victories.

We stand firm in our faith as we act on our faith (shield of faith). To defend themselves against flaming arrows, ancient soldiers soaked their wooden shields in water so that the fire would be quenched when the arrows struck their shields. Acting on our faith protects us from arrows of doubt, disappointment and discouragement, quenching them with the confidence that God is able to do amazingly more than all we can ask or even imagine (Ephesians 3:20). Acting on our faith strengthens our confidence that nothing we go through can separate us from his good character and good plans for us (Romans 8:28-38).

We stand firm in faith as we renew our minds with the Scripture (helmet of salvation). Paul wrote that we are to be transformed by the renewing of our mind (Romans 12:2) and that we should measure every thought we have by the truth found in Scripture. If our thoughts do not match the truth found in Scripture, then we reject our thoughts, taking them captive to the obedience of Christ (2 Corinthians 10:5). Taking a thought "captive to the obedience of Christ" means simply that all thoughts are to be submitted and subservient to the truth of Jesus Christ's obedience in death and power in resurrection. No thought that we have is to supersede the reality of Christ's life.

We stand firm in faith as we speak the Scripture (sword of the Spirit). This is the only piece of armor that is clearly offensive in nature. The writer of Hebrews compares the Word to a sharp, double-edged sword that pierces and cuts at our inner man (Hebrews 4:12). God's Word cuts away the worldly, fleshly and demonic ties that bind us.

Every soldier who carries a sword realizes that they must swing the sword if it is going to have any real effect on the enemy. For this reason, we must speak Scripture. It must come out of our mouth to be effective in our lives. When the Scripture is spoken, God hears his Word and acts accordingly. Scripture spoken out loud, brings God's character and presence to bear upon a situation. In Romans we learn that it is when people hear God's Word spoken, that faith rises up (Romans 10:17).

Ten Commandments

The Ten Commandments reflect God's lifestyle expectations for his people. After being miraculously redeemed (i.e. set free) by God from Egyptian slavery (Exodus 7-12), the Israelites travel to Mt. Sinai where Moses received the Ten Commandments from God (Exodus 19-20). Through the Ten Commandments we learn how the redeemed are to reflect their Redeemer. The Ten Commandments are listed in Exodus 20:3-17.

1. You shall have no other gods before me.
2. You shall not make for yourself any idol.
3. You shall not take the name of the Lord in vain.
4. You shall remember the Sabbath day, to keep it holy.
5. Honor your father and mother.
6. You shall not murder.
7. You shall not commit adultery.
8. You shall not steal.
9. You shall not bear false witness.
10. You shall not covet.

While it is true that Christians are not justified before God (i.e., saved) by keeping the Ten Commandments, the commandments continue to serve as a guide for how the redeemed are to live. We are justified before God only as we trust in the death and Jesus Christ for the forgiveness of our sin (Galatians 2:16). Unfortunately, many Christians mistakenly believe that God's grace offered through Jesus mysteriously cancels God's expectations outlined in the Ten Commandments, but the Ten Commandments continue to define holy living for God's people. Too often it seems that Christians have not simply been saved by grace, but that we have been paralyzed by it, believing that nothing is expected of those whom God has redeemed. Jesus said,

> Do not think that I have come to abolish the Law or the Prophets; I have not come to abolish them but to fulfill them. Matthew 5:17 (NIV)

The word "fulfill" means literally "to give full meaning." In other words, Jesus was a perfect example of how to live out God's righteous requirements found in the Ten Commandments. We see in the character, conduct and concerns of Jesus Christ a living demonstration of God's holiness. In fact, it was the perfect law keeping character of Jesus that made him an acceptable sacrifice for the sins of God's people, and as we trust in Jesus Christ for the forgiveness of our sin we affirm, as Paul did, that the law is good (Romans 7:16).

Too many Christians have interpreted God's provision of salvation by grace alone, apart from anything we do (Ephesians 2:8-9), to mean that God does not care how we live. But Paul explains that it is only those in whom the Spirit of Jesus lives, those who are saved by grace through faith in Jesus, that will be enabled to live a redeemed life by God's Spirit's presence (Romans 8:3-4).

The same Spirit that descended upon Christ at his baptism, dwells in those who have been born again. This means the same Spirit who enabled Jesus to fully meet the righteous requirements of the law, will enable Christians to live not according to the sinful nature, but according to the character of Jesus Christ, which is holy. Thus, keeping the Ten Commandments is not a means of redemption, but a demonstration that we have already been redeemed.

Temptation

Temptation is the act of enticing someone to sin. Satan is the first recorded tempter in Scripture (Genesis 3:1-13), and his work of temptation is recorded throughout Scripture (Job 1:1-2:10, Acts 5:9, 15:10, 1 Corinthians 7:5, 2 Corinthians 12:7, 1 Peter 5:8). Matthew even describes Satan as "the" tempter (Matthew 4:1-11). For this reason, we are to avoid situations in which we might be tempted (Luke 22:40, Galatians 6:1), and look for the provided way of escape (1 Corinthians 10:13).

Temptation is brought by the evil one.
And lead us not into temptation, but deliver us from the evil one. Matthew 6:13 (NIV)

Temptation can be avoided through prayer.
"Watch and pray so that you will not fall into temptation. The spirit is willing, but the body is weak." Matthew 26:41 (NIV)

Temptations of all types are common and can be escaped.
No temptation has seized you except what is common to man. And God is faithful; he will not let you be tempted beyond what you can bear. But when you are tempted, he will also provide a way out so that you can stand up under it. 1 Corinthians 10:13 (NIV)

Temptation was experienced and resisted by Jesus.
For we do not have a high priest who is unable to sympathize with our weaknesses, but we have one who has been tempted in every way, just as we are—yet was without sin. Hebrews 4:15 (NIV)

Temptation is not experienced or caused by God.
Let no one say when he is tempted, "I am being tempted by God," for God cannot be tempted with evil, and he himself tempts no one. But each person is tempted when he is lured and enticed by his own desire. James 1:13-14 (ESV)

Tithing

The word "tithe" means a tenth part (10%), and the Israelites were commanded to annually give one-tenth of their produce (ex. fruits, grains, livestock, etc.) to the Levites (Leviticus 27:30-33), who otherwise had no source of income (Numbers 18:8-32). The Levites were the tribe within Israel designated by God to care for the Temple. In many cases though, the Israelites failed to tithe as they had been commanded by God (Malachi 3:6-12).

Unfortunately, the command to tithe in the Old Testament, and the failure of the Israelites to keep the command, has become the linchpin for a theology called "prosperity theology," which teaches that if Christians will give 10% to the Church, then God will "open the floodgates of heaven" and prosper them financially (Malachi 3:6-12). While this was clearly God's promise to the Israelites, this promise does not hold true for us today in the same way.

We must remember that this promise was spoken to a particular people—that is the people of Israel—who were under a particular covenantal agreement with God—that being the Old Covenant put in place by Moses. To miss the importance of the specific context in which these words were spoken leads one to miss apply the Scripture in our context.

The Old Covenant was based upon blessings and curses. If Israelites kept the covenant law they were blessed. If they broke the law they were cursed, which Malachi points out in verse nine that they were in fact inheriting a curse, because they were robbing God. Malachi's call is for God's people to keep the law by faithfully tithing so that they can experience God's blessing! There is simply no such command, or promise of blessing or curse, in the New Testament. At the same time, there is a New Testament verse that does promise blessings to those who are generous financially. But the blessings cannot necessarily be assumed as financial. Paul writes:

> Remember this: Whoever sows sparingly will also reap sparingly, and whoever sows generously will also reap generously. 2 Corinthians 9:7 (NIV)

Paul goes on to promise that God will provide a harvest of righteousness to those who are financially generous. So there *is* a biblical principle of financial generosity that is encouraged among Christians and will be rewarded by God, but this principle should not be twisted to mean that God will make us rich.

Now unfortunately, while many Christians have rightly understood that we are no longer required to tithe, many have also wrongly interpreted this to mean that we should not tithe. It is true that we do not have to tithe in order to keep the law—that is to say we do not have to tithe in order to stay in right relationship with God. But it is also true that every example of giving cited in the New Testament goes well beyond the tithe. For example, Jesus applauds the widow who gave away 100% of her income (Mark 12:41-44). Paul does the same in praise for the Macedonians, who did not simply give what was expected of them or what they could afford, but he says they "gave beyond their ability" (2 Corinthians 8:3).

It is true that we are free from the law because Christ has paid the final sacrifice, but we are not free from the responsibility to keep those portions of the law that reflect the unchanging character and nature of God. For some reason, many Christians are prone to believing that because of God's grace shown toward us in the New Testament we are free to hoard our wealth and give very little. But Christians are to follow the New Testament example of generosity and sacrifice and go far beyond the tithe because of the grace we have been shown through Jesus Christ. It is inconsistent with New Testament living to acknowledge that Jesus is Savior and withhold our money (Matthew 6:24).

Transgender

Transgender is an umbrella term that describes the person who identifies with or expresses themselves as a gender other than their genetic gender. In other words, transgender is a psychological and emotional sense of self that does not match with one's gender at the time of birth. For this reason, being transgender is separate from one's physical makeup (i.e., not having to do with one's genitalia), as well as a separate issue from one's sexual orientation (i.e., not having to do with one's sexual preferences/desires). One can be transgender and heterosexual, homosexual, bisexual, etc.

While the psychology of transgender thoughts and feelings is not directly addressed within the Bible, the activity of crossdressing (transvestitism) is condemned (Deuteronomy 22:5). The reasons given for condemning these activities is that they are detestable to God, in that they are a departure from design. A biblical response to those experiencing transgender thoughts and feelings includes:

- affirming all people are created in the image of God (Genesis 1:27, Psalm 139:13). Everyone has dignity as image bearers, regardless of their struggles.
- affirming God's design of all individuals as male and female (Genesis 1:27). The Bible is clear that our sexual identity is something with which we are born and a part of God's work of individual design in our lives. This means that one's gender identity is not a matter of personal preference, but a matter of God's providential care of each of us.
- acknowledging that sexual confusion is faced by everyone to some degree. When sin entered the world, our sexuality, as one part of our personal identity, was negatively impacted and everyone will face sexually confused thoughts and feelings in some fashion.

- noting that an individual's identity is primarily defined by one's relationship to their Creator. The temptation is to equate one's physical characteristics (i.e., genitalia), or one's thoughts or feelings or experiences sexually with one's identity. While our identity is in part reflected in our sexuality, it is not the primary part of our identity. In short, we are far more than maleness and femaleness.
- comforting, supporting, and encouraging anyone carrying these burdens to honor God with their body (1 Corinthians 6:20). God's call upon the lives of all people, regardless of one's sexual thoughts and feelings, is to submit to his authority in their lives by embracing his design as expressed in nature and his will as expressed in the Bible.

Trials and Suffering

Trials and suffering are a common part of the world in which we live, and God's people are not immune to them. Some of the trials we experience and the suffering we endure are the result of our own sinful decisions, the just consequence of ungodly actions. At other times, trials and suffering are brought upon us because of no fault of our own, but rather simply by living in a fallen world.

Jesus was even described as a "man of suffering," someone who was familiar with difficulty and pain (Isaiah 53:3), and the first disciples were promised difficulties by Jesus (John 16:33). Rather than being caught off guard by difficulty, Christians are encouraged to make the most of every trial and all suffering by seeing them as an opportunity for maturity in faith (James 1:2-4).

Trials and suffering were common for Jesus Christ.
"You are those who have stayed with me in my trials. Luke 22:28 (ESV)

Trials and suffering were foretold for Christ's followers.
"I have told you these things, so that in me you may have peace. In this world you will have trouble. But take heart! I have overcome the world." John 16:33 (NIV)

Trials and suffering are an opportunity to mature.
Count it all joy, my brothers, when you meet trials of various kinds, for you know that the testing of your faith produces steadfastness. And let steadfastness have its full effect, that you may be perfect and complete, lacking in nothing. James 1:2-4 (ESV)

Trials and suffering are overcome by the Lord's rescue.
If this is so, then the Lord knows how to rescue godly men from trials and to hold the unrighteous for the day of judgment, while continuing their punishment. 2 Peter 2:9 (NIV)

Trials and suffering can be endured by God's grace.
But he said to me, "My grace is sufficient for you, for my power is made perfect in weakness." 2 Corinthians 12:9 (ESV)

Trials and suffering were common in the early church.
We sent Timothy, who is our brother and God's fellow worker in spreading the gospel of Christ, to strengthen and encourage you in your faith, so that no one would be unsettled by these trials. You know quite well that we were destined for them. In fact, when we were with you, we kept telling you that we would be persecuted. And it turned out that way, as you well know. 1 Thessalonians 3:2-4 (NIV)

For it has been granted to you on behalf of Christ not only to believe on him, but also to suffer for him. Philippians 2:29 (NIV)

Trinity

Trinity means "tri-unity." Although the word "Trinity" does not appear in the Bible, it is used to describe God's "three-in-oneness." Scripture teaches there is only one God (Deuteronomy 6:4), and that he exists in three distinct persons (i.e., Father, Son and Holy Spirit). Although each person within the Trinity is distinct (i.e., a unique individual), being three-in-one means that each person is of the same essence and fully shares in all of God's attributes (e.g., eternality, omniscience, omnipresence, omnipotence).

While "three-in-one" can be difficult to fully understand, to deny any part of Trinitarian theology, whether the 1) distinctness of each person, or 2) the deity of each person, or the 3) oneness shared among members of the Trinity, results in false teaching. *Modalism*, for example, falsely teaches that there is one God who appears in three different forms, or modes. Modalists deny the reality of three distinct persons being united in the Trinity. To do so, however, Modalists must deny the work of the Trinity at the baptism of Jesus (Matthew 6:16-17), and must also ignore the command given by Jesus to baptize his disciples in the name of the Father, the Son and the Holy Spirit (Matthew 28:19-20). Other false teachings regarding the Trinity include *Arianism*, which denies the deity of Jesus and teaches that he was created by the Father, *Subordinationism*, which affirms Jesus' deity but denies his equality with the Father, and *Adoptionism*, which denies Jesus' deity and teaches that he was a man who was simply adopted by the Father at the time of his baptism.

While it can be hard to understand God's "three-in-oneness," if Jesus is not fully God, then we should question whether his death on the cross was sufficient payment for our sin (Romans 3:21-26). If the Holy Spirit is not fully God, then we should question whether his presence and counsel are truly helpful (John 14:26).

The Trinity was alluded to in the Old Testament.
Then God said, "Let Us make man in Our image, according to Our likeness." Genesis 1:26 (NKJV)

Also I heard the voice of the Lord, saying: "Whom shall I send, and who will go for us. Isaiah 6:8 (NKJV)

The Trinity was revealed in the life of Jesus.
At that moment heaven was opened, and he saw the Spirit of God descending like a dove and lighting on him. And a voice from heaven said, "This is my Son, whom I love; with him I am well pleased." Matthew 6:16-17 (NIV)

Go therefore and make disciples of all nations, baptizing them in the name of the Father and of the Son and of the Holy Spirit, teaching them to observe all that I have commanded you. And behold, I am with you always, to the end of the age." Matthew 28:19-20 (ESV)

The Trinity is referred to by both Peter and Paul.
May the grace of the Lord Jesus Christ, and the love of God, and the fellowship of the Holy Spirit be with you all. 2 Corinthians 13:14 (NIV)

According to the foreknowledge of God the Father, by the sanctifying work of the Spirit, to obey Jesus Christ and be sprinkled with His blood. 1 Peter 1:1-2 (NASB)

The Trinity makes up only one God, with three persons.
For there is one God, and one mediator also between God and men, the man Christ Jesus. 1 Timothy 2:5 (NASB)

You believe that God is one You do well; the demons also believe, and shudder. James 2:19 (NASB)

Wisdom

Biblical wisdom is a God-given understanding for living that enables a person to honor God and enjoy life. Being a God-given understanding, biblical wisdom is different from earthly knowledge and greater than human intelligence. Wisdom always results in goodness and is demonstrated in one's actions and shapes one's character.

Throughout the Old Testament book of Proverbs, wisdom is often described using terms of personification, as if wisdom itself has a character and purpose. For example, in Proverbs we read that "wisdom calls aloud" to us, raising its voice in the square (Proverbs 1:20). Wisdom is also described as "dwelling" with prudence and "possessing" knowledge (Proverbs 8:12), as if wisdom is alive. Wisdom is even described as being born as a human, taking on flesh, as if God's divine character was physically present on earth (Proverbs 8:22-31).

Of course, this is exactly what happens in the New Testament. The Old Testament description of wisdom becomes a reality in the New Testament birth of Jesus Christ (1 Corinthians 1:24). Ultimately, all who follow Jesus possess a God-given understanding for living that enables them to honor God and truly enjoy life.

Wisdom is given by God to all those who ask.
If any of you lacks wisdom, let him ask God, who gives generously to all without reproach, and it will be given him. But let him ask in faith, with no doubting, for the one who doubts is like a wave of the sea that is driven and tossed by the wind. For that person must not suppose that he will receive anything from the Lord. James 1:5-7 (ESV)

Wisdom from God is personified in Jesus Christ.
It is because of him that you are in Christ Jesus, who has become for us wisdom from God—that is, our righteousness, holiness and

redemption. Therefore, as it is written: "Let him who boasts boast in the Lord." 1 Corinthians 1:30-31 (NIV)

Wisdom is proven wise in the rightness of its actions.
For John came neither eating nor drinking, and they say, 'He has a demon.' The Son of Man came eating and drinking, and they say, 'Look at him! A glutton and a drunkard, a friend of tax collectors and sinners!' Yet wisdom is justified by her deeds." Matthew 11:18-19 (ESV)

Wisdom begins with fearing God and leads to shunning evil.
"But where can wisdom be found? Where does understanding dwell? And he said to man, 'The fear of the Lord—that is wisdom, and to shun evil is understanding.'" Job 28:12, 28 (NIV)

The fear of the LORD is the beginning of knowledge; Fools despise wisdom and instruction. Proverbs 1:7 (NIV)

"I, wisdom, dwell with prudence, and I find knowledge and discretion. The fear of the LORD is hatred of evil. Pride and arrogance and the way of evil and perverted speech I hate. I have counsel and sound wisdom; I have insight; I have strength. Proverbs 8:12-14 (ESV)

Women in Ministry

The two theological positions on women in ministry are "egalitarian" and "complementarian." Egalitarians hold that God created men and women as equal in all respects, that both were charged by God with the responsibility to rule over creation, and that sin's entry into the world corrupted God's design for equality. This resulted in a harmful hierarchy, where men oppress women and women resent and resist male leadership. Christ's work however aims at removing the effects of the fall and restoring God's design of equality and mutuality between men and women. For egalitarians, Galatians 3:28 expresses the ideal for all relationships.

Complementarians hold that God created men and women equal in value but with distinct roles, that men are given the responsibility of leadership in home and church and women are charged to offer support and assistance to men. Sin's entry into the world corrupted God's design, resulting in oppression of women by men and rebellion of women against male authority. Christ's work aims at restoring male and female relationships and Ephesians 5:22-28 represents the ideal, which was evident in God's design at creation in.

- created order – Adam was created before Eve (Genesis 2:18-25).
- responsibility before the law – the prohibition against eating from the "tree of the knowledge of good and evil" was given to Adam (Genesis 2:17).
- authority within the Garden – Adam named the animals and Eve (Genesis 2:20, 2:23, 3:20).
- women's specified role of helpmate – Eve was given a distinct role of support (Genesis 2:18).
- responsibility for sin's entry into the world – God came looking for man first (Genesis 3:9).

- God's judgment of Adam – Adam was judged by God in part for his failure to lead (Genesis 3:17).
- sin's destructive impact upon marriage – Adam and Eve's roles were negatively affected (Genesis 3:16).

As one studies the New Testament, hierarchy and role differentiation is clearly identified in the:

- Trinity – God is the head of Christ, and the Son submitted to the Father (1 Corinthians 11:3, Philippians 2:6-7).
- nature of ministry – Christ is the head of man and man the head of woman (1 Corinthians 11:3).
- work of salvation – Jesus is the second Adam, overcoming the first Adam's sin (Romans 5:12-21, 1 Corinthians 15:22, 45-49).
- church's relationship with Christ – Male headship in marriage represents Christ's headship in the Church (Ephesians 5:25-31).
- ministries of the Church – prayer, prophecy, teaching, and leadership are all guided by the doctrine of hierarchy (1 Corinthians 11:2-16, 14:34-36, 1 Timothy 2:11-12, 3:1-7, Titus 1:5-9)

While egalitarians dismiss the above New Testament references to hierarchy as culturally bound, the New Testament authors clearly support and teach a hierarchical interpretation of Genesis 1-3, and God would certainly not allow the New Testament to misinterpret the Old Testament. The complementarity of men and women is transcultural and demonstrated by the:

- testimony of Scripture - The plainest reading of the New Testament supports male headship within the church (1 Corinthians 11:2-16, 14:34-36, 1 Timothy 2:11-15, 3:1-7,

Titus 1:6-9). In addition, the Israelite priesthood was male (Exodus 28, Leviticus 9) and all twelve apostles were male.
- practice of the early church - While the role of women in ministry was elevated in the New Testament, and while women ministered within the early Church, neither Jesus nor Paul removed male headship and there are no examples of women elders.
- link between male headship in home and church – the headship of husband at home implies that headship of men at church (1 Corinthians 11:3).

The most difficult part of this discussion is distinguishing between directives that are culturally bound and those that are transcultural. While Paul's prohibition against a woman praying or prophesying with her head uncovered (1 Corinthians 11:3-5) is often seen as culturally conditioned, his prohibition against women teaching and exercising authority over a man (1 Timothy 2:12) is seen as transcultural, even though both are linked to God's intended design of hierarchy (1 Timothy 2:13-14).

Complementarians make this distinction for a couple of reasons. First, the primary purpose for wearing head coverings was to demonstrate an acceptance of God's hierarchy in male headship. At the same time, head coverings are not an essential "ministry" of the church, and the underlying principle of submission to male authority can be upheld in other modern and more culturally appropriate ways. On the other hand, the primary purpose for prohibiting women from teaching and exercising authority over men, was to reserve those functions for male leaders, and there are no substitute means for upholding the principle of male headship in these areas. Further, the permanent validity of the prohibition against women teaching and exercising authority of a man is tied directly to the:

- Nature of God, as reflected in the Trinity (1 Corinthians 11:3, Philippians 2:6-7).
- Design of God as established at creation (Genesis 2:18-25, 1 Timothy 2:13).
- Salvation of God as illustrated in the family and church (Ephesians 5:25-31).

At the same time, we know that Paul does not have in mind the complete "silence" of women (1 Corinthians 14:34), in that he gives permission for them to pray and prophecy (1 Corinthians 11:3-5). Thus, it appears that Paul's dual prohibition in 1 Timothy 2:12 is aimed at reserving a specific type of authoritative teaching role within the church just for men, a role that is most clearly identified in the weekly preaching ministry of the local church.

This seems apparent because 1 Timothy 2:12 includes two separate, but mutually interpreting, verbs (to teach or exercise authority) whose meaning is best understood when interpreted together, communicating a single coherent idea. A paraphrase of the verse might read, "I do not permit a woman to hold the authoritative teaching position in the church." In other words, not all teaching positions within the church are equally authoritative, and Paul limits the most authoritative teaching position to men, namely that of weekly preaching ministry of the local church.

Second, the focus of 1 Timothy overall and of the Pastoral Epistles in general is not to exclude women from all teaching positions, but to strengthen the elder's role of authoritative teaching. The apostle Paul writes to Timothy, the leader of the church in Ephesus, calling him to "command certain men not to teach false doctrine" (1 Timothy 2:3), and to make sure that those approved as elders are in fact able to "teach" (1 Timothy 3:2). Setting apart for the elders a specific authoritative teaching role, which in our contemporary setting is most closely associated with the weekly preaching ministry of the church, was aimed at strengthening the doctrinal integrity of the church.

Beyond 1 Timothy 2:12 there are other Scriptural indications that women are to play a vital role in the teaching ministries of the church. For example, when Paul describes the corporate assembly in worship he writes, "Each one…has a teaching" (1 Corinthians 14:26), which is without gender restriction. Further, women actively participated in teaching men in the early church. For example, Priscilla's teaching of Apollos (Acts 18:24-26). Luke even lists Priscilla's name before her husband, Aquila, suggesting she was the more prominent of the two.

Finally, passages addressing the "silence" of women (1 Corinthians 11:2-16, 14:34, 1 Timothy 2:8-15) cannot mean that women may not "utter any sound" in a church since that would conflict with Paul's recognition that a woman may prophesy (1 Corinthians 11). When Luke announces the Spirit's arrival, he affirms that both "sons and daughters" will prophesy (Acts 2:17), and in Acts the four daughters of Philip the evangelist were named as "prophetesses" (Acts 21:9), and the apostle Paul even gives guidelines for women when prophesying in public worship (1 Corinthians 11:5).

Therefore, women may address co-ed adult audiences through prophecy. This gift of prophecy most likely included spontaneous "inspired" communication, as well as prepared instruction and exhortation from the Scripture. The implication is that women can prepare a message to be delivered in the corporate assembly, which might include reading or quoting Scripture, as well as explaining Scripture and offering examples of application for the Christian community. Thus, women can exercise their gift of prophecy, as long as they demonstrate a posture of acceptance toward male headship (1 Corinthians 11) and submission to the elders who continue to bear the responsibility for leadership, teaching and care within the congregation.

Work

Work is not described as evil in the Bible, but rather as mankind's natural occupation within the world. Even before sin entered the world, mankind was given work to do in the Garden of Eden (Genesis 2:15). In the Bible, work is described as a means to utilizing the abilities God has given to us, as well as an opportunity to bring him glory, in the effort to provide for our physical needs.

The notion that work was given for our fulfillment, as well as God's glory, runs contrary to much of what we hear from popular culture. Work is often described by the broader culture as a burden to be avoided, or even escaped if at all possible. For example, vacation and retirement are often presented as the highest goal of working. While it is true that because of sin's entry into the world the effectiveness of our work has been undermined, causing greater difficulty in our labor than God intended, (Genesis 3:17-18), we are still enabled, as well as called by God, to enjoy our work and to bring him glory through our work (1 Corinthians 10:31).

Empowered by the Spirit of God, Christians are to view work as a divinely appointed task, through which they can honor him, and enjoy contributing to their own care, as well as meeting the needs of others (Romans 12:11). One of the greatest blessings of work is being able to share with others (Ephesians 4:28).

Work is an activity in which God himself participates.
By the seventh day God had finished the work he had been doing; so on the seventh day he rested from all his work. Genesis 2:2 (NIV)

Work was assigned to mankind in the Garden of Eden.
The LORD God took the man and put him in the Garden of Eden to work it and take care of it. Genesis 2:15 (NIV)

Work became toil as a consequence of sin.
And to Adam he said, "Because you have listened to the voice of your wife and have eaten of the tree of which I commanded you, 'You shall not eat of it, 'cursed is the ground because of you; in pain you shall eat of it all the days of your life; thorns and thistles it shall bring forth for you; and you shall eat the plants of the field. By the sweat of your face you shall eat bread, till you return to the ground, for out of it you were taken; for you are dust, and to dust you shall return." Genesis 3:17-19 (ESV)

Work is enabled by God and is for his glory.
The LORD said to Moses, "See, I have called by name Bezalel the son of Uri, son of Hur, of the tribe of Judah, and I have filled him with the Spirit of God, with ability and intelligence, with knowledge and all craftsmanship, to devise artistic designs, to work in gold, silver, and bronze, in cutting stones for setting, and in carving wood, to work in every craft. Exodus 31:1-5 (ESV)

So whether you eat or drink or whatever you do, do it all for the glory of God. 1 Corinthians 10:31 (NIV)

Work is an expected activity for survival.
For even when we were with you, we gave you this rule: "If a man will not work, he shall not eat." 2 Thessalonians 3:10 (NIV)

Worship

Worship is the act of recognizing the worthiness (lit. "worthship") of an individual to receive special honor. Although in our contemporary context expressing worship most often includes the act of singing together in a group, worship is far more than singing. Worship is ultimately a lifestyle of honoring God for who he is and what he has done for us through Jesus Christ.

For this reason, both the first and the second commands within the Ten Commandments flatly condemn false worship (Exodus 20), and Israel was firmly punished by God when they participated in idolatry (Deuteronomy 8:19). In the New Testament, the Church is defined as a worshipping community, charged by God himself to be a people offering praise to God (1 Peter 2:5).

Some of the essential acts of worship for the Church include reading publicly the Scripture (1Timothy 4:13), praying with and for others (James 5:16), singing with and to one another (Ephesians 5:19, Colossians 3:16), sharing in Communion (1 Corinthians 11:17-24), and celebrating new life in Christ through baptism (Matthew 28:20).

Worship is sought by God the Father.
But the time is coming—indeed it's here now—when true worshipers will worship the Father in spirit and in truth. The Father is looking for those who will worship him that way. John 4:23 (NLT)

For God is Spirit, so those who worship him must worship in spirit and in truth. John 4:24 (NLT)

Worship requires our bodies being offered in sacrifice.
And so, dear brothers and sisters, I plead with you to give your bodies to God because of all he has done for you. Let them be a living and holy

sacrifice—the kind he will find acceptable. This is truly the way to worship him. Romans 12:1 (NLT)

Worship is offered through the Spirit and Christ's Word.
Don't be drunk with wine, because that will ruin your life. Instead, be filled with the Holy Spirit, singing psalms and hymns and spiritual songs among yourselves, and making music to the Lord in your hearts. And give thanks for everything to God the Father in the name of our Lord Jesus Christ. Ephesians 5:18-20 (NLT)

Let the message about Christ, in all its richness, fill your lives. Teach and counsel each other with all the wisdom he gives. Sing psalms and hymns and spiritual songs to God with thankful hearts. Colossians 3:16 (NLT)

Worship was received by Jesus while he was on earth.
When he reached the place where the road started down the Mount of Olives, all of his followers began to shout and sing as they walked along, praising God for all the wonderful miracles they had seen. "Blessings on the King who comes in the name of the Lord! Peace in heaven, and glory in highest heaven!" Luke 19:37-38 (NLT)

Wrath of God

The Apostle Paul wrote that "The wrath of God is being revealed from heaven against all the godlessness and wickedness of people, who suppress the truth…" (Romans 1:18). God's wrath is his anger toward, as well as condemnation and punishment of, human sin. God's wrath being revealed because we ignore the revelation of God's "eternal power and divine nature" that is clearly seen in what has been made (e.g., the sun, moon, stars, oceans, mountains, trees, etc.) (Romans 1:20). In short, when we walk outside and see the beauty of the day, we know that we are not God, but we sinfully refuse to acknowledge that we owe him a life of worship. As a result, our minds become darkened, and although we claim to be wise, we act like fools by worshipping idols our hands have made, rather than the Creator of our hands (Romans 1:21-23).

Of course, this is not to say that there is no one who does good. There are many morally impressive people. Yet, still no one is perfect. Even highly moral people sin, and for every good person who does good like Ghandi, or Mother Theresa, or Martin Luther King Jr., there is a Hitler, Stalin, Mao Zedong, Mussolini, Saddam Hussein, Kim Jong-Il, and Idi Amin. Clearly, humanity is not going to solve the sin problem on their own, which means God's wrath remains on us apart from God's care of us. And in case we're tempted to think that the notion of God's wrath is simply a holdover from Old Testament stories like the destruction of Sodom and Gomorrah, Jesus himself said, "whoever rejects the Son will not see life, for God's wrath remains on them. John 3:36 (NIV)

Predictably, some have asked, "Why is Jesus the one in whom we are to trust? Why can't we place our faith in Allah, or Buddha, or Krishna?" We can't place our faith in Allah, or Buddha or Krishna, because they aren't offering help. Islam, Buddhism and Hinduism each teach that humanity must overcome sin through moral discipline, while Christianity invites us to trust in another man's righteousness, namely Jesus'. In Christianity we are trusting in God's Son, Jesus, to do for us what we can't do for ourselves, namely living a morally perfect life, dying as a sin sacrifice, being raised from the dead, conquering death and providing eternal life for all who will believe. Only in Christianity is God himself providing a remedy for own wrath toward humanity.

Sadly, realizing that humanity can't provide a remedy for sin, but still not wanting to trust in Jesus, some decide to simply deny a theology of God's wrath. They will say something like, "I just can't believe in a God of wrath. I can only believe in a God of love." What they fail to understand though is that God's wrath toward sin, *reflects* God's love. Imagine if God didn't feel wrath toward crimes like murder and rape, then how could he claim to be loving? The truth is that if you like justice, then you want a God who reveals his wrath against sin. Ironically, in refusing to acknowledge God's wrath toward human sin, our experience of God's love is jeopardized, as it is only in Christianity that both justice and mercy are upheld. The gospel is good news because it offers us mercy through faith in Jesus' who absorbed God's wrath toward human sin.

GLOSSARY

Amen. An affirmation of agreement said at the end of prayers or in response to Scripture that means "may it be" (Psalm 41:13).

Antichrist. The "man of lawlessness" appearing prior to Jesus' return and bringing great sin and suffering (2 Thessalonians 2:13).

Apocrypha. A collection of books included with the Bible by the Roman Catholic Church but not considered as equal to the testimony of Scripture.

Arianism. A heresy denying the full deity of Jesus Christ and the Holy Spirit.

Catechism. From the Greek word *katecheo*, meaning to instruct, this is a formalized system of Bible training. Augustine and Martin Luther both wrote catechisms, and parents are instructed to teach their children (Ephesians 6:4).

Compatibilism. The Reformed theology that teaches God's sovereignty is compatible with man's freedom to make real choices (Philippians 2:12-13).

Covenant. Any binding agreement that establishes a relationship. God entered a covenant with Abraham (Genesis 15:18). Jesus Christ was the fulfillment of God's agreement with Abraham and the beginning of the new covenant (Luke 22:20, Hebrews 8:6).

Creed. A formal statement of belief. The Bible contains several early creeds (Philippians 2:1-11; Timothy 3:16), and several were written by early Christians (Apostle's Creed, Nicene Creed).

Docetism. A heresy that denied Jesus' full humanity (Hebrews 4:15).

Doctrine. A truth or system of truths from Scripture (1 Timothy 4:6).

Doxology. A combination of the Greek *doxa*, which means glory, and *logos*, which means word, this is a short hymn of praise to God.

Ecclesiology. From the Greek *ekklesia*, meaning assembly, this is the study of the Church and its function (Ephesians 3:10).

Evangelical. From the Greek *evangelion*, which means good news, this term describes anyone who believes the gospel is the "power of God for salvation" (Romans 1:16) and makes it a priority to proclaim the gospel.

Exegesis. The activity of interpreting and applying a passage of the Bible. Often includes grammatical and historical studies.

Fundamentalism. Strictly adhering to essential beliefs. Originally referred to a theologically conservative response to liberal theology of the early 20th century, the "fundamentals" included an affirmation of the Bible's inspiration and inerrancy and the historical reality of the miracles reported in the Bible.

Gap Theory. The belief that a large gap in time exists between Genesis 1:1 and Genesis 1:2, during which God judged an earlier creation, making it "formless and empty" (Genesis 1:2), and clearing the way for another creative act as described in balance of Genesis 1.

General Revelation. Knowledge of God's existence revealed to all through creation (Romans 1:20).

Gloria in Excelsis Deo. The title of a well-known Christmas carol this Latin phrase means "Glory to God in the highest," and is quote taken from the angels who met shepherds in the field on Christmas Eve (Luke 2:14).

Great Commission. A command of Jesus to his disciples, just before his ascension, to go and make more disciples (Matthew 28:18-20).

Hallelujah. Transliteration of the Hebrew word meaning "praise God."

Hermeneutics. The theory and/or rules governing biblical interpretation and application.

Heterodox. Any teaching or practice at variance with the historic orthodox teachings and practices of Christianity. Heterodoxy often leads to heresy.

Hosanna. A cry for salvation, literally "save us now" (Matthew 21:9).

Hypostatic Union. From the Greek *hypostasis*, meaning substantive reality, this is a technical term describing the unique union of Jesus Christ's humanity and divinity (John 1:1, Hebrews 1:3).

Imputed Sin. The transfer of sin from the first humans, Adam and Eve, to all of humanity (Romans 5:12). The good news of the Gospel is that just as sin is transferred from Adam and Eve to all humanity, the righteousness of Jesus Christ is transferred to all who believe (Romans 3:22). This is the theological principle of "imputation."

Justification. The doctrine that God declares sinners to be "just" on the basis of faith in Jesus' death (Romans 3:24-26).

Kenosis. From the Greek *kenoo*, which means emptied, this word refers to the activity needed for God, as Jesus Christ, to become fully man, while maintaining his deity (Philippians 2:7).

Maranatha. An ancient Aramaic word beckoning Jesus' urgent return (1 Corinthians 16:22).

Maundy Thursday. Also known as Holy Thursday, it is the Thursday before Easter, commemorating the Last Supper of Jesus (1 Corinthians 11:23-26).

Mercy Seat. The cover, or lid, made of gold that was on top of the Ark of the Covenant. On top of the mercy seat were two gold statues of Cherubim, which are heavenly beings. Once a year, on the Day of Atonement, the blood of from a bull was sprinkled on the mercy seat, as the people sought God's forgiveness for sins committed (Leviticus 16:11-19).

Millennium. A thousand years, most often designating the period of Jesus' reign on earth, whether literal or figurative (Revelation 20:1-7).

Modalism. The heretical teaching that denies the Trinitarian teaching that God exists in three distinct persons, but rather that he simply appears in different modes.

Monergism. A combination of the Greek words *mono*, which means one, and *erg*, which means work, refers to the belief that the Holy Spirit is the singularly active agent in regeneration.

Occult. A term that refers to "hidden" knowledge. In an effort to discover hidden knowledge, occultists may attempt to speak with the dead, or cast spells, etc. These activities are condemned in the Bible (Deuteronomy 18:10).

Original Sin. The doctrine that all humanity is inherently corrupted by the sin of the first humans, Adam and Eve (Romans 5:12). The good news of the Gospel is that just as sin is transferred from Adam and Eve to all humanity, the righteousness of Jesus Christ is transferred to all who believe (Romans 3:22). This is the theological principle of "imputation."

Orthodoxy. A combination of the Greek words *ortho*, which mean right, and *doxa*, meaning opinion, this term refers to the historically approved beliefs within the Christian faith.

Orthopraxy. A combination of the Greek words, *ortho*, which means right, and *praxis*, which means deed or action, this terms refers to historically approved actions within the Christian faith.

Panentheism. The heretical belief that God is *in* everything that has been created, that he permeates and penetrates all things.

Pantheism. The heretical belief that the universe *is* God and/or that everything in the universe is a part of God.

Parousia. A Greek term referring to someone coming or someone's presence, which is used in reference to the future arrival of Jesus Christ. (Acts 1:11).

Pentecostalism. A denomination that was birthed in the American revival of 1901, and believes that the a subsequent baptism in the Holy Spirit is needed after one is born again and teaches that speaking in tongues as a necessary evidence of saving faith.

Pietism. A movement within the Lutheran denomination during the 17th and 18th centuries that called for individual discipline in pursuit of holiness.

Predestination. God determining and assuring who will be saved by faith in Jesus Christ (Ephesians 1:11).

Propitiation. The doctrine that God's wrath toward sin was appeased through Jesus' death (Romans 3:25, 1 John 2:2, 4:10), making possible our forgiveness by grace through faith.

Protestant. That branch of Christianity that separated from the Catholic Church as a result of the Protestant Reformation.

Protestant Reformation. A reforming movement that broke from the Catholic Church and aimed at correcting doctrinal error and abuses of power. It began in 1517 with the Catholic priest, Martin Luther, and resulted in the birth of Protestantism.

Purgatory. The place in which Roman Catholic doctrine teaches souls of Christians are held for further purification before heaven.

Soteriology. From the Greek *soteria*, meaning salvation, this is the study of God's saving work through Jesus Christ.

Theistic Evolution. The belief that God used evolution in his work of creation.

Transubstantiation. The Roman Catholic doctrine that the bread and wine of Communion literally becomes the body and blood of Jesus.

WAIT...WHAT?
Biblical Teachings Worth Repeating

Jesus described himself as the Good Shepherd and those who follow after him as his sheep (John 10:11). Being compared to sheep is not flattering, as there are stories of sheep walking into an open fire. There are also stories of sheep stuck on their back and unable to right themselves. It's called being "cast." The short of it is that sheep can be too weak to care for themselves and too stubborn to change course, a deadly combination. Yet, I must be honest. I certainly find within myself a lot of sheep-like tendencies.

Jesus is the Good Shepherd, but he also gifts some to help him in his work (Ephesians 4:11-12). That's my passion. I love helping other sheep follow the Good Shepherd. Toward that end, this book is a collection of sermon excerpts from the last couple decades.

The title, "Wait...What?" came from my teenage children, who daily remind me of the value of repeating important messages. The chapters are short, which can be read in under 12 minutes.

FOLLOWING JESUS
Defining Discipleship in the 21ˢᵗ Century

Whether you are a non-Christian, wanting to understand better the beliefs of Christians, or a Christian wanting a succinct definition of discipleship, *Following Jesus* is for you.

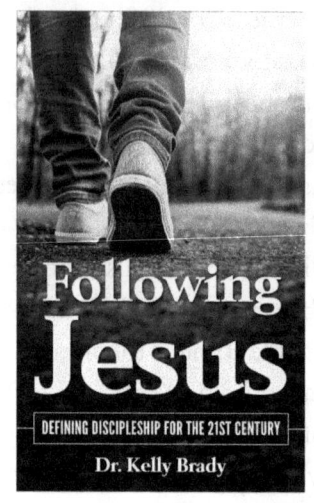

In that first-century world disciples were those who detached themselves from their own way of life and reattached themselves to a *rabbi* (teacher), committing themselves to his service and to becoming like him in every way.

When following a rabbi, first-century disciples would pay attention to every word he spoke and every move he made, sometimes even trying to mimic his mannerisms. So complete was a disciple's commitment to the rabbi that it became the defining element of their character, and the nature of what it means to be a disciple has not changed in over 2000 years.

Following Jesus is aimed at defining discipleship in order to help those following after Jesus better understand his call upon their lives.

RESTORE
Experiencing The Power of a Healing Fellowship

The Apostle Paul wrote about those entangled in sin that "You who live by the Spirit should **RESTORE** that person gently (Galatians 6:1). The Greek word translated as "restore" has in mind the work of repairing what has been damaged. Sin damages us. It leaves us in need of repair, and by God's design, we are to play an active role in restoring one another, and we do that as we gently bear one another's burdens, which is what Christ has done for us through his death on the cross.

RESTORE is a gathering for those who want to heal from their wounds caused by sin, whether their own sin or someone else's sin, as well as gain freedom from the sinful behaviors those wounds have fueled in their life. RESTORE is a gathering for those who want to talk about experiences that cause feelings of shame, anger, fear, and anxiety. RESTORE is a time and place to share our stories of trauma, temptations, and unwanted sinful behaviors, as well as our hope for increased freedom and joy in life. RESTORE is a gathering for those who want to act courageously by sharing with and listening to one another, and by persevering in prayer for God's healing.

SHEPHERDING
The Elder Notebook of Glen Ellyn Bible Church

The Apostle Paul appointed Elders in each church he established (Acts 14:23), and he wrote that serving as an Elder is a noble task (1 Timothy 3:1). In fact, having a desire to serve as an Elder is one of the first qualifications for service. In an effort to strengthen the office of Elder at GEBC and equip the men who have a desire for service, we have put together this notebook.

Shepherding is the product of a community effort, as both the Elders and the staff of Glen Ellyn Bible Church have contributed countless hours in research, prayer and study to provide this written record of our theology and philosophy of ministry. It is our desire is to strengthen not only the people of GEBC by providing competent and godly leadership, but to share what we've learned with other churches in order to advance God's Kingdom around the world. Toward that end, you are free to reproduce any portion of this notebook for educational purposes, provided you do not change the content or charge others for the content. Finally, proceeds from the sale of this book go to the Benevolence Fund of Glen Ellyn Bible Church, which is dedicated to meeting the needs of physically and spiritually impoverished.

EQUIPPED
2 Timothy 3:16-17

Why should I use a journal? The short answer is that journaling takes our learning to a whole new level. Reading Scripture daily is valuable but writing about what we read forces our mind and heart to process God's Word in a much more thorough way. Research shows that writing our thoughts out "longhand" engages both the right and left hemispheres of our brain, which is a more robust learning experience.

A common complaint among those who journal regularly is feeling aimless. Many are unsure what they are to write about from one day to the next. It's not uncommon to string a few good days of journaling together only to feel like you have soon run out of things to write. However, this journal is uniquely designed to guide our reflection day to day, keeping us focused on processing the message and meaning of Scripture.

Each journal entry is guided by five simple prompts. Begin by selecting a passage of Scripture. Read the passage several times, then follow the prompts. Journal entries can be long or short, but you will always be guided through a process of Scripture reflection, prayer and application.

www.ingramcontent.com/pod-product-compliance
Lightning Source LLC
Chambersburg PA
CBHW070723160426
43192CB00009B/1295